R0061512208

01/2012

W9-AXB-148

Praise for Ariel Sabar's *My Father's Paradise*

"Graceful and resonant . . . A personal undertaking for a son who admits he never understood his unassuming, penny-pinching immigrant father, a man who spent three decades obsessively cataloging the words of his moribund mother tongue. Sabar once looked at his father with shame, scornful of the alien who still bore scars on his back from childhood bloodlettings. This book, he writes, is a chance to make amends."

—*New York Times* Sunday Book Review

"If Ariel Sabar's *My Father's Paradise* were only about his father's life, it would be a remarkable enough story about the psychic costs of immigration. But Sabar's family history turns out to be more than the chronicle of one man's efforts to retain something of his homeland in new surroundings. It's also a moving story about the near-death of an ancient language and the tiny flicker of life that remains in it. . . . "

—*Washington Post*

"A wonderful, enlightening journey, a voyage with the power to move readers deeply even as it stretches across differences of culture, family, and memory."

—*Christian Science Monitor*

"A powerful story of the meaning of family and tradition inside a little-known culture."

—*San Francisco Chronicle*

"A biography, a memoir, a meticulously reconstructed history of a largely vanished people and place, and a meditation on one of the world's oldest languages. Transcending mere reportage, it acquires a novel-like warp and weft."

—*Los Angeles Times*

"A remarkable new memoir . . . Sabar's *Paradise* is especially noteworthy because of its multilayered narrative. While it begins with a young man's personal and familial crisis, it ends up exploring universal themes about the linguistic origins of culture and about the vital importance of tradition to the health of any community."

—*Philadelphia Inquirer*

"Sabar offers something rare and precious—a tale of hope and continuity that can be passed on for generations. . . . Readers can only be grateful to him for unearthing the history of a family, a people and a very different image of Iraq."

—*Publishers Weekly*, starred review

"Be forewarned: you will lose sleep over this book. . . . [Sabar] mesmerizes with the very first sentences. . . . In the tradition of the famed storytellers of Zakho, Sabar narrates a saga so touching, so amazing, so miraculous that the reader will feel awe for the resiliency of the human spirit. . . . Unlike many memoirs flooding the book market these days, *My Father's Paradise* is both unique and universal."

—*Roanoke (Va.) Times*

"With the novelistic skill of a Levantine storyteller . . . Sabar explores the conflicting demands of love and tradition, the burdens and blessings of an ancient culture encountering the 21st century. A well-researched text falling somewhere between journalism and memoir, sustained by Mesopotamian imagination."

—*Kirkus Reviews*

"[Sabar's] a lovely writer, slyly adapting his voice as needed to write about the different generations, shifting from the mode of a storyteller to the mode of a journalist. One of the best recent memoirs I've read."

—*Huffington Post*

"Taut and extravagant. A sweeping saga with the cadence of a Biblical tale."

—**Daniel Asa Rose, O. Henry Prize winner and author of** *Hiding Places: A Father and His Sons Retrace Their Family's Escape from the Holocaust*

"An enchanting combination of history, family and discovery—Ariel Sabar's chronicle of his journey is flat-out wonderful."

—**Rabbi David Wolpe, author of** *Why Faith Matters*

"Excellent. . . . The story is told with novelistic attention to narrative and detail, but its heart is Ariel's heart, that of a son searching with love for the meaning of his relationship with his father."

—*The Providence (RI) Journal*

"Written with a reporter's flair for people and places . . . Recommended."

—*Library Journal*

"An involving memoir that works as both a family saga and an examination of a lost but treasured community."

—*Booklist*

HEART *of the* CITY

Nine Stories of
Love and Serendipity
ON THE
Streets of New York

ARIEL SABAR

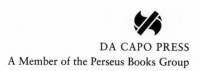

DA CAPO PRESS
A Member of the Perseus Books Group

Designed by Brent Wilcox
Set in 11 point Fairfield Light by the Perseus Books Group

Library of Congress Cataloging-in-Publication Data
Sabar, Ariel.
    Heart of the city : nine stories of love and serendipity on the streets of New York / Ariel Sabar.—1st Da Capo Press ed.
        p.   cm.
    ISBN 978-0-7382-1379-8 (alk. paper)
    1. Love—New York (State)—New York.   2. Love stories.   3. Environmental psychology.   I. Title.
    BF575.L8S313 2011
    947.7_10430922—dc22
    [B]
                                                    2010029916

Published by Da Capo Press
A Member of the Perseus Books Group
www.dacapopress.com

10 9 8 7 6 5 4 3 2 1

For Meg,
who first caught my eye
in the mess-hall slop line

"A city is, properly speaking, more poetic even than a countryside, for while Nature is a chaos of unconscious forces, a city is a chaos of conscious ones. The crest of the flower or the pattern of the lichen may or may not be significant symbols. But there is no stone in the street and no brick in the wall that is not actually a deliberate symbol—a message . . . as much as if it were a telegram or a post-card."

—G. K. CHESTERTON

Contents

Introduction   ix
A Note on Method   xxxv

Nine Stories

Green | CENTRAL PARK   1

Collision | THE STREET   27

Navigation | GRAND CENTRAL TERMINAL   49

Freestanding | LIBERTY ENLIGHTENING THE WORLD   69

Depths | THE SUBWAY   89

Elevation | EMPIRE STATE BUILDING   111

Crossroads | TIMES SQUARE   137

Renovations | THE METROPOLITAN MUSEUM OF ART   161

Sightlines | WASHINGTON SQUARE PARK   183

Epilogue   205
Postscripts   211
Acknowledgments   233

Introduction

In its original telling, the story of how my parents met has a tidy simplicity. Yona Sabar was born to an illiterate mother and peddler father in a mud hut in the mountains of Kurdish Iraq. Stephanie Kruger was born to a Manhattan CEO and his fashionable wife, holders of season tickets to the Metropolitan Opera. Yona, twenty-seven, had been in America for less than a year, for graduate school at Yale. He was depressed, homesick, and lonely, and was in New York for a long weekend to see friends from back home who now lived in the East Village. Stephanie, twenty-eight, was a caseworker at a foster agency in upstate New York. But her relationship with a boyfriend was on the rocks, so she drove to Manhattan for a few days to be with her parents.

It was Labor Day 1966, late morning. Yona's friends had gotten up early to see a parade, but Yona was too dejected to join them. He wandered the streets and eventually walked under an arch into a leafy refuge of curving paths in the heart of Greenwich Village. A sign said Washington Square Park. Yona wanted only to clear his head, to think.

But then a woman caught his eye. She was in a raincoat and was photographing people—beggars, unwashed street musicians—on benches around the central fountain. Her subjects reminded Yona of his countrymen, hard-luck immigrants to Israel who struggled for a sense of belonging in their new country.

He did not know then that the woman's name was Stephanie Kruger, or that she was an amateur photographer whose parents lived just a few blocks away. Watching her flit through the park with her camera, he knew only that he wanted to talk to her, to see if she knew something about this country and its people that he had yet to grasp.

He closed his eyes for a moment, then opened them. Then, his legs moving as if by a force not wholly his own, he approached.

"Pardon me," he said. "Are you a tourist?"

Four months later, they were married.

|||

IT SEEMED like a quintessential New York story: two vastly different people brought together by chance in America's greatest city. It said a lot about our country, I thought. It showed how immigrants here could leap borders of culture and class in ways unthinkable back home. It showed how in a society as fluid as America's, any two people could fall in love, anywhere. It was Horatio Alger recast as love story.

I thought I knew their story well, having told it in my first book, about my father's immigrant journey. But not long ago, when I asked my parents to tell it again, my mother injected a detail I had not heard before.

"Yona, didn't you actually see me before I entered the park?"

"Em, aha, Stephanie, maybe," my father said, in his gentle Middle Eastern accent.

"Yes," my mother persisted. "You said you saw me on one of the side streets and started following me."

"Eh, possibly. Into the park?"

"Yes, into the park! Where else? You followed me for a while on the street, and I remember what you once said."

He looked suddenly guilty. "What, Stephanie? What did I say?"

"You said that it wasn't until I was inside the park that you had the courage to walk up to me."

"Correct," my father said, with a nonchalance he often used when he knew he'd been cornered.

"So, wait a second," I said, turning to my father. "You mean if she'd never gone into the park, you wouldn't have tried to talk to her?"

"Correct." The streets were too exposed, he said. Attractive as she was, it would have felt improper to strike up a conversation there. The park, though, was different.

I scratched my head. But how?

It was, he said, like stepping into a village. The park shrank the city. It slowed time. With its roving paths, its fountain and trees, it filtered away the facelessness and noise of the street. Once inside, he said, people ceased being strangers. For a fleeting moment, they were on common ground. They were *sharing* something: not just the leaves and grass and water, but the human carnival. The park's habitués in those days—raffish New Yorkers sprawled on benches, picking at guitars, sipping from brown bags—were a sight to see. But so were the reactions they inspired in other people. Like Stephanie Kruger. From the way she photographed people, up close and with obvious empathy, Yona felt as though he already knew something about her. She sees the image of God in human beings, he thought, even when they are not at their best.

"The space was very important," my father told me during a springtime visit to our house to see his grandkids. "The first thing I thought about when all my friends left that day was, Where can I go where I can be around other people? And friendly people. People who are open to communication. Whereas the rest of the city was tall buildings and all the noise and subways and buses and people rushing everywhere, Washington Square Park was the opposite. Here you could just be with people without all the commotion. This was a place where you could be yourself. You didn't have to hide behind some mask."

More than four decades had passed since they'd met. My father, a resident of Los Angeles since the early 1970s, hadn't set foot in the park for almost as long. I was surprised at the intensity of feeling. "What was so bad about the rest of New York?" I asked.

"The rest of the city alienates you in a way," he went on. "If you are not with somebody when walking on the streets, you feel just smaller and smaller. The park was a small place where even if people didn't know each other before, they behaved like family."

My mom, sitting across the kitchen table from him, couldn't resist a jab. "In that park, especially, there were a bunch of odd-balls. You probably felt like you could fit right in."

"So what about you, Mom?" I asked. "Did the park do anything for you?"

She assured me that for her, it was all business. She was there, she said, as a photographer. "I went because I liked to take pictures of the characters."

My father, seeing his opening, cracked a smile. "Were you also open to *meeting* a character?"

In the coming months, I couldn't stop thinking about our conversation. I felt it contained some important truth, but I couldn't quite put my finger on it. I always knew I had America to thank, at least in part, for my parents' meeting. But had I overlooked the role of Washington Square Park? Could a vibrant public space, in some subtle but essential way, play matchmaker?

||||

WHEN I turned to books on the history of cities, I saw that their builders understood from the start the power of the built environment over how people think, feel, and act. The walls that Gilgamesh built around civilization's first city, Uruk, in what is now southern Iraq, in 2700 BCE, were both physical and symbolic. They were markers of the city limits. But they were also a kind of rope line between the lowly farmers outside and the craftsmen, religious leaders, and other elites inside. They were a potent signal to both subjects and enemies of the stability and power of the new city-state.

"Esthetically," Lewis Mumford wrote in his landmark history of cities, the earliest urban wall "made a clean break between city and countryside; while socially it emphasized the difference between the insider and the outsider, between the open field, subject to the depredations of wild animals, nomadic robbers, invading armies, and the fully enclosed city, where one could work and sleep with a sense of utter security, even in times of military peril."

In the Epic of Gilgamesh, the narrator is downright swaggering on the subject of walls. "Behold its outer wall, whose cornice is like copper / Peer at the inner wall, which none can equal! . . . / Go up and walk on the walls of Uruk, / Inspect the base terrace, examine the brickwork: / Is not the core of kiln-fired brick? / Did not the Seven Sages lay its foundations?"

The Sumerians, for their part, erected ziggurats—terraced temple compounds—so their priests would feel closer to their gods. The Greeks built agoras, open gathering places at the center of cities, so citizens of every class (except, to be fair, women and slaves) could trade, mingle, and debate the issues of the day. New Englanders planted greens at the center of town to instill in residents a sense of communal obligation.

Not long after Nazi warplanes bombed the British House of Commons in 1941, leaders began proposing new designs for its replacement. Winston Churchill was adamant in his opposition, grasping at a gut level the psychology of the original. He wanted the chamber to remain oblong—rather than semicircular—so that members of Parliament would continue to have to "cross the floor" to vote against their own party. A switch of allegiance should be conspicuous, he felt, so that it gives pause. He also wanted fewer seats than there were members, so that the chamber would seem bustling, even with members absent. Cramped was good.

"If the House is big enough to contain all its Members, nine-tenths of its debates will be conducted in the depressing atmosphere of an almost empty or half-empty Chamber," Churchill warned Parliament during a debate on rebuilding in 1943. The conversational style of parliamentary debate, he said, "requires a fairly small space" that projects "a sense of crowd and urgency. There should be a sense of the importance of much that is said and a sense that great matters are being decided."

Whether they actually were, it seemed, was beside the point, so long as the design made it appear so. Churchill knew the stakes. "We shape our buildings," he told Parliament, "and afterwards our buildings shape us."

|||

SURE, I thought. But is there any hard evidence? Any architectural theorist could say that a wall antagonizes, or that a tower exalts, or that a green unites. But could any of this be measured? Where were the social scientists? I was particularly interested in landmarks and public spaces, like Washington Square Park, where people find themselves in close proximity to strangers. Were some such places more likely to induce friendly glances than others? Could some actually encourage people to take the first steps toward falling in love?

After muddling through card catalogs and online databases at a few research libraries, I discovered writings in a field I had never before heard of: environmental psychology. The discipline came of age with the social movements of the late 1960s. Architects and psychologists began discussing how the design of everything from rooms and buildings to streets and cities might be contributing to social ills like poverty, crime, mental illness, overcrowding, and isolation. But soon the conversation shifted to a more universal question: how do the physical places in which we live, work, and play shape us?

One of the field's founders was a maverick psychologist named Roger Garlock Barker. A small-town Iowa boy who earned a PhD from Stanford, Barker landed early teaching jobs at places like

Harvard before growing irritated by what he saw as a major flaw in psychological research: psychologists of his era were great at running experiments in labs, but they rarely studied human behavior in the real world. This was in sharp contrast to natural sciences like chemistry and, say, entomology. "Although we have daily records of the oxygen content of river water, of the ground temperatures of cornfields, of the activity of volcanoes, of the behavior of nesting robins, of the rate of sodium iodide absorption by crabs," Barker wrote in the introduction to his seminal 1968 book *Ecological Psychology*, "there have been few scientific records of how human mothers care for their young, how teachers behave in the classroom (and how the children respond), what families actually do and say during mealtime, or how children live their lives from the time they wake in the morning until they go to sleep at night."

Barker, whose rounded shoulders and oversized eyeglass frames made him the picture of the bookish Midwesterner, set out on just such a task. No sooner had the University of Kansas recruited him in 1947, to chair the psychology department, than he told the dean that he didn't intend to live in the college town of Lawrence, the lone real city amid vast tracts of farmland. Instead, he was interested—for scholarly reasons—in settling in one of the rural outposts. Such towns were ringed by farm fields and largely immune to outside influences. They were naturally occurring laboratories. "My idea," he once told an interviewer, "was to settle in one of these towns and study the children as biologists study the animals of nature preserves."

In retrospect, his words might have been better chosen. But the impetus was sound: to study an organism in its native habitat. He and his wife, Louise, who collaborated on his research, settled in Oskaloosa, a place of some 715 souls more than twenty miles north of campus. They set up their "Midwest Psychological Field Station" there and spent the next twenty-five years studying the behavior of Oskaloosans—particularly children—in their own environments. (In his research Barker gave Oskaloosa the fictional name "Midwest.")

An early book, *One Boy's Day*, published in 1951, was a minute-by-minute stenographic record of an ordinary day in the life of a boy named Raymond Birch. Barker called it a "scientific document . . . of what a seven-year-old boy did and of what his home and school and neighborhood and town did to him from the time he awoke one morning until he went to sleep that night." Soon Barker was recording the behavior of scores of Oskaloosans in drugstores, Sunday school, 4H club meetings, and football games.

"It was during these studies that we shed the blinders of individual psychology, and it became clear that how a child behaves is not only determined by what he or she wants to do but by where he or she is," Barker told an interviewer in the late 1980s, a few years before his death. "For example, Raymond could not ride his bicycle, as he clearly wanted to, in the courthouse where his mother worked (the stairs and the 'rules' were absolute barriers). We also observed that there was more similarity in the behavior of Raymond and Roy in arithmetic class than between Raymond in arithmetic and Raymond in recess. How could we account for this? Obviously, recess 'did something' to Raymond. We had the idea that we should station observers in various places in the town and make a record of Raymond in each place so as to understand him. But then we began to see that the 'places' were dynamic entities into which children (and adults) were incorporated. I don't know why it took us so long to see that the drugstore was not only a building with equipment but also a particular pattern of behavior. We later called these places behavior settings."

Barker's notion of "behavior settings" gave birth to the field of environmental—or ecological—psychology. If you want to know how someone is acting, Barker said, don't tell me who they are—tell me where they are. "All inhabitants of the genotype Drugstore behave drugstore, and all inhabitants of a Tavern behave tavern," he declared in *Ecological Psychology*.

As early as the 1950s, some behavioral researchers were going further. A setting could not only predict with some certainty what people were doing. It could also, in some cases, tell you how they were feeling. For their classic study in *The Journal of Psychology*, professors Abraham Maslow and Norbett Mintz divided a few dozen Brandeis University undergraduates among three rooms and told them (falsely) that they were part of a study of facial types. The "beautiful" room had large windows, a soft armchair, and a mahogany desk, and was decorated with a large Navajo rug, paintings, and other art objects. The "ugly" room had two half-windows, battleship-gray walls, an overhead bulb with a grimy lampshade, and furnishings like mops and pails that evoked a janitorial closet. The "average" room fell somewhere in between.

Interviewers, also unaware of the study's purpose, entered the rooms with a series of close-up photographs of faces and asked the subjects to rate the faces on scales of "energy" and "well-being." On average the subjects in the beautiful room rated the faces as having nearly 20 percent more energy and well-being than did their counterparts in the ugly room. Over the course of the three-week study, the rooms' aesthetics even took a toll on the interviewers, who had not been briefed on the actual purpose of the study. Maslow and Mintz noticed that the interviewers assigned to the beautiful room reported liking their work and feeling happy, energetic, and comfortable. The interviewers in the ugly room, meanwhile, suffered from fatigue, boredom, headaches, and irritability. "The dungeon is all yours," one interviewer said, glumly, to another at the end of her ugly-room shift.

Over the years, scholars would take the insights of Barker, Maslow, and Mintz in new directions. Places were not just "behavior settings," these new thinkers said, but "stage sets" on which people acted out life's dramas or "containers" that framed our conduct. Soon, theorists would try to apply some of the emerging principles to design. If physical settings shaped behavior, they reasoned, shouldn't changes in design trigger changes in behavior?

Books with names like *People and Buildings*, *Design for Human Affairs*, and *The Human Context: Environmental Determinants of*

Behavior appeared in the 1970s suggesting socially minded design tweaks for everything from urinals to entire cities. The more carpets in a psychiatric ward, for example, the less anxious the patients. The more natural scenery that postoperative patients see from their recovery room windows, the less pain medication they request. The more car traffic on a street, the less neighbors socialize. The wider the aisles in a department store, the longer female customers linger. The fewer the buildings on a school campus, the more interaction between teachers and students. The closer together the chairs in a waiting room, the warmer strangers feel toward one another.

One of the most consistent findings across decades of studies was that the closer any two people were—whether in dorms, offices, classrooms, or neighborhood streets—the more likely they were to become friends or at least think well of one another. As the authors of one environmental psychology treatise concluded, "the architecturally determined and accidental arrangements of persons can have dramatic effects on their relationships." But why leave those effects to chance? A group of renegade psychologists, sociologists, and urban designers soon felt that by working together, they could build their way to a happier, healthier, and more productive society. "The rather obvious principle that people who don't come in contact don't become friends seems to offer the designer an intriguing new assignment," the architect C. M. Deasy, who employed a sociologist in his practice, wrote in his 1974 book *Design for Human Affairs*. "[We] can draw on a considerable arsenal of design devices to increase the probability that chance encounters will occur, not only in the formal settings design usually deals with but in the myriad informal settings where so much of life occurs: parking lots, bus stops, elevator lobbies, laundry rooms, supermarkets and gas stations."

Perhaps no figure associated with the field would leave a deeper imprint in the concrete than William Hollingsworth Whyte. Known as "Holly" to friends, Whyte was a Princeton-trained urbanist who wrote the 1956 bestseller *The Organization Man* before turning toward problems of public space in his adopted city of Manhattan. A marine veteran who worked for a spell as an editor at *Fortune*, Whyte shunned the aloofness of his academic colleagues. He preferred plain talk to academic jargon and street-level observation to theory. In the 1960s, the New York City Planning Commission began trying a new style of zoning that gave developers financial incentives to include public space in designs for new buildings. The more square feet developers set aside for outdoor public plazas, the more stories they could build.

The assumption was that such plazas were an unqualified public good. Set aside open space in the crowded center of New York City, the theory went, and harried Manhattanites would flock there—to lunch, stroll, soak up the sun, or meet friends. But after looking at some of the plazas, Whyte had his doubts. All but a few were wastelands, forbidding deserts of concrete that people, at best, speed-walked through on their way somewhere else. Whyte was an admirer of Jane Jacobs, the author of the influential 1961 book *The Death and Life of Great American Cities*, a critique of her era's urban renewal policies and an homage to the "sidewalk ballet" that unfolded each day outside her Greenwich Village apartment. "That the sight of people attracts still other people is something that city planners and city architectural designers seem to find incomprehensible," Jacobs had written. "They operate on the premise that city people seek the sight of emptiness, obvious order and quiet. Nothing could be less true." But as Whyte looked out over the vacant plazas, he saw none of the impromptu public life that Jacobs had argued was essential to great cities.

In 1970, Whyte set out to understand why some public spaces in New York worked as gathering places while others did not. Calling his study "The Street Life Project," he mounted time-lapse cameras atop neighboring buildings and sent Hunter College students into the plazas with clipboards to carefully plot the activity. Where were people sitting? How long did they stay? Did they come alone or in groups? Did sunlight matter? Did they prefer the backs or the fronts of the plazas?

Some of Whyte's findings, however often neglected by builders, seem obvious. The best public spaces had sunlight, water, trees, food vendors, and, most critically, many different places to sit. But among his most surprising discoveries was that people beget people, just as Jacobs had theorized. Contrary to the notion that the best-used parks and plazas are hideaways from the urban rush, Whyte found that people often sought out the busiest areas of a public space to lunch, chat with colleagues, or snuggle. He called it "self-congestion."

"What attracts people most, it would appear, is other people," he wrote in *The Social Life of Small Urban Spaces*. "People didn't move out of the main pedestrian flow. They stayed in it or moved into it, and the great bulk of the conversations were smack in the center of the flow—the 100 percent location, to use the real-estate term." People often chose the most visible spot—on the front steps of a plaza, for instance, or among closely spaced outdoor tables—even if it meant some jostling.

The most popular plazas didn't cut themselves off from the streets, he found, but opened into them. And if you want strangers to talk, give them something to talk about: an unusual sculpture, a mime, a juggler, a musician, a street character. A spectacle, even a minor one, "triangulates," Whyte wrote. It takes two strangers with ostensibly nothing in common and, through a shared, immediate experience, links them, even if just for a moment. New York City officials were so impressed with Whyte's findings that they incorporated many of them into the zoning code.

||

I HAD set out to find the invisible forces at play in great public places, and felt now that I was getting warmer. I had discovered that for ages, builders had an abstract sense of the effects of the built environment on people. By the middle of the twentieth century, scholars had begun quantifying those effects. And more recently, a few visionaries, like Whyte, were urging cities to apply the insights about people-friendly design to real public places.

But did any research go further? Had any settings been found to stoke, well, lust?

Arthur P. Aron was a graduate student in psychology at Berkeley in the late 1960s—and newly in love with a woman he'd one day marry—when he grew curious about the causes of intense attraction. Poets had long cloaked the phases of love in mystery. What drew two people together was ineffable, unknowable. That was its magic. True, it was the Summer of Love, and Berkeley its capital. But few grant-making institutions were funding scientific research on the psychology of love, viewing it as too frivolous for academic study. Leave it to the poets, they seemed to say.

But Aron persevered. He holed up at the University of California library and scoured the stacks for every single research study on love. There weren't many. But before long, he wrote, "I had several clear ideas about what ought to generate love, or at least attraction, between people. All these ideas were based on the notion that there was more to falling in love than just the right combination of personalities (the main theory up until then)." What also mattered, Aron said, were "the circumstances under which people met." From a smattering of clues in the available research, he theorized that people were more likely to be attracted to people they met during unusual or "boundary breaking" experiences—"those involving power, mystery, isolation, or strong emotions."

For his dissertation, Aron conducted an experiment in which he asked fifty-two male undergraduates to take part in a role-playing game with the same attractive woman. Though the woman had been coached by Aron, the men were told the woman was just another subject. In one scenario, Aron asked the male subject to pretend he was a captured soldier being tortured by the woman, who dripped a painful "acid" (actually water) on him from an eye-dropper until he confessed military secrets. Aron encouraged the male subjects to really get into their roles, acting as if they feared for their lives as the imaginary acid burned through their skin. In the control scenario, the subjects were asked to play the same roles but without the torture or high emotion. Afterward, the male subjects were asked to complete a Thematic Apperception Test (TAT). A fixture of psychological studies, a TAT depicts an ambiguous scene and asks subjects to describe what is happening. The men who had been through the high-emotion role play were far more apt than those in the control group to describe the scene as sexual. On a separate questionnaire, they were also more apt than those in the control to say they wanted to kiss the woman. Interestingly, there was no difference between the high-emotion and low-emotion groups in the number of men who wanted the woman as either a work partner or friend. It was, for Aron, a eureka moment. An emotionally stimulating situation didn't necessarily make you want to be friends or colleagues with attractive strangers. But it could make you hot for them.

Aron wanted to see if he could repeat the experiment outside the lab. The result—a 1974 study titled "Some Evidence for Heightened Sexual Attraction Under Conditions of High Anxiety"—would become one of the most talked-about papers in social psychology. In it, Aron and a colleague, Donald G. Dutton, of the University of British Columbia, enlisted an attractive female student to stop men as they crossed one of two footbridges over Vancouver's Capilano Canyon. The first bridge, a long and narrow span made of wobbly wooden boards suspended from wire cables, was some 230 feet above rocky rapids and had low handrails and a tendency to sway underfoot. The second bridge—the control—was wide and solid, had high handrails, and was just ten feet above a small stream.

The woman stopped unaccompanied men who looked between eighteen and thirty-five years old and said she was doing a project for a psychology class on the effects of scenery on creativity. She showed the men a TAT drawing of a young woman covering her face with one hand and reaching out with the other. Then she asked them to write a short story about the scene. When they were done, she said she could say more about the experiment if they called her later. She wrote her name and phone number on a scrap of paper. (On the shaky bridge, she gave her name as Gloria, on the control bridge, Donna, so the researchers would know where the interviews had taken place if the men called.)

The findings were striking. The men on the shaky bridge had 75 percent more sexual imagery in their stories than those on the stable one. Moreover, half the men stopped on the shaky bridge called the woman, whereas just 12 percent of those on the solid one did. To rule out the possibility that the bridge crossers were self-selecting—perhaps the rickety span tended to attract thrill seekers with more testosterone—the researchers swapped the female student for a male one but otherwise left the experiment unchanged. Without a potential love object (and assuming, as the researchers seemed to do, that most of the men stopped were heterosexual), men on the shaky bridge were no more likely to write racy stories or call the interviewer later. (In most of these early experiments, men were cast as the pursuers and women as objects, but later studies, with the roles reversed, confirmed many of the findings.)

Researchers soon turned up more evidence for the aphrodisiacal effects of "arousal," which psychologists define as any state of heightened physiological activity, from a racing pulse to a rush of adrenaline. The stimulus, it turned out, didn't have to be anything as drastic as make-believe torture, a walk across a rickety bridge, or the anticipation—as in yet another experiment—of an electric shock. Physiological arousal could just as well come from listening to a Steve Martin comedy tape, being surprised by a loud noise, or even just running in place for a few minutes. In a 1989 study, researchers watching couples leave a theater observed more touching after a suspenseful movie than after a dull one. A headline in *Psychology Today* in the 1970s distilled the emerging findings: "Adrenaline Makes the Heart Grow Fonder."

When I tracked down Arthur Aron at Stony Brook University, where he now teaches, he said that one theory sees the arousal-attraction link as a cousin of the fight-or-flight response. When we're worked up—excited, upset, euphoric, jealous—we are more at the mercy of our most basic drives, not least the urge to reproduce. "You're not thinking as clearly," Aron told me, "and you focus on those biological responses to a situation that from an evolutionary standpoint are most prominent, and mating is one of them."

Advances in brain science would later identify another key chemical as dopamine, a pleasure-inducing neurotransmitter associated with reward-seeking, gambling, and drug addiction. It is closely related to adrenaline, and its levels in the body tend to rise and fall with those of testosterone, in both men and women. "Anything that's novel, scary, interesting, or new drives up dopamine in the brain, and that brain system is associated with feelings of romantic love," Helen Fisher, a renowned biological anthropologist at Rutgers University who has used brain scans to study the neural circuitry of love, told me when I called her on a recent spring day. "If a person you find attractive walks by at just such a moment, then, boom, you have love."

But is this good for evolution? I asked. Should you really be choosing a mate when you're, well, high? Fisher told me that the evolutionary value of the arousal-attraction link was the subject of debate. But she sees benefits. "The dopamine system may have originally developed to give you the energy and focus and motivation you need to cope with a new situation. Romantic love may have piggybacked on that, so that when you're suddenly in a situation of real danger, you fall in love with somebody, and then you have someone to get you through the situation." She pointed to a recent article about the brisk business among wedding planners in Iraq. "In wartime," Fisher said, "people really fall in love."

Aron was blunter: "There's a huge evolutionary advantage to *anything* that gets people together." From a strict Darwinian perspective, he seemed to be saying, the quality of a relationship matters less than the quantity of offspring. He shakes his head now when he thinks about those grant makers in the 1960s who thought love unworthy of scholarship. "From a scientific point of view, understanding initial attraction is enormously important," he said. "Who we are today is determined by who our ancestors were *and* who they were attracted to. If your mother and father weren't attracted to each other, you wouldn't be here."

Sobering thought. But was there anything besides arousal that fanned attraction among strangers? The environmental psychologists Albert Mehrabian and James A. Russell sifted the fairy dust and found a few other ingredients. For a place to make strangers want to "affiliate," it should be not just arousing but "pleasant" and at least a little "dominance-eliciting." That is, it should make us feel good and, to a lesser extent, in control. Water-skiing across a mountain lake on a warm day, dancing to a band at a wild party in an old barn, and riding a motorcycle down a country road at sunrise were the sorts of scenarios that put subjects in the mood, they found. Walking into your apartment and finding dirty dishes or cooking in a steamy, foul-smelling kitchen with shouting children underfoot were not. A shortcoming of the Mehrabian-Russell experiment, however, was that it didn't look at actual places. Instead, the researchers asked a few hundred University of California undergraduates to read short descriptions of hypothetical settings, imagine they were actually there, and then answer a questionnaire about their "desire to affiliate."

Later researchers, however, took such studies to the street. In the early 1980s, a pair of social psychologists in Australia, Paul R. Amato and Ian R. McInnes, sent assistants to twelve places, among them a public beach, a small park, a shopping mall, and a construction site. The assistants initiated eye contact with strangers, smiled, and said hello. Then they recorded the strangers' responses. Did they return eye contact? Smile? Speak? The results raised immediate doubts about the then-fashionable theory of "cognitive overload." That theory had gained ground in the years after a young bar manager, Kitty Genovese, was stabbed to death near her home in Queens, New York, while not one of thirty-eight bystanders called the police. In an influential 1970 article in *Science* magazine, the psychologist Stanley Milgram had argued that the noise, traffic, and crowds of cities were so overwhelming that residents adapted to the overstimulation by tuning out the needs of strangers. Hence, the archetype of the brusque New Yorker, too busy to give you the time of day.

Amato and McInnes, however, found that people in highly stimulating settings could be very amiable, so long as the setting was pleasant. Take, for example, a party, a pickup basketball game, or a downtown pedestrian shopping mall. "Of course, urban settings that are congested, noisy, and dirty (such as the construction sites in the present research) are unpleasant places to be, and hence unlikely to be 'friendly,' places," they wrote. But "people are often attracted to . . . large cities because of the high level of stimulation that they offer. To the extent that complex, highly loaded, arousing environments make people feel good, they should facilitate, rather than inhibit, affiliative and prosocial forms of behavior." Nor, they noted, should anyone idealize the social lives of country folk. "Indeed," the researchers wrote, "complaints about living in rural areas frequently include the comments that life is boring, there is little to do, and that nothing ever happens."

What makes a setting pleasant, of course, is somewhat subjective. But studies have found a few near-universals. We like a moderate level of complexity—a mix of shapes, textures, and activity. We like focal points that command the eye and help organize our surroundings. We like water. We like mystery: a feeling that just out of sight there is more to explore. This explains our yen for winding paths and rolling hills. But we also like "legibility." That is, we want a sense of our bearings so that even as we wander, we never feel wholly lost. We also like some feeling of enclosure, a sense of containment, as in the streets of old European cities. Contrast the uplift you feel in Venice's Piazza San Marco or Paris's Luxembourg Gardens with the vulnerability you feel in Boston's City Hall Plaza, and you get the picture. "I think it's instinctual," Steve Lopez, a Los Angeles architect, told me. "It's the same reason early man lived in caves. You're protected. You're not all alone on a plain unsure of when a lion might pounce."

In 2005, Andrew Stuck, an urban design consultant in London, began leading groups of single people on walks through major cities. "Together we will devise an index of romance that anyone can apply to any town or city, so they can create a place that generates passion," he wrote in a newspaper ad seeking recruits for one of his first "Romantic Walkshops," in Toronto. He paired the men and women and urged them to pay attention to their surroundings. Afterward, he asked participants to identify turn-ons in the physical environment. In cities as diverse as Barcelona, Zurich, and Melbourne, he found a remarkable consistency. People liked hidden spaces and shifting elevations (mystery), fountains (water), and contrasts of lighting, ground surfaces, and building styles (complexity).

Helen Fisher, the expert on the brain chemistry of love, is a native New Yorker who lives on the Upper East Side. A devotee of what she calls "urban hiking," she told me she knows "every inch" of Central Park and spent many hours in Washington Square Park in the mid-1960s as an undergraduate at New York University. It is no surprise, she said, that people visiting Manhattan landmarks should meet and fall in love. "Those are supremely good places," she said. "They're open, they're full of street life, they're exciting, they're full of novelty and adventure— and that drives up dopamine in the brain and can push you over the edge into falling in love."

Ever mindful of biology, she flirted with an idea I had yet to consider: busy public spaces, of the sort found in Manhattan, are excellent places to size up the Darwinian fitness of prospective mates. How does an object of attraction assert himself in a crowd? How does she react to stress? Is he physically coordinated? In public settings, away from the comforts and crutches of home, "you see more of the person."

|||

IN MARCH 2009, I went to see Fred Kent, the founder and president of Project for Public Spaces, a Manhattan nonprofit that advises clients around the world on people-friendly design. Kent is a disciple of Whyte's, and his organization, a few blocks from Washington Square, is acclaimed for the life it has injected into tired parks and plazas. I wanted to road test the studies I was reading, and I knew that the Project for Public Spaces had succeeded in large part by discounting arid academic research in favor of intuition, pragmatism, and observation.

Kent, looking in his blue fleece vest and open-collared dress shirt like somebody's fun uncle from Minnesota, joined me at a circular table outside his office. Was there any basis in the real world, I asked, to the notion that great public places could kindle attraction among strangers? Or was I just working myself into a lather over nothing?

Kent was one of Whyte's young assistants on The Street Life Project, and he recounted some of the researchers' least expected findings. Lovers, they saw, kissed not in the secluded back areas of parks and plazas, where one might have guessed, but right out front, in the most visible spots. Also, the most crowded public places had far higher ratios of women to men than did the emptiest, which tended to be dominated by men. Women, it turned out, were more discriminating. The ratios were a barometer of a place's comfort and safety.

Over the course of hundreds of projects, however, Kent had gone Whyte one further. His staff, he said, had developed an unofficial metric for judging the success of a public place: the number of people publicly displaying affection. Kent doesn't always share this litmus test with clients, who tend to want harder data. But it is nearly infallible.

"We're always asked to quantify what is a good place: you've got to have economic numbers, you've got to have statistical analysis," Kent said. "But we know right away if a place is good if people are kissing, if they're affectionate."

That affection—whether between lover and lover, parent and child, or dog and owner—is a goalpost in the Project for Public Spaces's approach to urban design. "We've always thought about, Well, how do you create a little place that people will come into and drop their guard and smile at someone else? How do you create that little opportunity, that little incident that then helps you start connecting?"

A key, he said, borrowing one of Whyte's terms, is "triangulation."

"You need what we say is the Power of Ten. If you enter, say, Central Park, and you have ten little things going on there, from flowers, to a little sign, to a bench, to a coffee cart, it's a sense of richness that gives you that little 'aha.' You can just see people: they might be walking faster, but then they slow down, and then they start taking things in and they've changed. You can almost feel a smile coming onto their body. I think there are probably more proposals to marry in public places than anywhere else."

||||

AFTER A few months of research, the notes I'd taken from dozens of studies began to gel into a coherent picture. I started to glimpse a nexus between passion and place, between architecture and attraction. The findings were tantalizing. But I began to feel that something was missing. The results had been gleaned from lab experiments or anonymous observation. They lacked the warp and weft of real life. The experiments registered the first stirrings of attraction. But then what? Most of the undergrads used as guinea pigs in those studies no doubt went back to their lives, embarrassed to realize that the experiment's "attractive subject" was actually a "confederate" of their professor. Whyte made remarkable discoveries. But what became of the chance meetings he observed? What of those people the next day? The next year?

I knew what psychologists had surmised. I had read the sociologists' treatises and the architects' manifestos. But I am a storyteller by trade. What if I found couples who had actually met in public? What if those chance encounters had led not just to an exchange of smiles and a batting of eyelashes, but to a wedding day? What might the long and winding path of real life tell us that no amount of academic study could?

I wanted to find out. I chose New York City as my laboratory and began a search for couples. I plumbed decades of wedding announcements. I scoured online newspaper archives. I posted details about my search on Craigslist and on blogs about Manhattan and weddings. I spread word among friends and acquaintances. I took out a classified ad in *The New York Review of Books*. I enlisted a summer intern to buttonhole staff at Manhattan landmarks and ask, "Do you know any great love stories that started here?" I called priests and rabbis, wedding planners and wedding photographers. Several who wanted to help told me I was wasting my time. These days, they said, many people were meeting online, through dating websites. But I persevered. And soon I had more stories than I could fit in this book.

Why New York City? Some reasons, to be sure, are personal. I've already mentioned my mother and father's meeting in Washington Square Park, and the many years my mother's parents lived there. I was born in Manhattan, and though my family moved to Los Angeles when I was a toddler, we visited often. In the monotony and sprawl of Southern California, I often longed for the compactness and vertical grandeur of New York. Manhattan is also where my mother's grandfather, Chaim Boris Kruger, entered the United States, in 1902. With just nine rubles in his pocket, H.B., as he was known, settled in the Bronx and worked his way up from newspaper deliveryman to Harlem newsstand owner before opening a shirt company. Writing in his diary a few days after his ship landed, H.B., then twenty-one, sounded like so many newcomers before and since. "I would like to fall in love or to get into a noble cause for all mankind," he wrote. But H.B. was downcast and lonely—"sometimes I suffer without any reason"—until he met one Dora Rubin. An entry on the very last page of his dairies, from May 1904, which I discovered only recently, stopped me cold. It wasn't just that Dora had proposed marriage to H.B.; it was where she did it. "On Williamsburg Bridge," H.B. had written, "we confessed the words of everlasting love."

But there are other, more legitimate reasons. New York is America's most populous city, and its best-known. Even before Ellis Island opened its doors to the world's unwashed, the city served as America's immigrant gateway, an enclave packed with people of every tongue and color. More so than in any other American city, routine contact with strangers is a fixture of public life. Squares, parks, landmarks, museums—even the subway— were in some ways perfect laboratories for the questions that had captivated me. Unlike schools, offices, or houses of worship, public places often draw people with little in common. In big cities, they attract so many tourists that any two strangers—or "unacquainted dyads," in psychology lingo—could well share nothing so much as citizenship, let alone a ZIP code. They were good spots, I thought, to isolate the romantic effects of place.

|||

NEW YORK City was not built to be beautiful. The commissioners who drew its seminal 1811 street plan rejected the rounded forms of places like Washington, D.C., in favor of a simple grid of narrow streets and wide avenues. New York was a financial capital, and its layout, they felt, should reflect economic exigencies. The commissioners wrote that they considered whether "to confine themselves to rectilinear and rectangular streets, or whether they should adopt some of those supposed improvements, by circles, ovals and stars, which certainly embellish a plan, whatever may be their effects to convenience and utility." In the end, they decided that "they could not but bear in mind that a city is to be composed principally of the habitations of men, and that straight-sided, right-angled homes are the most cheap to build, and the most convenient to live in. The effect of these plain and simple reflections was decisive."

Because the city was ringed by water, they reasoned, residents would have plenty of fresh air. So why waste precious space on parks or public squares?

But by the mid-nineteenth century, as New York became the country's most populous city and its financial stronghold, its elite clamored for equal footing with the grand capitals of Europe. Great cities, they saw, needed great public spaces. Civic leaders and philanthropists pressed. Soon, a pantheon of visionaries built: Frederick Law Olmsted, Calvert Vaux, Whitney Warren, Richard Morris Hunt, Stanford White, Frédéric Auguste Bartholdi, and Ignaz Anton Pilat. Before long, the grid sprouted one of the country's most impressive collections of landmarks and public spaces: Central Park, the Empire State Building, Grand Central Terminal, the Metropolitan Museum of Art, the Statue of Liberty, Times Square, Washington Square Park. I was drawn to these places not just for their outstanding design. It was also that, in a city determined to remake itself every few years, these places were survivors. Over a yearlong search, I tracked down couples who had met by chance in each of those seven places and in two others—the subway and the street—that I saw as cornerstones of New York's public landscape. The couples' stories are this book's heart.

Olmsted was rhapsodizing about his newly built Central Park and Prospect Park in an address to social scientists in 1870, but he might as well have been talking about any of New York's extraordinary public places. Inside, he said, you will find people "with an evident glee in the prospect of coming together, all classes largely represented, with a common purpose, not at all intellectual, competitive with none, disposing to jealousy and spiritual or intellectual pride toward none, each individual adding by his mere presence to the pleasure of all others, all helping to the greater happiness of each. You may thus often see vast numbers of persons brought closely together, poor and rich, young and old, Jew and Gentile."

These places not only bind people of widely different circumstances. They also hurry heartbeats and flood veins with adrenaline. Lean from the wind-lashed observatory atop the Empire State Building and look down, your stomach dropping, at a city becalmed. Steam across New York Harbor until the sheer mass of the Statue of Liberty overhangs you, upsetting every sense of earthly proportion. Wade into the permanent sunshine of Times Square at midnight and lose yourself, for a moment, in the madness of crowds. And pleasure? It is everywhere. It is in the sight of Alice of Wonderland in Central Park, and in the voices of folk singers in Washington Square Park. It is in the flutter of whispers along the arch at Grand Central Terminal, and in the sanctuary hush of the back galleries of the Metropolitan Museum of Art.

People. Adrenaline. Pleasure. The makings of attraction are all there.

|||

THE COUPLES in this book hail from across America and the world. Most don't live in New York City. Some never did. What mattered to me was that they met there, in one of its iconic public places. Each of the nine stories begins just before that chance meeting—when they are strangers, oblivious to how, in moments, their lives will irrevocably change. The stories, each a separate chapter, span from the early 1940s to the present. A look at where the couples are now appears in a set of postscripts at the end of the book.

I am deeply indebted to the couples for their good humor and patience with what must have seemed like an onslaught of questions about some of the most intimate moments in their lives. Their willingness to make their stories public, I discovered, often had nothing to do with vanity. Several saw their first encounters as an affirmation of the everyday miracle that is New York. Others said they simply wanted to set something beautiful in the world.

Surveys show that even with the rise in Internet dating, most people still meet their partners through their circle of friends. In one recent study, just 6 to 9 percent of married people reported meeting their spouses in a public place, though what share of those meetings were chance encounters is impossible to tell. Still, there is an undeniable poetry to love born of chance. And for such a chance, there remains a stubborn yearning. To find believers, you need look no further than the "Missed Connections" or "I Saw You" listings that fill the back pages of newspapers and websites.

In Shakespeare's *As You Like It*, Rosalind says of the chemistry between her sister and Orlando's brother, "No sooner met but they looked; no sooner looked but they loved."

For many of us, such meetings will never overspill the banks of fantasy. Then there are the few—might it be you?—with the luck, or sense, to be in exactly the right place.

A Note on Method

To write these stories, I conducted hours of interviews with each of the couples. In most cases, I first spoke with husband and wife separately, by phone, to capture the start of relationships from each spouse's point of view. In some cases, I also talked with friends and relatives to help flesh out parts of the story. Then I visited each couple in person—trips that took me to California, Illinois, Indiana, Virginia, and across New York. Most of the couples were unflinchingly generous, sharing not just the details of their lives but photos, notebooks, newspaper clippings, letters, drawings, timelines, and diaries. I complemented the interviews with library research on New York City architecture and history and with extended visits, with a camera and notepad, to the places where the couples met.

In the interviews, I pressed the couples for details of conversations during their first meetings. I asked about their thoughts and feelings at turning points in their stories and about their broader values, fears, and aspirations. I also wanted the specifics of key scenes: what places looked and smelled and sounded like. In some cases, however, many years had passed since the events. Where memory fell short of perfect, I allowed myself to imagine plausible dialogue and minor scenic detail. In every instance the imagined dialogue or detail was an outgrowth of what I knew of the couples, the places they inhabited and their times. In the interest of bringing these stories to life and deepening their larger meanings, I permitted myself this small artistic license.

For reasons of privacy, couples were given the option of changing their names. Three of the nine chose to do so; the use of pseudonyms in those cases is noted in the postscripts at the end of the book. The names of minor characters in some of the stories were changed.

Green

CENTRAL PARK

The 843 acres of winding paths,
rolling meadows, and water at the heart of Manhattan
offer an illusion of unspoilt wilderness—of an island
before the invasion of bricks and people and concrete.
But in truth, Central Park is as man-made as the
surrounding city. It is not an original landscape, but the
painstaking articulation of a social philosophy: that a
city riven by economic stratification owed its masses an
oasis from the ravages of toil. "It is one great purpose of
the Park," wrote Frederick Law Olmsted, its chief
designer, "to supply to the hundreds of thousands of tired
workers, who have no opportunity to spend their
summers in the country, a specimen of God's handiwork
that shall be to them, inexpensively, what a month or
two in the White Mountains or the Adirondacks is, at
great cost, to those in easier circumstances." Olmsted's
partner, Calvert Vaux, was more succinct: he wanted to
"translate democratic ideas into trees and dirt."

The chill fingers of fall touched down in the city, and Joey Filip, eighteen, pulled her jacket tight as a gust of wind rattled the awnings over the store windows on Fifth Avenue. Shivering, she paid a street vendor a nickel for a box of cigarettes. She had never smoked before, but on this cold September day in 1941, with clouds unfurling across the sky, she liked the thought of drawing hot smoke into her lungs. Of burning inside.

"You're going to hell," her mother had shouted a few weeks before, as Joey ran down her driveway in Passaic, New Jersey, with a sack of clothes. Her father, the only person she felt had ever understood her, had died in July. Her mother, an observant Catholic, had demanded she follow her older sisters into a convent. Joey ran away from home instead.

Her first night in the city, she slept on the subways. She needed a job, but would anyone in this big city hire a mill hand with little education and no one to vouch for her?

On her left, the stores with glittering things in the windows gave way to the arching trees of Central Park. Joey, her feet throbbing, turned onto a path that dipped through greens planted with tall elms.

There must be benches here, she thought. Maybe even a hiding place, where I can lie down for the night. She studied the spaces between the trees, some so close together they shrouded the understory in shadow.

A cackle from somewhere behind her right shoulder made her jump. She turned to see a pair of women in fur coats, with jewels at their throats and gentlemen on their arms.

"Charlie, you in the mood for a highball?" one of the women said.

"When is Charlie *not* in the mood?" said the other, as the group exploded in a howl of laughter.

Joey ducked away to let the group pass. They showed not the slightest awareness of her.

|||

EVERYWHERE Quartermaster Third Class Willis Langford looked in Central Park, there were girls. And the variety! Rounded and thin. Some with the rouged cheeks of angels, others with the darkened eyes of devils. There were broads and dames. Sweet patooties and shebas.

"Swell to be back on land," Willis said, shimmying his chest so his uniform straightened over his tall, lean frame.

"And how," said his shipmate, Joe.

It was hard to tell from the proud, ruler-straight way Willis carried himself, but he'd grown up poor on the outskirts of Victoria, Texas, the son of subsistence farmers. With no other prospects—his grades, at an unaccredited high school, would impress no college—he answered a postcard from the Navy that arrived a few days before graduation. The Navy promised adventure and, more important, a living. Enough money to send home to his nine younger siblings—all girls—who spent summers barefoot because there was no money for shoes.

Serving on a coastal gunboat off South China for the past two years, Willis had sent his family fifteen dollars a month, out of his salary of twenty-one dollars. Liberty was cramped enough in Asia, with its different customs and language. But it could be downright frustrating if all you had in your billfold was six dollars. While shipmates were drinking themselves into a stupor in bars in Hong Kong or the Philippines, Willis often found himself on solo walking tours through town. And so yes, back in America for a few weeks, awaiting new orders, Willis, twenty-two years old, with dark hair, thick eyebrows, and a leading man's smile, was ready to have a little fun.

Liberty came early on September 11, 1941, and sailors at the Naval receiving station on Manhattan's Pier 51 didn't have to be back until eight the next morning. "This could be a long night," Joe said, jutting his chin at a pair of smartly dressed young women who were just then passing. "Ready to start the hunt?"

"How about the lake over there," said Willis, nodding to a green crescent of water visible through some trees where couples in rowboats were paddling.

"Fish?" Joe smirked. "I thought you boys from the country liked big game."

|||

JOEY SAT on a bench at the edge of a curving walk, just before it dropped and wound under a short bridge. Every time a man who looked like Steve walked by, she felt the fury inside her. A crumb. A cad. A heel. There was no word strong enough for him.

She had met Steve at the woolen mill in Passaic that had hired her as a spool girl after she ran away from home. She fell in love with him—he was older, a supervisor at the mill, but what did that matter? He was a gentleman. He even bought her a ring. Then, one morning, another girl whispered that Steve was married. He'd preyed on other spool girls before, she told Joey, seducing them with false promises of marriage before throwing them over for someone new.

Joey had felt so sick at the news that she left the mill in the middle of a shift, never to return. She scampered, sobbing, to her boardinghouse, where she persuaded a young man she cared nothing for to take her to a bar. After three glasses of beer, she returned to her room and opened a bottle of iodine that some other boarder had left in a closet. Priests said that people who took their own lives went straight to hell. But hell, whatever it was, couldn't be as bad as the past few months of her life.

The liquid stained her lips blue and burned the back of her throat. Before the dizziness set in and she heard the bottle crash against the floor, she thought, Was my father the only good man in the world?

The sky over Central Park was darkening, and the wind shook the trees. Joey felt a twinge in her stomach, and gulped down the bile at the back of her throat. She hadn't eaten since the night before, but she would make herself wait. There was no money for food. The wind was blowing so hard now that she could not keep the match burning. She left her sack on the bench and walked into the underpass of a short footbridge. There, shielded from the wind, she struck another a match and, with a trembling hand, raised it to her lips.

|||

THE SAILORS rounded a sharp curve beside the lake. A flotilla of ducks glided over the rumpled surface, trailed by a lone swan.

"Any scoop on where Uncle Sam's gonna ship you?" Joe asked.

"Heard an officer talking about one of those new net tenders," said Willis.

"You mean the ones with the horns? Those things give me the heebie-jeebies."

"Look like walruses."

"Beats me how Roosevelt thinks we'd ever bag a German sub with one of them."

"Trapping subs? Officer told me we'd just be primping buoys."

Ahead, where the walk sloped down, a girl in a beige coat was leaning against the abutment of a low bridge. Willis elbowed Joe in the arm and nodded. The girl's face was pale. She was so skinny it was hard to make out her age. The sailors slowed down.

"What's she doin'?" Joe whispered, leaning in.

"Think she's trying to light a cigarette." Willis put his hands in his pockets and strode toward her.

"Ma'am, can I help you with that?"

The girl jumped at the sound of his voice, took him in with a flash of fluttering eyelashes, then turned away, toward the darkness of the tunnel. She pulled her coat around her.

"It's just that, you see, ma'am, the fire stays better if you cover the match with your hand. Something you learn real quick on a ship."

Looking over her shoulder, and seeming to take his measure, the girl sputtered, "Why should I care? I don't even smoke."

"You are holding a cigarette, ma'am."

Silence.

"Okay, so you don't smoke. What about eat? You do that?"

She turned around, backing into the abutment, and narrowed her eyes into a scowl. "Don't be a goof."

"It's just, you look hungry, ma'am, like a starved kitten I once found," Willis said. "I'd like to buy you dinner is all."

She turned her head away and raised her chin. "You don't even know my name."

"I was about to ask."

"You want a cigarette? Is that why you're talking to me?"

Willis took a few steps back and glanced over his shoulder at his friend, who had taken a seat on a bench a few paces up the path. "I'll leave you be, ma'am. Good evening."

"It's Paula, if you must know."

"Pardon?" Willis had already turned to leave, but pivoted now.

"My name. But they call me Joey because my middle name's Josephine, and the kids in school used to say I was a tomboy."

"My name's Willis, or Bill's okay, too. And if you don't mind my saying, ma'am, you look like no boy I've ever met."

She felt heat rush to her face. Before she could think the better of it, she pinched the sides of her jacket and did a small curtsy.

"Gosh, I sure am hungry," Willis said, putting on his best smile.

Joey pointed her elbow at the bench. "Who's your friend?"

"Who, that fella? Oh, that's just Joe, just met him down at the pier."

Joe lifted his cap and hollered. "Glad to meet you ma'am."

"Joe was about to hit the silk," Willis said, winking at his shipmate.

"He's right, ma'am," Joe said. "Got someplace I need to be."

Joey raised a delicate-looking hand and gave an emphatic wave. "Farewell," she said, smiling. Then, without warning, she wound a small scarf around her neck, brushed past Willis and strode down the walk, plucking her sack from the bench. "I don't eat much," she called without looking back.

Catching up with her, Willis said, "I know just the place."

||||

AT A diner off Fifth Avenue, the waitress brought two plates of chicken with cream gravy and two glasses of beer.

Joey heaped forkfuls into her mouth, barely looking up from her plate.

"You make a habit of lollygagging in parks alone?" Willis asked.

She swallowed a mouthful of chicken and let her glance fall on the spoon beside her plate. "It's not what you think," she said. "I'm a good girl."

"How about I talk for a spell," Willis said. "You eat."

He told her doozies about being the only boy in a houseful of girls. He told her about reading every Zane Grey book he could get his hands on—had she ever heard of him? "He's the best scribbler in the U.S. of A.," he said. He talked about how his Texas hometown during the Great Depression wasn't so unlike the Old West. He said his grandfather, a genial old man who loved regaling his grandchildren with cowboy stories, had been working on a construction site when for reasons no one ever figured out someone cut him down with a shotgun.

"That's awful," Joey said, with a look Willis took for genuine sadness.

"He was a good man. A real good man. I miss him."

When Willis looked up, he saw that Joey was in tears.

"What is it, darlin'?" Willis said. He wondered if the beer had gone to her head.

"My poppa," she said, and the tears ran harder now. Willis reached for the napkin dispenser. "He died just a while ago," she said, pressing the napkin to her cheeks.

"Was he old?"

"No. Young. The doctor said it was lead that killed him. He mixed rubber at the tire plant. The gases, they say, were something awful."

"If he raised you up, Joey," Willis said, "he must have been a good man."

"A saint," she said. Then came another round of tears and more of the story. She had been the youngest of six in their small home in Passaic. Her older sisters tormented her. And when her father, her only protector, died, no one understood how she felt. Instead, her mother seemed to live to make her life miserable. She demanded Joey quit school and follow her older sisters into a life of chastity at a nunnery. When Joey refused, her mother raged, calling her "boy crazy" and destined for the agonies of hell. Joey ran away from home, found a mill job, and fell in love—only to discover that the man already had a wife.

"I wanted to die. I didn't do that right, either."

"I thank God you didn't, Joey, or else this would have been a pretty lonely dinner," Willis said, trying in vain to make her laugh. The skin around her eyes, he saw, was so pale that he could make out the blue veins underneath.

"I was two weeks in the hospital," she said. "You know how many times my mom and my sisters visited?"

Willis shook his head.

"Not once." The day the hospital discharged her, she said, she took a train to New York, hoping to find a job that would let her live on her own.

The more she spoke, the more Willis found himself drawn in by her helplessness. He was miles from Victoria, but he had seen the same broken look on the faces of sharecroppers back home, the ones beaten down by hurricanes and hard times. Something about her—he wasn't sure what—reminded him of the feral cats he'd taken to pouring bowls of milk for on the farm. Maybe it was a product of being a big brother to so many sisters, but he'd always been drawn to helpless things. And because of his height and sympathetic face, it seemed, they'd been drawn to him.

The waitress set down two tin cups of vanilla ice cream. Joey pecked at hers joylessly, then set down her spoon. "I won't fail next time," she said darkly. "I won't."

"Joey, please listen to me," Willis said. "I know troubles. My mom and pop are farmers, and dirt poor to boot. We got through the Depression by the skin of our teeth and because weak folks leaned on stronger ones until they could stand again on their own. It's only right that you let me help you."

"The food," she said, waving at the empty plate. "You already have. I don't need anything else."

"Let me give you some money for a room," he said. "The streets are no place for a pretty thing like you."

Fear clouded her face. "No," she said, shaking her head and pushing back her chair suddenly. "No."

"Oh, golly, Joey, it's nothing like that," he said, excoriating himself for his choice of words. He reached into his pocket and pulled out ten dollars. "Take it and leave. I'll stay in this booth. There's a cup of uneaten ice cream to keep me company for at least another half hour. Don't tell me where you're going. Just go somewhere safe."

"No," she said. "No, no. Thank you—it's swell. No."

He took a deep breath and looked over his shoulder at the streaking headlights of passing cars. "All right," he said, patting the table with a note of finality. "Then I'll stay up with you. We can walk the streets together. All night if we have to."

Pushing a loose curl behind her ear, Joey gave a half smile and choked back a laugh. "You're loony, you know that? You've got rocks in your head."

|||

ON THE sidewalk outside, the throngs of businessmen were thinning and the shopkeepers were locking up for the night. The air felt warmer, and, looking up, Joey could see that clouds were parting, and there were stars. The sailor and the runaway walked together under the streetlights on Fifth Avenue, stopping in front of the closed shops and admiring the mannequins in high-stepping clothes.

"If only I were rich," Joey said, shaking her head at the mink stole in one window.

"Just make believe is what I do."

She gave him a quizzical look.

"Follow along," he said, stopping in front of the windows of a fancy dress shop. "Here! See that gown? I've just bought it for you. Why, the looks you'll get at the ball tonight! The dress is just as yellow as your hair and just as pretty."

Joey tittered.

"And this fur, and those shoes," he said, stopping at the next store window and turning to an imaginary sales clerk. "Wrap them in tissue, and add it to my account."

At the haberdashery down the street, Joey joined the charade. "Now, what do you think of this suit, Admiral Bill?" she asked.

"Aces."

"And that tie, in the corner, does it go with brown eyes?"

"If you say so, darling."

"Consider it yours."

She looped her hand through Willis's arm, and at times had to skip to keep up with his longer strides. They sauntered up and down Fifth Avenue for the next hour, putting together a complete trousseau for her, a swank civilian wardrobe for him, and, for both of them, a set of parlor- and dining-room furniture for what Willis called "our house." By midnight, they were punch-drunk from laughter. They stumbled back into the park and, after a few false turns, found the bridge where they'd met. The sky winked with stars, and the air was grass-scented and clean. From the lake, somewhere behind them, came an occasional plunking sound. Joey imagined toads springing off rocks into the water.

They lay down under a tree, in the shadows away from the path, and spread Joey's long wool coat over their chests. Joey curled into Willis, and, chastely, he cradled her head, a pillow of soft curls, against his chest. She fell asleep almost instantly. As he drifted off, Willis could hear short, rhythmic breaths that reminded him of his younger sisters', when they had been babies, in their cribs back in Texas, long ago.

|||

DAWN BROKE warmer than the day before, and the low-hanging sun fringed the buildings along Fifth Avenue in vermillion. Willis rubbed sleep from his eyes and, in a half-panic, glanced at his watch. It was 7:30 a.m. He was due back at the base in a half hour.

"Oh, darling," he said. "It's time."

Rolling out of his arms, she propped her elbow on the grass and rested her head on her hand. She wore a dreamy smile and reached over to finger a few blades of grass from Willis's hair. She felt happier than she had in a long time. It scared her a little, because the last time she'd been happy, it had been but a prelude to ruin.

"Time for what?" she said.

"Time for me to take a powder. Orders. Sailors gotta be back on base at zero eight hundred hours."

"Are you going somewhere? On a ship?" A smile clung to her lips, but it was fragile now. It was like one of those fallen leaves that look aflame with color, but break on touch into a million pieces.

"Darlin', the only thing sailors do at a receiving station is run in circles and twiddle our noses."

Joey laughed. "And such a pretty nose, too," she said, tapping his with her forefinger.

As Willis got up and brushed the leaves off his uniform, Joey's eyelids brimmed.

"Joey, I'm going to make you promise me something, okay?"

She nodded.

"That until I come back, you'll take care of yourself, you won't do anything stupid."

"You'll be back?"

"Yes, but you have to promise."

"I promise."

"Tonight, at six, as soon as we get liberty, all right?"

He pointed to a bench across the sloping lawn. It was at the edge of the path a few meters from the bridge they'd met under. "Where my friend Joe docked last night, remember? I'll meet you right there."

She touched the stubble on his cheeks, and then watched him—with that straight-backed, handsome frame—lope across the lawn and onto the curving path, until he was gone.

|||

NO SOONER had Willis passed through the security checkpoint at the pier than he sensed the air of commotion. Sailors were buzzing about with an intensity not often seen at a receiving station, where boredom and inaction were the rule.

"What's going on?" he asked.

"You haven't seen the paper?" A sailor tossed a copy of the *New York Times* onto his rack. A headline in large type said, "Roosevelt Orders Navy to Shoot First If Axis Raiders Enter Our Defense Zones."

Willis muttered, "Holy mackerel," and drew the newspaper close.

In his fireside chat to the nation the night before, President Roosevelt cataloged a series of unprovoked German attacks on U.S. vessels—including a recent torpedo strike on the destroyer *Greer*—and warned of an increasingly dangerous Nazi quest to conquer the Western Hemisphere through control of the seas.

"Holy moly," Willis said.

Roosevelt said he had ordered the Navy to destroy on sight any German or Italian submarines entering waters necessary for American defense. "The Nazi danger to our Western world has long ceased to be a mere possibility," the newspaper quoted the president as saying. "It is time for all Americans, Americans of all the Americas, to stop being deluded by the romantic notion that the Americas can go on living happily and peacefully in a Nazi-dominated world," he said. The time had come for America to tell the Germans, "You have now attacked our safety. You shall go no further."

That afternoon, an officer handed Quartermaster Third Class Langford orders for an immediate movement. He was to report that evening to the Philadelphia Naval Shipyard. Construction on an antisubmarine patrol craft was nearing completion there, and he was to join the crew.

Willis's first thought was of Joey, and their date that evening. "What about the net tender here?" he asked his officer.

"New priorities, sailor. Pack your sea bag."

Willis felt his heart in his chest. History was calling. He was ready. But the girl . . . With an hour left before his train to Philadelphia, he sat in the mess and composed a short note. "I'm so worried about you, honey," he wrote. "I'm afraid you'll die of pneumonia or hunger. But I don't blame you for not taking money. I respect you all the more. Keep your chin up, honey. You'll make a go. You have what it takes."

Willis ran into his friend Joe as he gathered his bags for the train. "I don't know what she'll do if she shows up and I'm not there," Willis said. "The girl's been through hell already."

"Gee, Bill, you'd hardly be the first swabbie to break a girl's heart."

"Just take this note to her, will you? Tell her what happened. That duty called. And that I'm sorrier than she'll ever know."

His note had no forwarding address.

||||

OVER THE next week and a half, Joey drifted through the streets of New York. Every day she felt more like a ghost. A lunch counter in the Bronx had given her a job as a waitress but decided after a couple of days that they didn't need her.

After a man had tried to grab her as she slept in the park, she took to spending the night on the subways. You could ride all night on a single token, she discovered, shuttling between Brooklyn and the Bronx. After a certain hour, the cars cleared out enough for a small woman to lie down on a bench and disappear under her coat. Tramps and loonies stalked through the cars in the wee hours, some staring, some muttering to themselves. Mostly, though, they left her alone. She slept until the start of the morning commute, when she was awakened by the sounds of serious men, with their stamping feet and clanking umbrellas and talk of stocks and the price of precious metals.

The clean clothes she had on when she arrived in New York were now streaked with grime. She had lost her scarf. The hem of her wool coat had started to blacken and unravel. Entering the washroom at Grand Central Terminal one morning, a matron in a fur coat looked at her and recoiled. Joey gazed at her reflection in the mirror and saw that her cheek was smudged black. Had she accidentally lain in something that night on the subway?

She had come with three dollars, and after the first week she was penniless. The nights grew colder, and, with no money for subway tokens, she returned to the bench in Central Park where Sailor Bill had told her to wait. She had managed to be angry for only a day. For a day, she had lumped him in with all the other scoundrels in her life, the ones who turned on her, who lied and left. But she couldn't keep it up. Not when she thought about his generosity, his restraint. If he wanted to give her the high hat, why would he have sent the note? Why, with no obvious advantage for himself, would he have tried to buck her up?

In her darkest moments, when she doubted the worth of her life, she reached into her stocking, where, against her ankle, she'd kept his letter. Sometimes she'd mouth the words aloud— "Keep your chin up. You'll make a go."—as if they might like a spell summon him back to the park, to this bench, beside her. For three nights in a row, she slept on the cold wooden planks. She looked in no more mirrors, for fear of what she might see. Early one morning, still half-asleep, she felt meaty fingers on her arm. She bolted up, shrieking, and swatted the air in front of her.

"Ma'am," came the man's voice. "Ma'am."

As her eyes adjusted to the light, she made out a tall man in a dark uniform standing over her.

"Ma'am," he said. "New York Police."

She stiffened, and frantically brushed flecks of dead leaves off her dress, now tattered at the sleeves.

"What do you want?"

"We've gotten some complaints, see. You got a place to stay?"

"No, sir."

"Somewhere to go to clean up, eat?"

"No, sir."

"Family, friends? Anyone to look after ya?"

She buried her face in her hands, shook her head, and began to sob.

"See, dollface, I gotta take you to the station on a charge of vagrancy," he said. "Central Park ain't a hotel, and, see, from what I hear you've been treating it like one."

She felt as though the ground was splitting beneath her.

"Don't be a pill, dollface, let's go." He hoisted her off the bench by her wrists, as thin as those of a girl half her age, and then guided her, a firm hand on her back, to a police car. She went along, rigidly at first, then without resistance, her eyes vacant, her face white as a shroud.

|||

AT THE Philadelphia Naval Shipyard, the imminent deployment Willis had hoped for never came. The patrol boat whose crew he was billeted for was still under construction. While other sailors, swaggering, headed off to sea on President Roosevelt's orders, Willis was mired in the kind of make-work that some sailors grimly called "shore duty."

He grew restless. The only true adventure since his return from the China seas was the night he'd met that sad and beautiful runaway on the streets of New York. A girl he knew he'd never see again.

|||

WHEN HELEN Worden entered the front office at the Women's House of Detention, in Greenwich Village, a guard by the door smirked and said, "Well, if it isn't our very own Girl Friday."

"Zip it, Charlie," Worden snapped. "The warden in?"

"What's hot?"

"I was hoping you could tell me. My editor's hungry for page-one color."

Possessed of an angelic face and big eyes, Worden studied art in Paris before joining the *New York World* as a society writer. Despite her Colorado upbringing—she was born in Denver—she styled herself a connoisseur of all things New York. She turned out no fewer than four books on the city from 1932 to 1939, with names like *The Real New York* and *Round Manhattan's Rim*, and prided herself on her nose for everyday human drama.

Her big break had come in 1938 with her story about the Collyer brothers, reclusive hoarders whose Harlem mansion was being slowly overtaken by their collections of thousands of books, newspapers, and musical instruments. Bent on getting their story, Worden staked out the house at night. When the younger brother—"a wisp of a man in janitor's overalls" with a "drooping Victorian mustache"—emerged briefly from a basement door, Worden cried out, "Good evening, Langley Collyer. Your neighbor tells me you keep a rowboat in the attic and a Ford in the basement. Is that true?" Worden's story about the "Hermits of Harlem" became a sensation and made her a star feature writer at the renamed *New York World-Telegram*.

Today, though, Worden was after smaller game: stories about women in the city lockup.

"Uh-oh, here she comes," the warden groaned. "Anything you know about my job that I don't yet?"

"Who, me?" Worden laughed, giving the warden a teasing glance. "I'm looking for human interest today."

"You mean like a sob story?"

"Why, you got one?"

|||

A POLICEWOMAN led Worden through an art-deco corridor to the cell block. Behind a row of iron bars, Worden glanced a wisp of a young lady slouched on a narrow bench jutting from the wall.

"Have at her," the policewoman said. "I'll be right outside."

The cell door clicked shut. The girl looked up expectantly. Worden gave a sympathetic smile and nodded at the bench. "May I?"

The girl nodded back.

"I'm a newspaper reporter, miss, and I'm writing about the jail and some of the women inside. I know a lot of the ladies never thought they'd wind up here. I'll bet a lot of them are good people who just had a patch of bad luck."

The girl's face brightened a little. "Yes, ma'am."

"Do you mind if I ask you a few questions?"

"No, ma'am."

"How long have you been here?"

"Four nights."

"How old are you?"

"Eighteen."

The girl, Worden noticed, was anxiously clasping and unclasping her hands.

"And, sweetheart, what's your name?"

"Josephine Filip," she said. "Or just Joey."

When the police had brought her to the station house a few days before, Joey refused to answer any of the desk lieutenant's questions. No name. No home address. No names of relatives. She didn't care what the police did with her.

But in the course of an hour, Worden had gotten the whole megillah.

|||

THE STORY ran that evening, on the *World-Telegram*'s front page. It would soon be transmitted by wire to newspapers across the country.

"Josephine Phillips"—the last name was changed somehow—"a thin, white-faced girl of 18, sat in the Women's House of Detention today and told how she came to be charged with vagrancy," it began.

The story told of Joey's fallout with her family, her ill-fated affair with a married man, her suicide attempt. And then the trip to New York, where she'd come in search of work and instead found a kind sailor named Bill, who was now somewhere far away. At the end of the interview, Worden wrote, Joey pulled out Bill's letter—"a worn sheet of paper covered with boyish handwriting."

"My life hasn't been a very pretty one," Joey told Worden. "You'd call it dull and sordid. About the only nice memory in it, outside my father, is Bill. My father's dead and Bill's gone. That's why I say 'memory.' Bill and I just saw each other one night, but I feel as if I'd known him always. I didn't have to explain things to him. He understood."

The two-column headline above the story read, "'It's Not Pretty'—Story of Girl's Life; Bill Found Her Hungry on Park Bench, Then His Ship Sailed."

It was a four-hanky weepie, if Worden's editor had ever seen one.

|||

WILLIS WAS on shore duty at the Philadelphia Naval Shipyard a couple of days later when a friend—a fellow sailor—approached in the afternoon with a grin and, folded under his arm, a Philadelphia newspaper. "That nutty story you told me, about meeting that girl in New York? The one I didn't believe?"

"Yeah."

"Looks like I'm eating crow. She spilled to the papers."

"Don't be a wise guy."

"The name Josephine mean anything to ya?"

Willis all but tore the paper from his friend's hands. Looking at the headline, he felt his knees go soft. The "Sailor Bill" in the story had no last name. But the way they met, the food they ate, his letter—it was all there. That night had felt so private, so seemingly unobserved, that he wondered sometimes whether any of it had happened. But here it was, all of it, down to the color of the sun as it rose the next morning, remade into a story.

"She's in jail," he stuttered, looking up, his voice hoarse with emotion. "If only I'd stayed in New York—"

"But she's alive, pal," his friend said. "And from the looks of the story, it's some thanks to you."

On the phone at the PX that evening, Willis's heart thudded in his ears as he asked the operator for the number for the *New York World-Telegram*.

The paper's switchboard made a few clicks. Then came a woman's staccato voice.

"Worden."

He told her he was the Sailor Bill in her story and wanted to know how to reach Josephine.

"Yeah, you and every other beard in this town."

"I swear on the Bible, ma'am," he said. "I'm a sailor. I'm not in New York. I'm here at the Philadelphia Navy Yard. What else you want to know?"

"Your last name." It was on the note Joey had shown Worden, but Worden had decided against putting it in the story.

He told her.

"Spell it."

"L-a-n-g-f-o-r-d."

"At ease, sailor," Worden said, her voice slackening. "All I can tell you is you made a real impression on this girl."

"Is she still in the brig?"

"Free as a bird, and looking better than ever. Some cousin in New Jersey saw my story, and got her sprung."

The cousin, one Blanche Kurowski, and her family had taken Joey in. They had already found her a job in the factory where Mrs. Kurowski had worked.

Willis had one last question for Worden: was there a phone number for this Mrs. Kurowski?

|||

WHEN MRS. Kurowski put Joey on the phone, Willis could hear the quiet sobs.

"You found me," Joey said, sniffling. "How I'd hoped it."

"I was so worried about you," Willis said.

"Are you still at sea?"

"Never got farther than Philadelphia."

"Oh, how I felt you were near."

"Are you with good people, Joey?"

"Oh, yes. Blanche is swell. One daughter, Phyllis, is my age. You'd like the whole family, Willis. They're already keen on you."

"I'd like to meet them."

That weekend, his first leave, Willis went to Philadelphia's Thirtieth Street Station and boarded a New York–bound train.

Blanche, an attractive thirty-six-year-old, opened the door to their small home, in Clifton, New Jersey, and threw her arms around Willis. "Oh, sweetie, we've heard so much—read so much—about you," she said. "Here, sweetie, come to the table, have some peach cobbler. Joey's still getting fixed up."

One of the youngest of Blanche's six children, Rosalie, a flirt at three, dashed over to Willis and hugged his knees. "Will you be *my* boyfriend?" she asked, looking up.

"You might be better off with someone your own age," Willis said, winking at Blanche.

When Joey stepped into the living room, Willis scarcely recognized her. She wore a crisp white calf-length dress, bright lipstick, and a relaxed smile. More than anything, she looked like she'd had a good night's sleep—perhaps several.

Willis stood up from his plate. As Blanche and her children looked on adoringly, he clasped both of Joey's hands. They stood there, fingers laced, for several minutes, studying each other's faces, grinning, and swaying slightly, as if dancing to a melody only they could hear.

Willis caught a late Sunday train back to Philadelphia but came back each of the next three weekends. With little money, they spent nearly all their time in the Kurowskis' apartment, gabbing with Blanche, playing games with her children, or snuggling on the couch. Joey is "with swell people now," Willis wrote to his mother in an October 15, 1941, letter. "They are her 'Mom' and 'Pop' in the real sense of the word and she calls them that. Mrs. Kurowski is thirty-six—a nice looking Polish woman. She treats everyone that will let her like they were one of her children. And she and the whole family are really swell to me, even the kids."

In another letter, to his cousin, he wrote that Joey "is beautiful and is a tomboy if ever there was one. She has a half-Nelson on my heart—all she has to do is put on a little pressure and who knows what might happen."

On a Saturday in early November, in the feathery evening light, Willis and Joey were talking near a washtub on the back porch. Willis leaned rakishly against the side of the tub, and Joey pressed her body against his, running her hands up his chest.

"Bill?"

"Let's get married, Joey," he said. "I know it's right."

"We'll make a family, okay?"

"Yes."

She gazed up into his eyes, searchingly, and, with her thumbs, smoothed away the creases on his brow.

Despite the sleep and the new clothes, Willis saw just how vulnerable she still was. He knew only that he wanted to protect her. "Yes, a family, Joey. A big one."

||||

WHAT THE young couple couldn't yet see was the approaching hurricane of publicity. Worden's story had landed on desks of important people on both coasts. In a country surfacing from the Great Depression and hungry for hopeful, all-American stories, the tale of the homeless waif and dashing sailor was irresistible.

David O. Selznick, the legendary movie producer who had recently won Academy Awards for *Gone with the Wind* and *Rebecca*, read the story in Hollywood. He saw it as a perfect match for a film he was planning, an anthology of shorts he called *Tales of Passion and Romance*. "It's a perfect episode as it stands,"

Selznick told the *World-Telegram* that October. "Jewel-like. Tiny, but complete. It seems to me to have some of the quality of O. Henry, some of the drama of New York." He didn't know when the movie would go into production, he told the paper, but he already had Gene Kelly in mind for the sailor and Ginger Rogers for Joey. Worden wired Willis a telegram with the good news.

In the meantime, the CBS radio show *We, the People* paid them fifty dollars each for an interview. The bandleader Harry James asked if Joey was available to appear with him on stage. *Life* magazine planned a two-page pictorial, with the couple re-enacting their romance for a photographer.

When word leaked of plans for a November 20 wedding—Thanksgiving—news reporters worked themselves into a purple-tinged lather. Glamorous portraits of the good-looking couple appeared in papers from the *Los Angeles Times* to the *Washington Post*.

"Sailor Prince Charming to Wed N.Y. Park Waif in Story-Book Romance," screamed the headline in *Philadelphia Inquirer*.

"Park Cinderella Weds Her Hero," the Associated Press said.

"Love Found a Way Today," said the United Press.

"Sailor, Park Bench Waif Marry Today." "Marriage Is Sequel to Previous Drab, Unhappy Life." "She'll Marry Her Bill, to End Modern O. Henry Yarn." "It's Like a Fairy-Tale." And for a few days, it was. For a few days, it felt as though the whole world were toasting their happiness.

More than three hundred people—among them celebrities and news photographers—crammed into the Garfield, New Jersey, City Hall to watch the "park bench Cinderella" and the "husky tar from the Philadelphia Navy Yard" exchange vows. The thirty-two-year-old mayor, John Gabriel, who had already played host at a wedding feast at the nearby Swiss Chalet, officiated. The Montauk Dress Shop of Passaic, Joey's hometown, donated a gauzy white wedding gown with Hungarian peasant touches and a fingertip-length veil (Willis wore his dashing dress blues).

A Philadelphia jeweler donated gold wedding bands carved to resemble interlacing orange blossoms. Tom's Flower Shop of Garfield contributed the wedding decorations and a pom-pom bouquet of white chrysanthemums. David Selznick sent a sixty-two-piece silver dinner set.

Blanche stood beside the bride as the matron of honor. With Joey's father gone and her mother conspicuously absent, Joey was given away by Joseph P. Luna, the mayor of Lodi, New Jersey. Someone in the audience thrust a stopwatch in the air when the couple fell in for a kiss. The length of the "clinch"—eleven seconds—would be reported in all the papers. Outside, hundreds of well-wishers pelted the bride and groom—and the police who had to carve a path through the crowd—with rice. An accordionist played "Anchors Aweigh."

The New Yorker Hotel donated its bridal suite for a three-day honeymoon. When the couple entered the lobby that evening, the bandleader Benny Goodman struck up *Here Comes the Bride*. In the hotel's Terrace Room, flashbulbs crackled as the couple shared lollipops and big bowls of ice cream. Willis toasted Joey as "the most wonderful girl I've ever met." Joey said, "I'm the happiest girl in the world."

|||

NOWHERE IS there evidence that their sudden fame changed them. If anything, it reinforced in them the fragility of existence. They saw, perhaps more clearly than most, that the road was never sure. They saw that as a guide to the future, the past was faithless.

The media glare, the movie interest, the crowds—it might have gone to some people's heads. But Joey and Willis made no new plans. They did not seek further attention or money for their story. Nor did they show any sign of higher expectations. "I was never one to make plans ahead of time, because they never come out," Willis told a reporter who'd caught them at breakfast at the hotel the morning after their wedding.

When the honeymoon was over, she was still a broke eighteen-year-old with a dead father and an estranged mother; he was still the son of impoverished Texas farmers, earning enlisted men's pay.

For Willis and Joey, it seems, it was enough to have found each other.

They rented a small two-room apartment on Fortieth Street in Philadelphia. And they used money from the radio show to furnish it. "She and I are determined to have a very happy life together," Willis wrote to his grandmother. "She wants a home of her own where she can have something she had never had before. A sense of security."

But security would be a long time coming. A reminder of life's inconstancy came less than two weeks after they'd left the New Yorker's bridal suite.

On Sunday, December 7, in the afterglow of their honeymoon, they slept in, reading the newspapers in bed and listening for hours to music on the radio. At around 2:45 p.m., the radio went suddenly silent. Then, in a moment, a news announcer's grave voice. Scores of Japanese warplanes had mounted a surprise attack on U.S. Navy battleships in Pearl Harbor. The damage was too great to tally, but authorities feared hundreds—if not thousands—dead.

Willis leapt out of bed, threw on his uniform, and raced to the Navy Yard. A commanding officer ordered him at once to the Delaware River. With sledgehammers and spikes and rope, he and the other sailors worked twelve hours a day, seven days a week, for nearly a month, draping a net across the river to repel submarines. Friday nights were his only liberty. Because of the travel time, that left just four hours with Joey—10 p.m. to 2 a.m.—before he had to start back for the river.

With the country at war, the sailor and his wife saw little of each other. In April 1942, Willis joined the crew of a PC-485 submarine chaser that landed troops on the Aleutian Islands. Joey cleared out of their Philadelphia apartment and moved in with Willis's family for a few months. Bereft without her husband, she moved to Seattle, to be as close to shore as possible when her husband's ship came in. She waited until the summer of 1943. They spent about a year together in Seattle before he was shipped out again. Their first child, a daughter, was born while Willis was at sea. He saw the baby for just three days, when she was nearly a month old, before shipping out for another year.

Their love story had vanished from the headlines as precipitously as it had appeared. A war was on, and the mood of the country had shifted. News reporters moved on to other, more pressing stories. Harry James never followed through. Selznick never made his movie.

Over the course of a nearly sixty-three-year marriage, they never returned to New York.

Collision

THE STREET

By the nineteenth century,
Manhattan was well on its way to becoming a
world center of high finance and culture. But at
least one part of the city was designed for ordinary
citizens: its streets. The grid plan of 1811 was
adopted on the basis of a "plain and simple"
reflection: that "straight-sided and right-angled
houses are the most cheap to build and the most
convenient to live in." The streets and avenues
wouldn't be named for city burghers but would
bear ascending numbers or letters. Moreover, they
would march across the island at fixed intervals,
regardless of natural topography.

Sofia Feldman couldn't remember the last time she'd ventured this far north of Twenty-third Street. A Gramercy girl who now lived in the East Village, she'd packed her viola and taken the uptown train to a dress rehearsal at Jazz at Lincoln Center. The performing arts center, at Sixtieth and Broadway, had asked the Greenwich Village Orchestra, an all-volunteer group Sofia was in, to play at the building's grand opening later that week.

It was early October 2004, and it was late—after 10 p.m.—when rehearsal ended. Sofia, twenty-six, had to be at her day job, at a lab, early the next morning.

She waved goodbye to the other musicians and made for the Columbus Circle subway station, just steps from the music hall. But when she stepped outside, she was overcome by a sense of dislocation. This part of Midtown had always conjured a single, unpleasant image for her: a zoo. During the day, it crawled with suits from the office towers and with fanny pack–wearing tourists window-shopping the luxury stores on Fifth Avenue. It was one of the reasons Sofia kept her distance.

But on this crisp fall night, she looked across Columbus Circle at row after row of nearly deserted streets. She could hear wind hissing through leaves in Central Park. The traffic lights ticked green, then red, then green again, with no one passing save a few lonely cabs and an old man on a ten-speed. When the breeze picked up again, she could hear the sound of a plastic bottle skittering along the pavement somewhere in the darkness.

She was born and raised in New York. But she felt at that moment like a stranger.

|||

MATT FITZGERALD, twenty-nine, left his therapist's office after another session of fruitless soul-searching. His love life had grown so complicated of late that if it weren't happening to him it would have almost been funny. He had been months from marrying Amanda, a colleague he'd dated for four years, despite obvious problems. The wedding invitations had already gone out when he discovered that she was cheating on him. He had to call each of the guests to explain that the wedding was off.

A week later, their wedding planner called. "I knew you two weren't right for each other," she'd said. "I could just tell."

Then *she* asked him out for drinks. The *wedding planner*. He was vulnerable and confused, and he accepted.

Earlier tonight was supposed to be his second date with the wedding planner. But she showed up with a man she described as a former boyfriend. "I told Ayden I was meeting you," she said. "And he insisted on coming. Ayden does this."

Matt finished his drink quickly. "I actually have to go," he said, forcing a smile.

"You just got here."

"I have a doctor's appointment."

"What kind of doctor is open at 9 p.m.?" the wedding planner asked.

Walking home along West Fifty-seventh Street after the shrink's appointment, he continued to brood. Why did he feel compelled to stay with Amanda all those years, even in the face of all those warning signs? Why didn't he stick up for himself more, be more open about his feelings? Did he really have a "nice guy complex," as his shrink suggested? He grew up in Rochester, in upstate New York, and still had some small-town values, but that didn't make him some hayseed. Nor could it explain why he kept winding up with the wrong women.

When it came to straightening out his career, he had been an ace. After a disillusioning stint in the music business, he spent nights and weekends teaching himself computer programming and had recently won a well-paying job as a software engineer at a financial firm. Why couldn't reordering his love life be as easy?

|||

THE INCONGRUOUS quiet of Midtown beckoned to Sofia, who had graduated from college four years earlier but in many ways still felt like a wanderer. Her degree was from Harvard, a place that was supposed to turn out graduates with a sense of their place in the world. But Sofia wasn't one of them. While classmates were heading off to law and medical school, she threw a few sets of clothes in a backpack and set off on a fourteen-month solo trek across Asia and Australia. She hitchhiked, shot down rivers in bamboo rafts, stayed in the homes of oddballs she'd met on the road. A walk though Midtown on a Tuesday night wasn't exactly a safari. But even after moving back to New York and taking the lab job, her thirst for adventure had persisted.

She decided to pass up the Columbus Circle subway station for a more distant one, several long blocks away. She walked onto Broadway and listened to the soft night music of a lonely city. She looked at the blurry pastel lights reflecting in the windows of the skyscrapers. A taxi sped past, then was swallowed in the darkness. For a long time, the only sounds were the clop of her old wooden clogs against the sidewalk.

She had no sooner turned onto Fifty-seventh Street than an old childhood memory caught her. She was eight years old and sitting in a row of chairs at Carnegie Hall, her violin in her lap. Her music school had brought students there on a field trip to see the auditorium and meet the violinist Isaac Stern.

Isn't Carnegie Hall near here? she thought. It *was*. But where? Then, out of nowhere, her name.

"Sofia," a high-pitched voice cried. "Sofia Feldman?"

Sofia wheeled toward the voice. Standing beneath the sign for the crosstown bus was a woman about her age who looked familiar but whom Sofia couldn't quite place. Next to her was a man—both were smiling.

"It's Emily, from Harvard," she said. "This is my husband, Sam."

"Oh, my gosh! No way!" Sofia shouted, dashing over to embrace her. She and Emily had been friends freshman year, but Sofia hadn't seen her in—what was it now?—something like eight years. The night, it seemed, was full of surprises.

|||

THE CAT-LIKE grin, the laugh, the expansive hand gestures— Matt wasn't sure what first drew his eye. But as he neared the woman talking with two friends at the bus stop catty-cornered from Carnegie Hall, he felt his legs almost involuntarily slow. An attractive, open face was framed by twirls of dark wavy hair. There was a tossed-off quality to her clothes that made her look approachable: olive corduroy pants, a threadbare hooded sweatshirt under a short brown corduroy jacket. He had once been a musician—he had gone to the Berklee College of Music before switching careers. He could tell she was carrying an instrument of some kind on her back.

He felt an aching somewhere in his chest. A conversation with her—or a woman like her—would save him the way no end of therapy could. He immediately recognized his irrationality. He knew nothing about this woman. But the way his life had been going lately, he couldn't help but feel everything deeply.

He was about five steps from her, passing on the inside of the sidewalk, when he was almost certain she looked at him. There was a weak smile, too, but was it meant for him or the people with whom she was talking? He had no idea. He kept walking, but his brain churned. Was there a way to cut into their conversation gracefully? Was there some clever thing to say?

Then a rush of self-doubt. Who am I kidding? he asked himself, feeling something tighten in his gut. And so he crossed to the other side of Fifty-seventh Street—which was closer to home—and kept walking. As he waited for the walk signal on Seventh Avenue to change, he stomped his heel against the pavement, disappointed in himself. "If you had bigger *cojones*," he told himself, "you would have said something."

|||

SOFIA SAID goodbye to her friends and quickly glimpsed a set of familiar-looking red banners: Carnegie Hall. The building, she could see now, was just across from where she was standing. She crossed to the other side of Fifty-seventh Street and turned left across Seventh Avenue until she was under its marquee. She pressed her face to the darkened doors. How earnest she must have seemed all those years ago, dutifully rosining her bow as Isaac Stern asked each eight-year-old to play him something. She shook her head and stifled a laugh.

The Fifty-seventh Street subway station was just a block away, and she returned to her regular walking pace—the supersonic clip of a native New Yorker. She was rapidly gaining on a man a quarter block ahead of her, and became suddenly self-conscious of the racket her clogs made against the sidewalk. They were the only two people on the block, and against the silence the clop-clop-clop of her shoes seemed to be caroming off the walls of buildings. A few steps from overtaking him, she tried to change the angle of her foot, to soften the clatter. But one of her heels caught on something, and she tripped. She stumbled forward, her viola bag thumping the man in the back.

"I'm so sorry," she stammered, worried what kind of dirty look this guy would shoot her.

But when she regained her balance and looked up, the man was looking over his shoulder and absolutely beaming. It was one of the goofiest, most cartoonish grins she'd ever seen—like something you'd see on some West Virginia coal miner who'd just been told he'd won the lottery and would never have to work again.

"What's in the case?" the man burbled. "A trumpet? A violin? Because I bought an electric violin a year ago, and have been trying to teach myself how to play."

"It's a viola." Sofia walked fast, looking at him warily over her right shoulder.

"A viola? Cool. You must be a musician. I was, too, a while back. Electric guitar. I went to music school, now I write software. Do you play in a band?"

"The Greenwich Village Orchestra."

"Okay. Yeah. I've heard of them. The electric violin I got, it's a Zeta, the same kind that Boyd Tinsley plays, you know, the violinist for the Dave Matthews Band? Well, every time I try to play it, it makes this super-weird noise, and I can't figure out why. Have you ever played electric?"

Wow, thought Sofia. A slow walker, but a speed-talker. She allowed herself a closer look: he was probably the same man who'd passed her a block before while she was talking with her friends. He'd smiled at her. She'd remembered the baby face, those apple-rubbed cheeks.

Oh, my God, she thought. He probably thinks I bumped into him on purpose. She was mortified, but unsure about how to pull away—or for that matter do anything—gracefully.

She slowed down a little, and said, "So if you can't play violin, what can you play?"

"Guitar," he said. "I was into rock and jazz guitar. I went to Berklee. The one in Boston. Have you heard of it?"

"I actually just dated a drummer who went there."

"Really? What's his name? Maybe I know him. I mean, I didn't know everyone, but I jammed with lots of guys."

She said his name, but the man, with a slight look of deflation, shook his head and said he didn't know him.

They had reached the end of the block and were under the light of a street lamp. "Well, this is my subway," Sofia said, nodding at the steps.

A look wrinkled the man's face that was the perfect opposite of the smile a few minutes earlier. If that first expression was the Greek theater mask for Elation, Sofia thought, the one now was Woe. "This is your subway?" he asked, as if the idea were beyond comprehension. "But, I mean, like, where do you live?"

"The Village." The light was bright, and she could see now that he was well dressed—was that a suede jacket?—and a little handsome. "What about you?"

"Gosh, just a couple blocks from here."

"People live here?"

"Why wouldn't they? I walk everywhere. It's one reason I'm surprised when people say they take subways."

Sofia let out a snort, then raised a hand to her lips to hide her smile. "Look, my orchestra is playing Saturday at Jazz at Lincoln Center. If you're interested in checking us out, come."

"Well, what are you doing now?"

"I was going to go home."

"Do you want to get a cup of coffee first? I'd love to keep talking, if you would."

"Coffee?" she said, eyeing him dubiously. "It's almost 11 p.m."

"There's like five Starbucks right around here. They're really nice."

This guy is pathetic, Sofia thought. There was an earnest quality that was so un–New York. The guys she'd met through online dating services were razor-edged with irony, attitude, intellectual one-upmanship. Many were aloof, hard to decipher, except maybe for when it came to expressing what they wanted in bed. Where the hell is this guy from? Maybe it was just that in strange lands—if you could call Midtown that—there roamed strange people.

He didn't offer much in the way of mystery. But if nothing else, he seemed safe. She was on safari, right? "Sure," she said, looking off into space and shrugging. "But I have to be up for work tomorrow, so I can't stay long."

|||

ALL FIVE coffee places he had in mind were closed, which she found amusing. "I thought this was your neighborhood," she said.

"It is. I swear."

"Well, we could just go to a bar."

They wandered for a while before finding a place with neon beer logos in the window, an Irish pub on Fifty-fifth Street called Cassidy's. There were maybe six other people inside. They found a seat in the back.

"How old do you think I am?" he asked, apropos of nothing.

"I don't know," she said, looking at his fresh-scrubbed face. "Twenty-five?"

"I turn thirty next month," he said. "But a lot of people think I'm older, because I have less hair than a lot of guys my age."

She hadn't noticed—his hair seemed fine. "Okay, so, like, you're *completely* not from the city."

He told her he grew up in a strict Irish Catholic household in Rochester—his dad was a family doctor, his mother a school-teacher. He was the third of four kids and, by the conservative standards of their family, the rebel. He started listening to classic rock on the radio at age five and by high school had started several bands.

"Oh, yeah," Sofia said, listlessly. "What were they called?"

"Earth Chick."

"Shut up."

"Yeah. And another one was Rare Picasso."

"That's pretty terrible."

"Oh, come on. It was definitely cool at the time."

"If you say so," she said, taking a sip of white wine. "So what happened after Berklee?"

He told her he'd moved to New York City in hopes of working his way into managing bands for major record labels. But it didn't work out. He got mired in low-level jobs in other departments and was turned off by the drug use endemic in the industry.

When he told her he'd reinvented himself as a successful soft-ware engineer, learning how to program from books, she sat up in her chair.

"Okay," she said, slamming her palm against the table. "The Internet. It makes no sense. Explain."

She got a rise out of pressing people's buttons. Asking a knuckle-head question was a good way of putting people on the defensive, of poking a hole through their pretensions as they bumbled their way through an answer. She wanted to see how he'd take it.

"That's a really good question," he said. "It can be confusing. I totally didn't get it at first. But let me draw you something."

He reached across the table for a stack of bar napkins and pulled a pen from his coat pocket. And like a teacher with his favorite pupil, he sketched a diagram with hubs and spokes and a few helpful notations in the margins. After this five-minute tutorial, she actually felt she'd learned something. But all she said was, "Hmmm."

He folded the napkin and handed it to her. "You can keep it."

"Tee hee," she said, covering her mouth and faking a coy laugh.

"So what do you do?" he asked.

"I chop mice's heads off in a lab." She told him about her detour after Harvard, about how she was helping to run experiments that her bosses hoped would help cure multiple sclerosis. When he asked about her name, she told him she was descended from Russian Jews.

"It's definitely a cool name," he said.

It was a quarter to midnight when Matt glanced at his watch and suddenly looked at her panicked. "Oh, my Gosh, I almost forgot."

"What?"

"It's 11:45. My sister. I have fifteen minutes to wish her a happy birthday." And so he excused himself to leave a message on his sister's voicemail. "The siblings, we always call," he said after hanging up. "Close shave tonight."

Is this guy for real? Sofia thought.

Some three hours had passed when Sofia started yawning. "I gotta get home," she said. She obliged his request for her phone number but refused when he dug into his wallet for cab fare. She was a few steps down the subway stairs when she turned around.

He was still there, at the top of the steps, with that goofy smile. "I'd ask for your phone number, too," she said, "but, like, I already forgot your name, so I wouldn't even know where to put it in my cellphone."

A perverse thrill seized her as his expression somersaulted, just as it had earlier in the evening, from a caricature of sublime joy to one of abject misery.

||

MATT TOSSED in bed that night. He thought he'd met the perfect girl: smart, pretty, quirky. On that empty street, it was almost like some supernatural force had handed her to him. Then, just like that, she turns on him. She bumps into me, she talks to me for three hours, and then, as a goodbye, she announces that she's already spaced my name. He replayed the evening a dozen times in his head. Everything had been going so well. When did he lose her? How?

Not long ago, he'd called a phone number a girl had given him only to discover it a fake. "Murray's Garage," some gruff-sounding guy answered, as Matt's heart sank. I won't make that mistake again, he told himself now. My ego can't stand any more dings. It was safest just to leave the thing alone, to sock away the memory as a trophy from the night he persuaded a random girl on the street to spend three hours with him at a bar. If he messed with it, if he called her, the memory was liable to turn into something else: a scar.

||

ON THE subway ride home, Sofia felt good about her rough handling of that guy. Pete. Dave. Matt. Whatever his name was.

Earlier in the year, she'd met a man through an Internet service. They had been dating seriously for four months—she thought they might have a future. Then she found out he had several other girlfriends, ones he'd never mentioned. To convince herself that she was desirable, that next time would be different, she plunged headlong that summer into online dating. A startling number of men were transparently after quick hookups. There wasn't so much as the pretext of romance. Her dates would rush her through dinner—"We'll split it," they'd say when the bill came, as if in some praiseworthy nod to feminism. Then it was off to a bar, where they drank so much that Sofia found herself kissing the boy—and going home with him—far faster than she'd intended.

The next morning, she'd wake up feeling cheaply used and in need of a hot shower. A few of the men she'd actually liked. She thought they were funny, intelligent, ambitious. Some she even saw again. But then, when their calls stopped, she began to hate herself.

Instead of withdrawing from the matchmaking services or more carefully screening suitors, at first she sought only more. She was like a compulsive gambler convinced that the jackpot was just one more roulette spin away. But after a long summer of betrayals, bunco, and bullshit, she felt something inside her go cold. "The nice person is always the one who gets hurt," she told herself. The next time, it wouldn't be her. The next time she met a guy she liked, she would comport herself like a zookeeper in a tiger's cage at mealtime—with quick reflexes and a high-voltage electric prod.

Meeting a nice guy on the street in front of Carnegie Hall was a charming story. She saw that. But if there was one thing she'd learned over the summer, it was to be careful around charmers.

||

AT WORK the next day, Matt told the whole story to Scott, who worked in the next cubicle.

"Dude," Scott said, "you're a total stud."

"Yeah, but I'm not going to call her."

Scott jerked his head from side to side in disbelief, looking like a dog drying himself after a swim. "What are you talking about?"

"I told you, she kind of dissed me at the end. The stuff she said, it was so random."

"Dude, the entire night was random. What did you expect? Chicks pull bullshit of that order all the time. She's testing you. Wants to know how big of a man you are."

"Or couldn't care less."

"Grow a pair, bro. Honestly, what do you have to lose?"

Matt agonized all week. Did she like him or not? Did he have her and lose her or did he never have her? He sifted and resifted her every word and gesture. He decided late in the week that he needed to know. Sure, he could have just let the memory be, but of what use was that? Memories were for people in nursing homes. In his last relationship, he had told his therapist, his passivity had been part of the problem. He had felt something was wrong for a long time but failed to act. Now he felt something was right. Had he learned anything?

At the end of a long day at the office, when the janitors began wheeling in their pails, he called her.

"Hi, it's Matt, from the other night, from outside Carnegie Hall."

There was a moment of silence. Had he lost the connection? He peeled the phone from his ear and looked at its display: the signal was still strong.

"Hi, hello? Is Sofia there?"

Another pause. "Who else did you think would answer my cellphone?"

Matt didn't understand the hostility. But he took a deep breath. He chose to ignore it, to blot out both this comment and the one by the subway about forgetting his name.

"Did you make it home okay the other night?"

"I survived," she said.

"I probably sounded like somebody's parent. 'It's late, you're a single woman.' But it really was late, and you told me you'd never been above Twenty-third. I didn't mean to be parental."

"I'm independent, that's all. But it was sweet of you."

"What are you doing next week? There's this cool restaurant. I wondered if you'd want to grab dinner there."

He had been thinking about HanGawi, a vegetarian Korean restaurant on Thirty-second Street near Madison Avenue. He was a red-blooded carnivore, but he remembered the place as romantic and was willing to forgo meat for the night: it was like some Buddhist temple, with its dark wood, antiques, and cubbies for shoes. Plus, Matt thought, the location was perfect, a midpoint between her place and his.

But before he could tell her any of this, she cut in. "It's a mouse bloodbath at the lab next week, so my schedule is a little crazy. But if you want, you can call me over the weekend. It's doubtful, but there's a chance things will change."

"Okay," Matt said, trying to mask his deflation.

He was about to hang up when she said, "Oh, wait."

"Yeah?"

"Since I've got your number in my cellphone now, I just need your full name. It's Matt what?"

"Fitzgerald," he said, suddenly smiling. "Matt Fitzgerald."

|||

TWO HOURS before the Greenwich Village Orchestra was to play at Jazz at Lincoln Center, Sofia sent Matt a text message. "Chk us out if u want," she wrote. "Shud b a gud show."

Matt looked at his cellphone, pleased at this small triumph. Then he decided not to go. He didn't want to sit through a concert, then have to hang around conspicuously for however long while the band packed up. For what? Only to say "Sounded great!" before she made some excuse about having to meet some other friends?

He ignored the text message.

"Are you running? Where are you?" Sofia asked the next afternoon, when he finally called.

"Playing a few rounds of golf with friends in Jersey. It's a beautiful day to be outside."

"I'm stuck on an overcrowded Metro-North and so wish I weren't."

"I was actually on par the last hole, if you don't count the three mulligans my friends let me take. Do you know anything about golf?"

She burst out laughing. "Sorry, no."

"City girl."

"Hey, about dinner, remember you asked?" Sofia said.

"I remember." Matt, feeling his throat muscles tense, hoped she would let him down easy.

"The mice have won a reprieve," she said. "How's Tuesday?"

||||

SOFIA WAS a half block from the restaurant and could see Matt standing in the middle of the sidewalk. His hands were on his hips, and he was pitched forward, wagging his head from side to side. He looked like a tourist puzzling over which direction was downtown and which up. Sofia looked at her watch. She was fifteen minutes late. She always was. To everything. But did he have to be so obvious? Oh, my God, she thought. What a dork.

When she got close enough and waved, she could practically see his face muscles unclench.

"Here," he said, handing her a small box of what she could see were gourmet chocolates.

She wrested them from his hand like a policeman disarming a suspect.

"What is *this*?" she said, with an incredulous smile.

"What do you mean, 'What is this'? It's chocolate."

"Why?"

"Because it's a thing people give other people." He looked at her as if she were half crazy. "You might even like them."

When Sofia opened the menu and saw it was entirely vegetarian, she felt her typically hypercharged nerves calm a little.

She'd never told Matt she didn't eat meat, and yet somehow this guy, who had a burger at the bar the other night, invites her to a vegetarian restaurant. She felt a tinge of guilt. Why was she giving him such a hard time? She let her guard down a little over dinner and just tried to talk normally, as she might to a friend.

She told jokes about her upbringing in Peter Cooper Village, the cluster of middle-class high-rises in Gramercy. Her parents— her dad was a solo architect, her mom a math teacher—grew up in the Bronx but were strivers.

"They gave me everything," she told Matt. Visits as a kid to museums and concerts, trips to Brazil as part of a peace-promoting summer exchange program, placement in two elite public city schools run by Hunter College. In return, she lived up to all her parents' expectations: straight A's, captainship of the high school soccer and volleyball teams, nice friends, admission to Harvard. She couldn't even cast her global trek after college as rebellion. The hallway of her childhood apartment was decorated with photos of her parents' journeys as newlyweds. Eager to leave the Bronx and see the world, they had spent months visiting places as far away as Turkey and Nepal.

"I graduate from college and am like, 'That's it, I'm going to the Himalayas, see ya in a year,' and they're like, 'Of course, Sweetheart.'"

"They sound nice," Matt said.

"Oh, please," she said.

They drank soju and laughed, and then walked more than twenty blocks to a downtown jazz bar where Sofia's cousin, a bassist, sometimes played.

"Do you want to come up?" she asked around midnight. Her walk-up studio apartment was a couple of blocks away. "I've got a few albums that I think you might like."

Matt sat down on her love seat—it was the one real piece of furniture besides her bed—and Sofia squeezed in beside him.

She spent the next four hours playing CDs and talking and, eventually, wondering when he would kiss her.

She had never been this close to him. He had full lips, she could see now, and liquid blue eyes, and fine light-brown hair.

But 4 a.m. flashed on her digital clock, and she was still kissless. Soon she started to get annoyed. How many clues does this guy need? After a moment's thought, she threw her leg over his, expecting him to respond as had other boys—like a jackal at the scent of meat. But all Matt did was smile, pat her knee, and stand up to leave.

"I have to be at work tomorrow," he said. "I should probably get home, change, shower, and try to get some rest."

This is ridiculous, Sofia thought. "Yeah, okay," she said. "Go home. You look exhausted."

Matt looked at her uncertainly, then left. She was already under the covers a moment later when she heard a knock. She opened the door to find Matt with his brow wrinkled and the fingers of his right hand at his temple, as if trying to puzzle out some heretofore unsolved computer programming problem.

"I just want to let you know," he said, "that I, um, wanted to kiss you. But I haven't brushed my teeth and I probably have bad breath, so. . . ."

"You came back to tell me that?"

He leaned across the threshold and pecked her on the cheek. "Good night," he said.

On their next date, a few nights later, Sofia didn't wait for the night to grow stale. As soon as they got barstools, she leaned in, pulled his head toward hers, and kissed him.

||

COLD SETTLED over New York, with dead leaves falling off branches and snow draping the city in lace. Sofia and Matt ate falafel in the East Village; they went to parties in SoHo and jazz shows in the Village. On Halloween, they dressed as Fred and

Daphne from Scooby-Doo. In early November, they celebrated Matt's thirtieth birthday.

Sofia was seeing Matt a few times a week but tried to hide her deepening attachment by grousing to friends about him.

"He's such a loser," she'd say. "Why are we still going out?"

"The guy bought you tacos," her friend Jessica said. "You *have* to go out with him."

It was true. He did buy her tacos. And noodles. And bagels. He paid for everything. And he brought her flowers, chocolates, and little gifts.

No boyfriend had ever done that before. The guys she'd met online had rarely even bought her a beer on their way to propositioning her.

So why did she keep fighting him? Their relationship had reached a point where she could stop worrying about self-preservation. Matt called her all the time. He showed no signs of bolting. If anything, he seemed more committed than ever. Maybe it was just that his small-town ways felt old-fashioned in a city as forward as New York.

"It's a little embarrassing," she told her friend.

"Why, because he's so nice?" Jessica said.

"Or something."

"What don't you get?" Jessica asked, exasperated. "He's courting you. That's what they call it in that itsy-bitsy part of America between Manhattan and L.A. 'Courting.' Alien concept, I know."

Weeks passed before Sofia came to understand the reason for her unease with Matt's open fondness: she didn't feel worthy.

|||

AT FIRST Matt had chafed at the callous things that flew out of her mouth. "I'm not warm and fuzzy," she'd blurted out the other day. "Don't expect me to cuddle with you." The way she stormed off sometimes, without any provocation, it was like she was trying to pick a fight. But after that kiss on their third date—when Sofia totally made the first move—he stopped getting his feelings hurt. "The jig is up," he told himself. She can be mean. She can make fun of me. She can laugh at me. But she shows up.

Her sharp edges, her neuroses, he began to see, were part of her character, and part of the city's. He decided to take them no more personally than he did the guff from the sandwich guy at the deli, the one who was always telling him he didn't have all day to wait for his order.

"I love you," Matt told Sofia over dinner one night that December.

Sofia stared at him for a long time, but said nothing.

"I think you love me, too, Sofia," Matt said after the silence, reaching for her hand. "You'd tell me if you didn't."

|||

SOFIA HAD begun applying to medical school that fall. Matt felt certain he'd dodged a bullet in the spring of 2005, when Sofia was accepted at New York University's School of Medicine. When he'd asked about the prospects for their relationship if she didn't get into any New York schools, she had been noncommittal.

"The long-distance thing rarely works," she'd replied, with characteristic bluntness.

But now that she'd made it into NYU, Matt had other questions. Will medical school change her? Will she be too busy for me? He thought about his father, a family doctor, who worked from six in the morning until ten at night, seldom seeing the family. Do I want to marry someone whose life may soon look like that? And if they did get married, she'd be in school and training for maybe ten years. Could he earn enough to support them both, let alone, possibly, a child?

The first year of medical school was difficult. Now five years out of college, Sofia wrestled with the volume of schoolwork and struggled to adapt to the rigors of academic life. She was older than most of her classmates, and because she lived off campus— she'd moved into Matt's apartment that summer—she felt cut off from them. When she came home at the end of the day, she needed solitude. Often she wanted nothing more than to lock herself in the bedroom for a half hour with a crossword puzzle, walling out the world. But no sooner would she walk in than Matt would pelt her with demands for attention. "Can I at least get a hug?" he'd say. In those first few months of school, she sometimes denied him even that. Why couldn't Matt understand that she needed a buffer between school and home? Why couldn't he see that she needed a half hour to decompress, to become herself again?

Matt, for his part, saw those first few months as confirmation of all his fears. Why didn't Sofia understand that he'd already had *his* quiet time? He spent his days in front of a computer. Then he was home, alone, for two hours before she returned from school. He wanted only to talk or cuddle or watch a movie. But Sofia no sooner came home than disappeared into the bedroom. He would accuse her of "going into crossword mode" and stew on the couch until she reappeared. After a half year of seeing each other all the time and staying out late at restaurants and concerts and bars, her sudden unavailability stung.

It was a long and trying year. Matt wanted signals that she was in the relationship to stay—"in it to win it," as he put it—but the signals were sometimes hard to see. He consoled himself with memories of their chance meeting in front of Carnegie Hall. *Something maybe we don't understand brought us together,* he told himself. *We can't just walk away from that.*

Then, by the spring of 2006, a thaw. Sofia grew more confident about school, and Matt began to accept that when Sofia needed time alone, it was about her, not him. They'd set up ten-minute dates to talk or a half hour for TV, and they treated that time as inviolable. Matt also learned that he had a secret weapon against "crossword mode." If he offered her a back scratch—she loved to be scratched—he could get her to break away from just about anything. These small changes were like the microscopic tweak of a television antenna that snaps a blurry image into focus.

Matt and Sofia had done what Matt had failed to do with Amanda, his onetime fiancée: they acknowledged to each other that they were going through a difficult stretch. Then they groped, together, for firmer ground.

Sofia came to see that Matt wouldn't hurt her. She came to see that he wasn't going away, that he was—what was his goofy phrase?—"in it to win it."

When Matt said, "I love you, Sofia," there was no longer silence. Now there was, "I feel the same way," and soon, "And I, you."

By the middle of 2006, Matt felt ready to marry her. He knew that the way Sofia threw herself into things—the way her minute-to-minute stress levels influenced even major decisions—the first years of med school were a risky time to ask. At the back of his mind, too, was his failed engagement to Amanda. He had rushed into it before either was ready, only to see it shatter.

So he waited and waited. Then, in February 2008, they were watching TV when an ad came on for laundry detergent. In one scene, a smiling mother cuddles a cooing newborn, swaddled in white.

"I want babies." It took a moment for Matt to realize he'd spoken the words, not just thought them.

"Excuse me?" Sofia looked at him sideways, her long curls falling across her eyes.

"Babies."

"Um, we can't have babies until we're married, Catholic Boy."

"Then, Sofia, let's get married. I've wanted to, but with med school and everything . . ."

Matt waited for the usual retort. But this time, none came. Sofia brushed the back of her hand against her eyelids and cleared her throat. She composed herself, but her voice had an unfamiliar softness. "You've wanted to marry me?"

"For two years now. It wasn't obvious?"

"Matt?"

"Yes?"

"I love you."

||

MATT STILL had the ring he had given Amanda. She had returned it when he broke off the engagement four years earlier. Now he took it to the jeweler for an appraisal. He hoped to trade it in, to unburden himself of it. He would need the money for a new ring, for Sofia.

"Sorry to say, my friend, but you overpaid," the jeweler said.

"But look how big the diamond is."

"Big, yes, but flawed."

The jeweler slid the microscope across the table, and Matt stared at the blaze of facets, which he thought looked like a dandelion head under glass. "Those specks, the lines," the jeweler said. "See? They're called inclusions. They cloud the stone. Some kinds of imperfection, you see only under a scope."

Matt nodded, feeling certain he'd understood. He thanked the man and walked out into the cool, gray-gold sunlight.

Navigation

GRAND CENTRAL TERMINAL

Even before Grand Central Terminal
opened in 1913, critics raved. The New York Times,
typically hard to please, called the cavernous Beaux-
Arts building "the greatest railway terminal in the
world." One national magazine hailed it as a singular
feat of both aesthetics and pragmatism and foresaw its
future as "a new city center" and a "vast theater of
great events." But it didn't take long for train riders to
notice a small problem with the astrological mural on
the ceiling of the main concourse. The zodiac, a blue
sweep of Mediterranean sky flecked with 2,500 gold
stars, was painted backward. The source of the
"mistake" was debated for decades, until historians
made a discovery: the artist, Paul Helleu, had intended
to depict the stars from the eyes not of man but of God.

From every corner of Grand Central Terminal, they came. Hundreds of sailors in dress whites careering across the concourse like caged doves bursting into flight.

Jean Westrum, tall, nineteen, and blond, tugged on her friends' sleeves, grinning. "What's happening?" she asked. "Someone declare war?"

"Oh, my goodness." Evelyn fanned her face with her ticket. "Just look at them."

The others giggled. "A Navy parade," Margaret said.

"Dear me," said Barbara, looking suddenly serious. "I wonder if it's our train."

Jean looked up at the display board and saw that Barbara, always the responsible one, was right: the 12:45 a.m. train to Boston, the Narragansett, was boarding.

"Run, girls," Jean said. "Run. Run!"

They would never have come were it not for that ad in one of the Boston papers: a spring special of $5.75 for weekend round trips, including tax, so long as you took the overnight train. No sooner had Jean clipped it from the paper than the five girls decided on a weekend in New York City. They had grown up together in Somerville, a working-class suburb of double-decker homes north of Boston. None had moved far after high school. It was 1951, and Jean, an only child, was working now as an auto-loan clerk at the Shawmut Bank near Fenway Park. Her friends had found similar office jobs around Boston. Like Jean, they lived with their parents. Manhattan was two hundred miles—and light-years—away.

"What will we tell our parents?" Mary had asked. New York, after all, was not the sort of place everyone approved of.

"Tell them we're going to Macy's," Jean said. "That's something they can't tell us we've already got in Boston."

"What ever will we buy?"

"Bathing suits," Jean declared, though the thought had only then occurred to her. And so it was agreed: with Memorial

Day fast approaching, they were going to New York for new swimsuits.

The weekend had been dizzy. The Rockettes at Radio City. Lunch at Billy Rose's Diamond Horseshoe. A snack at the Horn & Hardart automat, where for a quarter a machine would dispense a fully made sandwich. The tiny room the five shared at the Taft Hotel on Fifty-first Street. The drunks falling out of honky-tonk bars in Times Square. You saw every extreme in New York, Jean thought, and she was grateful for the steadier ways of her hometown.

But to get back—all five had work the next morning—they'd have to make this train.

||||

THE WEEKEND with his family had gone by too quickly, and now Danny Lynch, nineteen, was back at Grand Central Terminal. More than an hour remained before his 12:45 a.m. train north. It was a Sunday evening, and the terminal was empty enough to hear the tap of individual heels against marble. He dropped his Navy duffel against a wall near the ticket booths and flumped to the floor. Drawing his knees to his chest, he looked up at the massive vaulted ceiling. It sparkled, he saw now, with hundreds of gold stars. He had been here before but must have been too hurried to notice. Now the outlines of the fish, the twins, and the hunter seemed darkly alive.

Were these figures really the faces of fortune? Was fate etched in the patterns of faraway suns, cold and unknowable?

It was his first weekend liberty since boot camp. Instead of sticking around Newport with his shipmates, he had traveled nine hours home to Long Island. He couldn't stay near base, not after the accident. After those sailors drowned, Danny needed to be around people he knew: his parents, friends from Mineola High, his four younger siblings. He never thought he'd admit it, but he even missed his sister Alice, the one who was always calling him Fatso.

It was water—his love for it, and the fascination it held—that led Danny to the Navy. He was the shy son of a newspaper pressman. His father, hands streaked with ink, worked so much overtime to feed and clothe his five kids that they rarely saw him. Never was Danny more at peace than with a reel in his fist as the fish leaped in the ponds near their home in New Hyde Park. The place where land met water was a place where a boy could think. It was a place where a boy could see the everyday marvels of nature, mysterious and pure.

After high school, Danny won a concession at the pharmacy on Brian Street, selling sandwiches and shakes to folks in the neighborhood. The owner had offered to put him through pharmacy school if he came back to work for him. But Danny had other ideas. The conflict in Korea had been perfect cover for his decision to enlist, which had less to do with patriotic duty than with something else: a chance to be away from the rest of the world, inside a kind of floating observatory, with the sea as your mattress and for a nightlight the stars.

But water, he had recently come to see, had a kind of moral neutrality: it took life as readily as it gave. His neck twitched, and he lowered his eyes. A group of sailors was clowning around by the information booth. "You had a good time with that fuzzy duck, didn't ya?" one said, with an exaggerated wink. "That dog, not a chance," the other replied. Danny rifled through his bag for his corncob pipe, stuffed it with tobacco, and touched the bowl with a match. He inhaled and felt the heat in his lungs.

|||

THE FIVE girls picked up their bags and bounded across the concourse in a loose pack. "Hiya darlins," a sailor hooted as he dashed past. "Like that pretty blouse," cried another. But as they skipped down the ramp to the platform, there was only the thud of stampeding feet and a lightning streak of white uniforms. Jean soon began to curse herself for overpacking. She had stuffed her hard case with three choices of outfits for each day and four pairs of shoes. On top of that, she was toting a birdcage-shaped wire egg basket she'd bought at Macy's. A few months earlier, on a ski trip in New Hampshire, she had fractured the bones in her right palm when her pole struck the snow the wrong way. She hadn't felt pain in a few weeks. But now something in her palm was beginning to spasm.

"Go ahead, girls," she shouted, out of breath, as her friends, lighter packers, began to outpace her. "I'll catch up."

Mary turned her head, with a concerned look, but kept shuffling forward. "Toward the front," she shouted, nodding down the platform. "We'll save a seat. Hurry."

Jean gave a hard tug, trying to loft her suitcase above her knees for speed. Then came a sudden shudder in the muscles of her right arm. Then a feeling of something giving way. Her suitcase crashed to the platform and that silly birdcage basket tumbled after it.

She swallowed down a sob. She was sure now she'd never find her friends. To make the train, she might have to leave her things right there. Then, just as suddenly, a figure in white stopped to the right and in front of her. She turned only halfway, afraid of making eye contact. A sailor. He was on his knees collecting her bags.

"Where is your seat, ma'am?" came his voice, low and unhurried.

"My friends went ahead," she stammered, keeping her eyes on the platform, which, with most passengers now on the train, had started look forlorn. "That second car, or the third, up there, I think."

She stole a glance, long enough only to see dark hair, a sharp profile. A pipe jutted from the corner of his mouth.

"We'd better run," he said.

The inside aisle was a slalom course of sailors and their bags. Jean pardoned her way through and found the four girls at the end of the car, in two rows of facing seats, two to a side. They had thrown Mary's shawl over a pair of the seats on the other side of the aisle.

"Where are your bags?" Margaret asked.

"My word, what happened to you?" This, from Evelyn.

Jean gave a discreet sideways flick of the eyes, to indicate something behind her. Then she watched her friends' faces undergo subtle changes of expression. Mary looked into her lap. Evelyn gently tickled Barbara's elbow.

"Here?" The pipe in the sailor's mouth wagged slightly as he spoke.

"If you would, sir, please," Jean said.

He wrestled the suitcase into the overhead rack and gingerly handed her the egg basket.

"Thank you ever so much." Jean lifted the shawl and handed it to Mary. When she sat down, she smiled coyly at her friends.

From the corner of her eye, however, she could see that the sailor boy was still in the aisle. He had his arms on his hips and a look of concentration, as if studying the crowded train car for signs of an open seat.

"Ma'am, may I sit with you until Providence?"

Jean turned slowly, not sure at first if he was addressing her. Except, she saw now, he was. He was smiling and, with his pipe, gesturing toward the window seat beside her.

|||

A WHISTLE blew, and the train began clunking through a long, dark tunnel. When it surfaced, above rows of dimly lit tenement buildings, it picked up speed. But strangely, the sound of the wheels against the rails softened, as if the train had sprung a sail and were being carried by the wind.

Jean shifted in her seat. "Where is your ship?"

"Newport, ma'am," said the sailor. "Rhode Island. We have to report to duty at zero eight hundred hours."

"Is that the same thing as eight in the morning?"

"Yes, ma'am."

"Do sailors always cut it so close?"

"Yes, ma'am." He was smiling. "You don't get any stripes for showing up early."

"No medals?"

"Just infractions if we're late."

"And here *I* am talking your ear off. You must want to sleep."

"Not sure I can, ma'am," he said, looking out the window. A half moon hung in the sky, fringing the trees along the tracks in a spectral light.

"Well, if you want to talk, you're sitting next to the right person." Jean looked across the aisle at her friends, who were by now slumped in their seats, nearly asleep. "The thing about being an only child is we never get tired of hearing ourselves carry on."

"Danny Lynch," he said, nodding.

"Jean Westrum, of Lexington, Massachusetts."

Soon, with Jean leading the way, they were talking and talking. They discovered they were the same age. They both had working-class families. They both had fathers whose hard work had let them move to leafier neighborhoods—he from Hell's Kitchen to New Hyde Park, she from Somerville to Lexington.

When Jean said her father had been a farmer in Norway before immigrating to America, Danny smiled. "That sounds like a nice life," he said. He told her he had lived next door to a farm as a boy. After the harvest, the owner let the Lynch kids glean the fields for leftover potatoes, lettuce, and radishes. Once, they found rabbits living in the rhubarb field, and Danny taught his younger sister Ruthie how to feed them. "I had a business," he said, laughing at the memory. "I'd go over to the farm to fill my red wagon with topsoil. Then I'd wheel it over to the neighbors on the other side and dump it in their backyard."

"Clever," Jean said, giving him a playfully skeptical look.

"It's true," he said, defensively. "They paid me a penny a load. Whatever I couldn't sell, well, my dad would buy back from me."

|||

IT WAS 2 a.m. now, and the train was quiet except for the sound of a few sailors playing chess in the back and the buzz saw of some man snoring a few rows down.

Danny put his pipe in his bag and withdrew the newspaper he'd bought at Grand Central. He read for a while, then handed it to Jean. "Would you like a look?"

"Oh. Sure." She blushed. He must be tired of hearing me talk, she thought.

She read articles about Korea, air-raid sirens, Iranian oil. On one of the inside pages, she found an article about the life of sailors at Naval Station Norfolk, in Virginia. The city, it seemed, was a sewer of vice.

"Did you read this?" she asked, sliding the paper over the armrest. "It sounds just awful."

He picked it up and read silently.

"Is Newport anything as bad?" she asked, with a solicitous look.

"It hasn't been a real happy place, not after last week. You must have seen the papers."

"No," she said. "I haven't heard a thing."

The previous Thursday, he said, a Navy launch carrying more than 140 sailors to their ships in Newport Harbor had capsized in a storm. At least fifteen young men had drowned. "A few were newlyweds," he said, shaking his head. One sailor's wife learned of her husband's death while packing her bags for a move to his parents' home, where they had planned to await the birth of their first child.

The sailors were returning to their ships from overnight liberty in town, he told her. Too many crowded onto the launch, far more than was safe, particularly during a storm. All the same, the launch somehow steamed off, toward anchorages in Narragansett Bay. In the end, for no good reason, more than a dozen men were lost. It was one thing for men to die in battle, he said. But this?

Jean looked at him now, face downcast, and saw anguish.

"I'm terribly sorry," she said. "And how awful for those families. Had you been in Newport very long?"

"Less than a week." Newport, he said, was where the Navy
had sent him to await orders after boot camp. "I couldn't stay
there over the weekend. It's why I came home."

Jean felt moved by the story. You wouldn't know it from his
looks: he was over six feet tall, she thought, and as husky as any man.
But he was a gentle soul, introspective, without the roughness that
came to mind when she thought of what people said about sailors.

It was now 5:25 a.m., and when the conductor called out
"Providence, next station," Danny drew his pipe from his ruck-
sack and stuffed tobacco into the bowl. She could see from his
movements that he was exhausted.

"I get a bus from here," he said, the pipe wagging again.

"Try to get some sleep if you can."

He stood up with his duffel and set his cap on his dark hair.
"Miss Westrum?"

"Yes?"

"If I wrote you a letter, would you think about writing me back?"

She pulled a pen from her purse and wrote her address in the
margins of his newspaper.

"I would."

As soon as the train doors shut, she spread her long legs
across the seat, still warm, where Dan had sat. She was soon fast
asleep and dreaming.

|||

"YOU LOOK nice today, Barbara," the chubby man in the green
eyeshades said. Then he cupped his hand around one side of his
mouth. "But what happened to ya friend ovah heya?" he said in a
stage whisper. "She get into some kinda mix-up with a blendah?"

"A sailor." Barbara winked.

"Hubba-hubba."

"On a train."

"Ring-a-ding."

"We could hardly sleep for all the jabbering they were doing."

"Now, Barbara, you make it sound scandalous," Jean said, tiring of being talked about.

Jean's shift at the bank began at noon, and it was senseless to travel home to Lexington first. So after the train pulled into South Station, at 6:50 a.m., she went with Barbara to Barbara's job in the bookkeeping department at the *Boston Herald-Traveler*. When Jean went to the powder room, she saw what Barbara's supervisor was getting at. The curls on the right side of her head were crushed flat, while the ones on the left seemed to have gained volume. Her mascara looked like a tire skid.

She felt for an instant like she had as a little girl, when kids called her String Bean and asked, "How's the weather up there?" She was still a head taller than most of her friends, but she had grown into her height. She had dirty blond curls that inspired envy in some of her friends and a mirthful face that looked a little like Shirley Temple's. She splashed water on her cheeks and retouched her face and hair. Looking again in the mirror, she knew she had improved since her string bean days.

By about 3 p.m., midway through her shift at the bank, she was fighting to stay awake. The numbers on the loan amortization she was reading began to blur, and her eyelids felt leaded. Did she have to prattle on so? Did that poor sailor really need to know about her latest dance recital or the walk-in dollhouse her carpenter father had built her as a girl? Did he really care that the neighbors she baby-sat for had an atomic bomb shelter in their basement? If I'd only stopped talking an hour sooner, she thought.

||

A FUNEREAL air hung over Newport. Danny heard from his shipmates that the death toll had been revised upward to eighteen. The disaster had been the result of multiple errors: a seaman apprentice—someone of Danny's own low rank—was in charge of the fifty-foot launch, instead of the regular coxswain; the officer who sent the launch ashore told investigators he hadn't noticed the switch because the apprentice seaman "looked just like" the coxswain; at the landing in Newport, sailors ignored the seaman's request that some disembark; and on the way back to the anchorages, the seaman inexplicably barreled through a set of three breakers at full throttle.

At the mess, Danny overheard a senior enlisted man say, "We're supposed to have the smarts to beat the Communists in Korea, but we can't get our own guys back to ship in Newport?" Danny felt only more down.

His orders the next day couldn't have come too soon. His ship, the destroyer USS *Power*, was leaving Newport. It would be spending the whole summer in dry dock at the Boston Naval Yard, where it would be outfitted with new guns. *Boston*. Before taps that evening, he sat in his rack and stared for a long time at a blank sheet of paper.

"Dear Jean," he finally wrote. "As you can plainly see I wasn't joking when I told you I would write as soon as I had time."

He said he'd just learned he was heading to Norfolk for a week of training. Yes, that same "hell hole of vice and corruption" they'd read about in the paper on the train. Then—she'd never guess!—his destroyer was steaming to Boston.

"While we are in Boston I expect to get a good many liberties and would greatly appreciate it if you would show me around town," he continued. "You could never realize how much it means to a fellow to know someone in a strange place . . . I don't care too much for dancing, but I do like to go walking or to a stage show or movie and anything that you might like. I am sure I would enjoy anything you would suggest."

|||

IT WAS just after 11 p.m., and Jean was so spent from two nights of overtime at the bank that she almost stepped on the letter by her bedroom door. When she saw the return address—Daniel John Lynch SA, USS *Power*, c/o Fleet Post Office, New York, New York—she threw off her purse, shut the door, and curled up on her bed. It was a sweet note, she thought, and she smiled at the way the lines of blue ink tilted slightly, like waves beneath a ship. She found a piece of ordinary paper in her desk. She wanted to say the right thing. She used a pencil, in case she needed to erase.

"Dear Dan, As you can plainly see," she wrote, mimicking his first line, "I wasn't joking either when I told you I would answer your letter."

She told him she had to drink black coffee to survive the day after their train ride. She mentioned a friend named Lydia whose first anniversary passed with her husband fighting in Korea. Jean and her friends took her out alone to celebrate, but still, Jean wrote, "the poor kid . . . I wouldn't want to be alone on my first anniversary."

As for Danny's proposal that they meet, Jean decided to respond with nonchalance, as though such a meeting had already been decided but was of no special consequence. "I have been trying to think of things you might like to do," she wrote, "but we can talk about that when I see you." She reached into her vanity for her bubble gum–colored lipstick and rouged her lips. She puckered up and pressed them to the back of the letter. She thought for a moment about how that gentle sailor boy would react, and giggled.

The truth was, she was mostly a novice with boys. Up at her family's cabin in New Hampshire, counselors from the Boy Scout camp across the lake sometimes rode over on their horses to flirt with her and her friends. But the only kissing that went on was with "Prince Charming," a rock sticking out of the water that looked like some man's face in profile.

At Mosley's on the Charles, the dance hall just outside Boston, she had always liked when boys asked her to the floor. But they usually came over while she was seated, before they could gather that she was five feet ten. When she stood up, accepting, she could see some of them wince. Their partner was taller than they were. Danny, she remembered as she sealed her letter, was not just over six feet. He wore a uniform.

"Who's this Daniel Lynch?" her father asked over breakfast that morning, peering over the sports pages. "I know him?"

She explained.

"A sailor? I'd like to meet him."

|||

THERE HAD been no reply to her letter. So Jean was startled when she answered the phone on a Saturday in mid-June and heard Danny announce that he was at that very moment at the trolley stop nearest her home.

"The sign says *Orr*-lington Heights," he said. "Golly, Jean, I hope I'm in the right place. I don't know how I'll get back if I'm not."

"You mean *Ah*-lington Heights?"

"A-r-l-i-n-g-t-o-n," Danny said. "*Orrlington*."

"Your accent is something funny, Danny. Really, you should have let me know you were coming. Weren't you going to give me any notice?"

Her father snatched the receiver from her hand. "Who's this?" he said gruffly. "Who? Where? Right . . . Yes . . . Fine . . . Stay where you are. Yes. Fifteen minutes."

And then he hung up.

"Daddy!" She took stock of her plain dress and tousled hair. "I'm in no condition."

"Hurry, Jean," her father said impatiently. "The boy says he's never been to Boston. We don't want him, God forbid, getting lost up here."

They found him in his dress whites at the edge of the parking lot looking more than a little nervous. He shook hands with her father, a tall man with high Norwegian cheekbones and a steely face. Jean made it her business to keep up a stream of amiable chatter the whole way home. She was their only daughter, and she feared Danny would receive an interrogation.

Over lemonade in the living room, her parents got in only a few polite questions—about his ship, his family—before her mother remembered her bridge group over at her sister's house in Somerville.

"Why don't Dan and I drive you there?" Jean suggested. "Then I can drop Dan back at—what was it?—*Orr*-lington Heights."

She looked at her father, whose normally impassive face gave way to a grin.

"Do you see any problem with that, dear?" her mother asked her father.

"Not from where I'm sitting, Mabel."

"Just be sure to drop Dan off before dark," her mother said, "because I'll need you to pick me up before Auntie starts the roast. If I stay too long, she'll insist I eat."

"Of course, Mother," Jean said.

The twenty-five-minute drive to Somerville brought a few long silences. When Jean's mother finally got out and she and Danny were safely down the road, they broke into big smiles. Over ice cream sundaes at a nearby soda fountain, she scolded him again for not giving her more notice. "I would have put something nicer on," she said.

"You look nice to me," he said. "And anyways, I don't worry too much about clothes."

"Easy for a man in uniform to say."

He laughed, then began telling her about life on the ship. His eyes flashed when he mentioned the marine creatures and aquatic birds he'd spotted from the deck. She was surprised at how much he seemed to know about the natural world. He was something of a loner, she could see. But like Jean, who turned friends into the siblings she never had, Danny had found ways to fill the voids.

"Will you make a life in the Navy, Danny?"

"I'd like to give it my level best. Don't you have a dream? Something you've always wanted?"

"I like horses," she said. "I think sometimes about going west, somewhere with big open spaces, and raising them."

The more she talked, the more Danny liked the way he felt around her. She made him feel interesting. And she was so good at keeping a conversation going. With her, unlike with so many other people, he never felt at a loss for words.

|||

JEAN AND many of her friends saw their office jobs as way stations—and, it was hoped, brief ones. Every month or two at the bank, it seemed, another beaming girl announced an engagement or pregnancy and tendered her resignation, never to return. So when word spread of the surprise visit from "Jean's sailor friend from the train," there were titters and teasing.

"Now tell the truth, Jean," Margaret said. "When you saw him walking toward you, how did you know how far to throw your suitcase?"

"I heard something on the radio today," a friend at the bank said, in mock seriousness. "Drop a suitcase, pick up a sailor."

"No, no, I got it," said another girl at the bank. "What's the best way to land a husband? Toss a suitcase."

"Now, now, girls, no one's getting married," Jean said. "I've known Danny less than a month."

But she had to admit, he was dedicated. On each of the next two weekends, he came to see her in Arlington Heights, sometimes hitchhiking his way up Route 2. They mostly stayed at her house, talking with her parents or sitting beside the radio listening to shows like *Truth or Consequences*, *The Shadow*, and *The Lone Ranger*. When he came up that third weekend, he was a perfect gentleman: he helped her father mow the front lawn while she lay on a blanket in the backyard, sunning. But she could tell something was amiss. He was affectionate one moment, fidgety the next. Bouts of talkativeness were broken up by stretches of brooding silence.

That evening, a Sunday, before he was due back on ship, they parked her car at the bottom of Shade Street. The streetlights filtering through the tree branches turned his face into a study of shadows and light.

"Jean?"

"Yes, darling?"

"Instead of raising horses out west, would you raise children with me?"

"Danny, I don't understand."

"Well, what I mean is, Will you marry me?"

Jean felt for a moment as if she'd fallen through a trapdoor into some dark sea. She slid her hands under Danny's and, suddenly aware of her fast breathing, searched his face.

"Oh, Danny."

"Well?"

"It's so soon."

She looked at the windshield, her heart thrashing against her chest. At the neighbor's house at the dead end, a man was standing, backlit, in the frame of the open front door. The porch light flashed off and on, as if to signal that Shade Street was not a suitable place for couples in darkened cars. She turned back to the sailor in the passenger seat and dug her fingers into his wrist. "I am a little shocked, Danny. Do you think we know each other very well?"

"I know everything I need to know."

"Oh, Danny, I have to think."

|||

IN THE days ahead, she felt his absence more sharply than in any of the previous weeks. How often did men like him come along? How often did they propose marriage by asking a woman if they could raise children together? That is where his aim had been most true. Children were what she had wanted more anything. Her long-ing, she felt, was a symptom of growing up an only child. And here was a man who wanted the same thing. A picture took shape be-fore her eyes of a house filled with bright voices and little feet.

By the end of the week, she had made up her mind. She couldn't hide his proposal from her parents any longer. When she told them after work one day, she was nearly bursting. "I am going to accept," she declared. She stood with her purse in hand, legs firmly planted on the floor.

Her mother set her spoon back into her bowl and slowly turned to her.

"I've prepared some lentil soup," she said. "Would you like some?"

"Mother, I want to get married."

"Eat some soup," her father said.

"Why won't anyone answer me?"

After a dinner taken in silence, her mother spoke. "He seems like a very nice boy," she said. "But you have known him a few weeks only. It is too fast."

Her uncles had eloped with women they hadn't known well enough, she reminded her daughter. "You see their problems now."

"I am telling Danny yes." Jean was defiant. "I love him."

"What you tell him is your business," her father said. "But there will be no wedding for a year."

"But Daddy, his ship could sail," she protested, tears welling. "He could be halfway around the world then."

"All the more reason to wait," her mother said.

||

IN OCTOBER, the refurbished USS *Power*, with Danny on board, steamed out of Boston. It was the start of a long deployment that would take him around the world: Guantánamo Bay, Halifax, San Juan, Rio de Janeiro, Valparaiso, Glasgow, Cannes, Oslo, Lisbon, Gibraltar, Algiers. The destroyer rounded nearly every maritime

Everest: Cape Horn, the Panama Canal, the equator, the Arctic Circle. While other U.S. forces were at war in Korea, the USS *Power* cruised, showing the flag at friendly ports and taking part in training exercises. For a Long Island boy who had longed for a sea-faring adventure, it should have been one of the greatest years of his life. It turned out to be one of the loneliest.

In the letters they traded—as many as one a day some weeks—reports of the humdrum were salted with confessions of pained yearning.

"It isn't too bad during the day when we are working but after hours while I lie in my rack as I am doing now, I think about you constantly," Danny wrote. He lamented that "it isn't my good fortune to be able to express my feelings in a letter as my mother does when she writes to me."

"Dearest Dan, I feel no more like writing tonight," Jean wrote. "I just want you here with me, no distance between us . . . When we are married and your sea duty is over I want to go wherever you are stationed. I wouldn't care if I saw anyone if you were only with me."

New Year's 1952 came and went. A bitter New England winter turned to spring. They set a wedding date of December 4, 1952, soon after Danny's expected return. Jean began calling churches, ministers, and photographers. She put in for time off from work. But for a long while, all they had were their letters. Jean wrote about Red Sox games (a 6–3 win over the Senators!) and the age-old Lexington vs. Concord football match (Lexington lost 20–0). She cataloged the early wedding gifts—a covered casserole dish, a damask tablecloth, a pair of hurricane lamps, a pink nightgown—that she had already socked away in her hope chest.

In each letter she noted the days left until the wedding. She reminded him of any odd anniversary of the night he'd rescued her—and her suitcase—at Grand Central: the five-month anniversary, the fifteen-month.

Danny wrote of a plane that crashed on a nearby aircraft carrier and the water his ship took on during a refueling. He wrote of his "Shellback Initiation" into the "Kingdom of Neptune." It was a rite of passage, he explained, that all new sailors, or "pollywogs," undergo on their first equator crossing. ("Boy was my rear end sore.") And he wrote of the school of porpoises that had trailed the ship one day and the changing, deepening colors of the stars and sea.

He confessed to getting too drunk on liberty in Guantánamo Bay but vowed that he had been faithful to her, even in the face of temptation. "I wish there were some way to atone for it but at least I didn't give myself to any Cuban girls. I hope you believe me my darling because if I had I wouldn't have been able to write this letter to you. I suppose I got drunk because I kept thinking about how much I love you and how decent you are."

She replied with understanding. "Even if you had gone with one of the so called girls, Dan, I could and would have forgiven you," she wrote. "You don't have to tell me everything you do honey because I do trust you and believe in you."

He wrote that she was "crazy to put up with a guy like me."

Her parents, she saw, had been right to make her wait. The thousands of words that had spun out across the oceans during their separation were like threads that pulled them ever closer, forming a seam that life on land together would surely test. For Jean, that test came sooner than expected. In late September, Danny wrote that the Navy was extending his cruise. Their wedding would have to wait. How long, he couldn't say.

A few days later, when she read the letter, Jean could not contain her tears. She had already booked the minister and the photographer for December 4, and had gotten the time off work. She cried in her room for a half hour, shuddering, then folded her legs into her chest. Their wedding date had been sacrosanct. It was the fixed spot on the horizon she'd been gliding toward, the one that during their long separation had given her courage and hope. Now there was nothing except the prospect of telling everyone that the wedding was in limbo.

"My Darling, Please forgive me for not writing but I have been in such a state of depression," Jean wrote in early October 1952. "No one could even speak to me Friday in work or I would burst into tears."

She wrote again a few days later. "If I could just hear from you now tomorrow to tell me everything is definite, I could go along and make my plans all over again. It is just this awful indefinite feeling that gets you down."

Danny apologized in letter after letter. In one, he included an article from the *New York Times* about low morale in the Navy, so she knew not to take the postponement personally. The article made clear that the service wasn't great at keeping anyone happy.

Days passed with no news. The girls at work threw her a shower, but Jean couldn't shake a horrible feeling of uncertainty. What if he did give himself to some other girl? What if his ship was sent to war? Many nights, she awoke at some ungodly hour with a start, her hair damp with perspiration.

Then—yes, there it was at the foot of her door—a letter. And inside—she looked for it before she read anything else—the name of a real month and a real day. Danny wrote that his commanders were all but certain his ship would be home by December 5.

Cautiously, Jean began a new set of wedding preparations. For the ceremony, she chose Saturday, December 27, a date that left plenty of room for another extension of Danny's cruise. It also happened to be an "anniversary"—the nineteen-month, to be exact—of the night they found each other at Grand Central.

As she sat at her wooden writing table on a brisk fall night, wind rocking the window frames, she reread Danny's last letter. He told her he was passing Gibraltar, near the meeting point of two continents. And would she believe? From the ship's deck, he could see large apes—so humanlike—climbing the ragged bluffs along the coast. She fell asleep that night, her deepest sleep in weeks, thinking about how happy the sight must have made him.

Freestanding

LIBERTY ENLIGHTENING
THE WORLD

*The statue of "Liberty Enlightening
the World" was herself a kind of immigrant, crossing
the Atlantic in the hold of the French frigate Isère
and landing on Bedloe's Island in New York Harbor
in June 1885. The 151-foot statue was a gift from
the people of France to the people of America,
honoring the countries' shared ideals and the
centennial of the Declaration of Independence. But
the statue's symbolism was meant to have a far longer
reach. The seven spikes in her crown represent the
seven continents and seven seas; the broken shackles
at her feet, the universal human impulse to freedom.
In her sonnet "The New Colossus," etched inside
the statue's pedestal, Emma Lazarus called Liberty
a "Mother of Exiles" who asks the world to
"send these, the homeless, tempest-tost to me."*

Tina Wagenbrenner's friends Liz and Ron were consummate New Yorkers, the type who dispensed advice on all things Big Apple whether you'd asked for it or not. "The lines are so big, you gotta get there first thing in the morning," said Ron. "He's right, Tina," said Liz, whom Tina had known since those long-ago days when Liz had dated her brother. "Otherwise, fuhgeddaboudit."

So at dawn on that summer day in 1988, Tina and her son, Todd, boarded a train from her aunt's place in Long Island and got to the ferry at Battery Park early enough to have their pick of seats.

"Let's go up top," Tina told Todd, glimpsing the outlines of the Statue of Liberty through the haze of an August morning. "I want you to see what the immigrants saw."

Tina took a seat on an empty bench, but her son ran off.

"Not too far, hon," Tina cried out. His father hadn't been around much since the separation. Todd was a tough kid, ten years old now, a skateboarder who played it cool and never wanted for friends. But she could sometimes still see the hurt in his eyes, the kind that could make him seem like a little boy. She spotted him at the ferry's railing, gazing out over the harbor as the wind caught his hair. "He needs this," she told herself.

She thought for a moment of a favorite phrase of her late mother's. It was about the two things parents owed children. "Give them roots," her mother used to say, "and give them wings."

|||

AT GRAND Central Terminal, where he got off the train from the airport, Chris Holter felt shrunken by the city's immensity. Hundreds of people—or was it thousands?—were crossing the vast marble concourse with a seemingly choreographed efficiency. He cradled his small bag and sheltered against a wall near a row of ticket booths. How well had he planned for America?

Twenty-five and single, Chris had left home for a simple reason: escape. From sameness. From routine. For the past three years, he had worked the overnight shift on a factory assembly line in Straubing, Germany, a small city at the foot of the Bavarian Forest where his single mother had raised him and four siblings. The plant made television parts, and his work involved spinning copper wires onto plastic circuit boards. At quitting time, his fingers throbbed with another night's worth of nicks from where wire had caught skin.

In early August 1988, the plant shut for its customary summer furlough. Chris had always spent the three weeks off in Straubing, loafing with friends at the public swimming pool or beer hall. But this year somehow, that had no longer seemed enough.

His trip to America, he told himself, would be modest. He would visit New York and Washington, D.C., with a possible side trip to Pittsburgh. A friend of his Uncle Gerhard's allegedly lived there—a man his uncle had corresponded with through an international pen-pal program and had met only once, decades before. But that's where Chris's planning ended. How he'd get around, where he'd stay, how much things cost, whom he might call in a pinch—such details, it dawned on him now, might have been best sorted out in advance.

On the streets outside Grand Central, the air was heavy with a gritty heat and the vague smell of melting tires. Chris stopped in the first cheap-looking hotel, dabbed at the sweat on his forehead, and booked a room for two nights. At the front desk, he asked directions to the one thing he knew for certain was in New York.

"Which way," he said, "to the Statue of Liberty?"

||||

A HORN blew, and Tina gripped the sides of her seat as waves knocked the ferry into the pilings. "Hold on, Todd," she shouted across the deck, but her son was off in his own world.

Tina, forty, had spent the past year watching her marriage of two decades crumble. She had such a cheerful disposition that few of the other teachers at her school, in Newport News, Virginia, would have seen her suffering. But by the time she and Todd had moved out of the house, she felt isolated and at sea.

Her rock, as she put it, was her Aunt Helen, a no-nonsense Long Island woman who had taken on a maternal role after Tina's parents died. "If it's all right, I'd like to come up to Long Island for a few days with Todd," Tina had announced to her one day on the phone. "We need to get away." But that wasn't exactly it, Tina realized. What she needed was to come home—to a different home, where people could help her and Todd feel like part of a family again.

A few days before her trip, at a bookstore in Newport News, she came across a picture book on New York City. When she reached the photographs of the Statue of Liberty, she stopped. Her father had been born in Bavaria, and was sixteen and alone when he steamed past the statue in the 1920s on his way to the immigration center at Ellis Island. He came with little money and no English but had somehow cobbled together a new life. Her circumstances were different, to be sure, but wasn't she attempting a version of the same thing?

She pictured herself in his place, a boy from a faraway land, the son of a trolley operator, on a boat steaming into Upper New York Bay and the unknown. My God, Tina thought, how did he do it? I have friends, a job, people who care about me. Who did dad have?

William Wagenbrenner had met Tina's mother, a farmer's daughter from White Russia, at a dance on Long Island in the early 1930s. It was a glimmering moment, followed by a series of setbacks: his siblings never honored their promise to join him in America; a strike at his factory forced him into the bread lines. He served as a U.S. Army translator during World War II, only to receive the news one day that his parents—still in Munich—had been killed by a stray American bomb. But if these things left scars, he didn't let his family see. "Everything's going to work out," he told Tina after visits to the bread line. Then he'd pat his children on the shoulder and touch his fingers to his heart.

She hoped she had inherited some small measure of his resilience. But with the turmoil of the past year, she wasn't sure. She was still daydreaming when a warm voice with a foreign accent brought her back to the ferry deck. A man in shorts and a loose tank top was standing a couple of feet away, at a deferential angle, pointing to an open spot beside her.

"Ma'am," he said, but it came out sounding like "Mom." "Is this seat taken?"

||||

OFF BALANCE from the long journey, Chris awoke unsure of whether he'd slept for two hours or for ten. As the bus rolled through Midtown and Wall Street on the way to Battery Park, he marveled at the heights of the buildings. The tallest structure in Straubing was its five-hundred-year-old clock tower, which measured just sixty-eight meters, a dwarf by New York standards.

"This is an adventure," he told himself, smiling, as the city's sights and sounds rushed him.

For years, he had dreamed of visiting America.

Half of what he knew of it came from his Uncle Gerhard. A Falstaffian fellow, Gerhard had visited as a young man in the 1950s and came back prattling on about American-style freedom and singing songs with lyrics like "You say tomato" and "Hey, good-looking." The other half came from *The Terminator*, *Top Gun*, and other action movies, which had absorbed Chris in dubbed German in the two-screen cinema in the town square.

Still, the United States seemed a world away. Chris had never been farther from home than Austria. But with no wife or

children to support and free rent—he lived with his mother—
he eventually put aside enough money for a nonstop flight to
New York.

That morning, every seat on the ferry's bottom deck was
taken. So he climbed the stairs and quickly noticed two things: a
single empty seat and the woman sitting next to it. She had coal-
black hair and a slender figure, with a deep tan. She was exotic—
nothing like the blondes back home. She was alone, it seemed,
and looking at some distant point over the heads of the other passengers. A smile played on her face, as if in recollection of some
long-ago happiness.

When Chris asked if the seat beside her was taken, she
seemed almost to shudder. He hoped she hadn't misunderstood
his accented English. But then, just as suddenly, her smile returned and she waved him to the seat.

"Oh, please," she said.

"Thank you, ma'am."

Not five seconds passed before she spoke again. "So I hear
that accent, where ya from?"

Now it was his turn to be startled. Back in Germany people
tended to be reserved, particularly with strangers. He remembered from the Hollywood movies he'd seen in Straubing that
American women were often outgoing. But a direct personal
question to a stranger?

"Sorry? Me?"

"Yeah, you," she said, with a throaty laugh. "I hear something
in the way you speak. It's different."

"I am from Germany."

"Where in Germany?"

"Bavaria. You know where it is?"

"This is very funny." She shook her head. "You won't believe
this."

"I'm sorry?"

"That's where my dad's from, same part."

"Yeah?" Chris said, raising his eyebrows a little.

|||

WHEN TINA turned to face the strange man, she saw he was quite a bit younger than she was. He had blond hair, a broad mouth, and eyes that seemed to squint when they looked at you.

"So you just moved to the United States?" Tina asked.

"No," he said. "Here just two weeks. Vacation. Yeah?"

"First time to New York?"

"First time to America."

"Well, where's your group?"

"No group," he said, smiling. "Just me."

Is this man out of his mind? Tina thought. I need help in New York City, and I'm an American.

She shot him a look of concern but held her tongue. He probably didn't want a lecture.

"Okay, but what about a camera?" He was carrying nothing so much as a bag. "How will you remember your trip?"

"I take pictures in my head," the man said, tapping his temples with his forefingers. She laughed, and then he laughed, too.

With the boat slowing as it reached Liberty Island, Tina's son returned.

"Todd, this person is from Germany."

"Okay," Todd said. "So?"

"I am Chris," the man said. "Nice to meet you."

"Whoa, Mom, he sounds like the Terminator," Todd said.

"Honey, be nice," Tina said.

"Yeah, it's rad. It's like that guy, Arnold Schwarzenegger."

Chris looked at mother and son, paused for a moment, then deadpanned: "Ahl be bahk."

"Oh, whoa," Todd said. It had been a long time since Tina had seen her son with so free a smile.

|||

AS THE boat docked, passengers on the upper deck rushed to the exits. Everyone had been warned about the line into the statue. Chris stood up, but found himself lingering. Tina was the first American woman he'd met. She was in some ways a perfect likeness of the ones in movies: funny, extremely friendly, attractive in a wholesome way. He hadn't expected there to be a child. But there he was, which meant there probably was a husband somewhere.

Tina had lingered, too, rummaging for longer than necessary, it seemed, through her bag.

"You know you could get hurt in this city by yourself," Tina said.

"I'm not so worried."

"Are you sure?" Tina said. "I don't want to get in your way. But if you wanted to tag along with us for part of the day, you're really welcome to."

When he didn't respond right away, she said, "Wait a sec. I've got this book." She reached back into her bag. "*New York*," the title said. "*A Picture Book to Remember Her By.*" Turning to the pages on Chinatown and Wall Street, she said, "If you were planning to see these, you should come along."

He had never met anyone quite so direct. But wasn't adventure, a plunge into the unknown, the whole point of his trip? What could he lose?

"Okay," he said, shrugging. "Sure."

Tina and Todd stepped onto the lawn beneath the statute's granite pedestal and asked a tourist to snap a photo. Small waves splashed against the island's rocky shore, and Todd peered up at Lady Liberty, in her verdigris robes and spiked crown, arm outstretched.

"Todd, look at the camera," Tina said as the shutter clicked. "Okay, and now one with Chris."

"Me?"

"Who else? Get up here, you."

They climbed through the star-shaped pedestal and started up the narrow staircase that coils like a helix through the twenty-two-story steel skeleton. The inside of the statue was some twenty degrees hotter than the outside—there is no air-conditioning—and everyone was soon breathing hard and sweating.

"My feet, Mom," Todd said, giving his mother a pained look. "I can't do it."

"You can, Todd. Breathe, then step. Breathe, then step. Don't think about the top, honey, until we're there, okay?"

At last, her chest heaving, Tina staggered to the light streaming through the arc of windows that ring the base of the crown.

"Are you okay?" Chris asked.

"I cry easily," Tina said, laughing though the tears.

Chris handed her a handkerchief, and she touched it to the soft skin under her eyes.

"But Mom, we made it," Todd said.

"We did, honey. We did." She looked at the sun reflecting off the water and boats gliding silently below. Outside one window were Liberty's sturdy forearm and the handle of her torch, almost close enough to touch. Tina tousled her son's hair. "Just look at the view from here."

Later, after descending into the base of the statue, Tina told Chris about her immigrant father—how he built a modest life for his wife and three children as a bakery deliveryman. She had grown up, she told Chris, in a working-class town on Long Island called Bay Shore. The whole family had lived in a one-bedroom apartment above a clothing store on Main Street. Even after he'd moved on to a better-paying job at an aviation factory, she said, her father never lost his fellow feeling for new arrivals to America.

Whenever he heard that a newcomer to Bay Shore—an immigrant from some godforsaken country—was down on his luck, her father would go see him. "Stop by our house for dinner some-time," he'd say. And when the man and his family showed up, along with the food went a helping of advice on the makings of American-style success. Her father's impulsive charity vexed her mother, who wouldn't know until the last minute whether she was cooking for one family or three.

At a small museum inside the pedestal, Tina studied the sepia-toned photographs of immigrants disembarking at Ellis Island: men and women slouching under the weight of bundled possessions, awaiting a battery of inspections, their faces webbed with fear.

"Look at all these souls," she said, reaching for her son's hand. "They came with only the things on their back. When we go back home, we have to be grateful for the things we have. Like a place to live, our friends, our possessions."

They walked past a few black-and-white portraits of men who never made it past Ellis Island—the fabled 2 percent whom immigration officials sent back to their homelands, often because they seemed to have no means of support in America.

"I never knew my father," Chris said suddenly.

He told Tina that his father had died of kidney failure when his mother was seven months pregnant with Chris. His father was just thirty-three. To support the family after his death, his mother worked as a live-in cook and housekeeper for the owner of a local shoe factory. Chris's sister, eight years older, served as a kind of surrogate mother to her four younger siblings.

"The house had two rooms," Chris said as they stepped outside into the sunlight. "My sister got one to herself. The four boys had to share the other."

"Whoa, no fair," Todd said. "I could never do that."

Back in Manhattan, they walked through Chinatown and Little Italy, and visited the World Trade Center, Trinity Church, and the Federal Hall National Memorial. Soon it was 5 p.m.

An hour remained before Tina and Todd had planned to meet their friend Ron at his Wall Street office. Ron was going to ride the train with them to his house on Long Island, where Tina had parked her car that morning after driving over from Aunt Helen's.

"You hungry?" Tina asked Chris.

"Yes, okay, please."

She saw a sign that said "German Pub," and ducked down a few steps to a below-ground restaurant. A waiter waved them to a table.

"So what's next, Schwartzie?" she said.

"Schwartzie?"

"Schwarzenegger's too long," she said, winking at her son. "When you were in the little boy's room, Todd and I decided we're calling you Schwartzie."

"Yeah," Todd said. "Can't wait to tell my friends at school."

"As you wish," Chris said. "Maybe you can tell them you met Arnold's cousin."

"Isn't this great?" Tina said, tapping the top of his menu. "They've got knockwurst, bratwurst, wieners. Just like home, right?"

"Yes, just like home," he said. "That is why I will eat this," he said, tilting the menu toward her and running his finger under the words "cheeseburger with fries."

"Really?"

"I didn't come to New York for bratwurst," he said, smiling.

"Okay, so what kind of beer do you want?" Tina said, looking at the drink list.

"Beck's is good," he said.

"Ooh, I've never had that before."

"It's German."

"I'm usually a Budweiser gal. Mostly 'cause I can't afford anything imported."

"The Budweiser people I think were German, so you have been drinking German beer, just in American clothes."

"I never thought of that, Schwartzie."

The waitress brought out cheeseburgers and the bottle of Beck's, which Chris and Tina poured into separate glasses to share.

When the check came, Tina grabbed it. Chris protested, but she insisted. "As an American," she said, ceremoniously, as she straightened herself in her seat, "as the person who lives here and the host, I should treat you. It's only right."

"But you have already done too much I think—"

"So, anyway, Schwartzie," she said, cutting him off, "like I said, where you off to now?"

Chris said he was going to spend another day or two in the city before heading south to Washington and Pittsburgh.

"How ya gonna get there?" Tina said.

"Bus, train, whichever is costing least."

"You know," she said slowly, turning to Todd, "Washington's really not that far from us. It wouldn't be any trouble to give you a ride."

"Again, please?" He wasn't sure he'd heard her correctly.

"I mean, my friends Ron and Liz are driving back with us to Virginia on Saturday," she said. "We could pick you up in the city on our way out of town and then let you out in Washington."

|||

TINA'S FRIENDS thought she had lost her mind.

"What are you, insane?" Ron said at Aunt Helen's the next night.

Liz said, "You don't know this guy from Adam, and you're gonna spend five hours together in a car. I mean, this guy could be a serial killer."

"Who's a serial killer?" said Aunt Helen, emerging in her smock from the kitchen.

"Nobody," Tina said, flushing. "I met a nice German man at the Statue of Liberty yesterday who I offered to give a ride to tomorrow."

"What did he do, ask you out or something?" Aunt Helen said.

"I know what you're thinking, Aunt Helen, but please, I'm not rushing into things," Tina said. "He didn't ask me out. Didn't even make a pass at me. He doesn't have a lot of money and was thinking about how to get to Washington, and since we're going that way, I offered. Is that wrong?"

"Well, honey—"

"Do you know he's from Bavaria, near where dad grew up?" Tina added.

"Oh?" Aunt Helen said, her expression changing.

"He even knows Hans and Gerta," Tina lied, referring to her cousins in Munich.

"Then I doubt he's a serial killer," Helen said matter-of-factly, patting her on the hand and returning to her dinner preparations. "You're a big girl. You do what you feel is right."

Liz shook her head at Tina and rolled her eyes at the obvious deception.

Aunt Helen's son John, a thirtysomething Manhattan bank executive who heard the whole thing from the other room, could no longer contain himself. "Look, foreign men want just two things—one's a green card, and you know what the other is," he said. "New York's not Newport News, Tina. Don't be a rube. It's not going to last."

Though she didn't let on, their warnings gave her pause. She had always made small talk with strangers. In the supermarket line. On trains. At the park. That wasn't new. But why *had* she spent the whole day with this strange man? Why was she so quick to invite him on a long ride with her?

She had told herself at first that she was only doing what her father would have done. It was poetic, too, that they met on the way to the Statue of Liberty: here's this foreign guy who is coming to greet this lady who greeted so many foreigners. But there was something more. After a year of hurt and hostility, it felt good to be with someone who held doors, carried handkerchiefs, and laughed at her jokes. He was young, which made her feel less than her forty years. And he was playful with her son—so unlike her estranged husband, who could be strict, angry, and controlling. She felt safe because Schwartzie—she loved that he went along with the name—had been a gentleman. Back in Virginia, she'd been to three "Parents Without Partners" singles events, but they'd felt like meat markets. She knew that if Chris had touched her or made so much as the slightest pass, she would not have offered him the ride. All the same, she worried that prudence may have given way to impulse.

⫾⫾⫾

WHEN TINA was a girl, her mother would argue with the priests at their Catholic church about whether priests were really necessary. If worshipers wanted to talk to God, why should they need a go-between? Tina hadn't been to church much as an adult. But a more secular version of her mother's philosophy had endured. "If you put something out to the universe," as Tina had once phrased it, "the universe adapts to meet your needs."

In the weeks after her separation, she had closed her eyes and asked her parents—wherever they were—to watch over her and her son. "If there is someone for me, please let me find him," she whispered into the dark some nights. "If not, I'm okay being alone." She was in no hurry, she told herself. In fact, she needed time alone to recover the person she was before her marriage began to unravel.

Still, when the young man on the ferry said he was from Bavaria—her father's homeland—she believed the universe had winked at her. "It's like a fairy tale," she thought at one point. Then, just as soon, came doubt: New York in the summer was probably crawling with German tourists.

⫾⫾⫾

AT A rest stop on the New Jersey Turnpike, Tina said, "I'm tired. You mind driving for a while?"

She handed Chris the keys to her teal blue Volvo station wagon.

"Really?" he said. The open road had been another touchstone of the American movies he'd seen back in Straubing. "Wow."

Liz and Ron, vigilant, were right behind them in their own car. But by Baltimore, unbeknownst to them, the plan to drop Schwartzie in Washington had been scrapped.

Tina told Chris that a number of friends, including Liz and Ron, were converging on her house in Newport News for a week-end. "It's going to be like a gypsy camp," she told Chris, giggling. "We're going to go crabbing, drink some beer, listen to music. You want to see the real America? This will be it, baby." He could sleep on the couch and catch a bus to D.C. from Virginia on Monday, she told him.

That evening, by the York River up in Gloucester Point, Tina's friends taught Chris how to crab by tying a string around a chicken neck for bait. Later, back at the house, they taught him lines from *Saturday Night Live*'s "Hans and Franz" skit.

"We just want to pump! You! Up!" Chris repeated gamely, even though he'd never heard of *Saturday Night Live*. Everyone had had a few beers by then, and the room erupted in hysterics.

Tina was exhausted and went to bed early. Chris stayed up with the guys, who gathered in front of the VCR to watch *A Nightmare on Elm Street 3: Dream Warriors*.

|||

ON MONDAY morning, Tina dropped Chris at a Greyhound bus station and sent him on his way to Washington. He checked into a seedy hotel in a neighborhood he soon realized was the province of drug dealers and prostitutes. He spent lit-tle time in the room. Over a couple of days, he saw the Capi-tol, the Washington Monument, and Arlington Cemetery, and took a jog around the Mall. In Pittsburgh, he saw his Uncle Gerhard's old acquaintance, an elderly man named Ralph who showed him Three Rivers Stadium and spun stories about the good old days.

America, with its kaleidoscope of people and its dramatic history, fascinated Chris. Still, at the back of his mind was Tina. He loved how fluid she was with people. She was friendly, not just to him but seemingly to everyone she met—waiters, other tourists, the people who stopped her on the street for directions, mistaking her for a native. She had a way of making everyone around her feel good. "Full of life!" Chris knew it was a popular American expression—he may have heard it on a TV commercial. He thought it fit her perfectly.

It had been nearly a week since they'd parted. He was anxious about how she might react if he got back in touch now. A week was plenty of time for chemistry—if you could even call it that—to dissipate. His return flight to Germany was now just two days away. But he had an open-ended ticket, and he didn't have to be back to work at the factory for another week and a half.

On his last night in Pittsburgh, he worked up the courage to call her. "Hello, um, Tina," he said.

"Schwartzie!"

She told him she was going camping in the mountains for a week with Todd and his friend. Did he want to come?

From her voice, it was as if six minutes had passed, not six days.

|||

THEIR WEEK in the Adirondacks was a turning point. They hiked up Blue Mountain, a grueling four-hour trek, and stayed in a cabin that belonged to one of Tina's college friends. It was an isolated spot in the wilderness, without electricity or plumbing. Chris canoed and picnicked with Todd and his friend during the day, and accepted their invitations to play manhunt in the woods. "I want Schwarzenegger on my team," one would shout. "No fair, he was on your team yesterday," the other would say.

While Tina was away for her evening bath in a nearby pond, Chris built a fire so the cabin would be warm when she returned.

At campfires after dark, they talked more about their families and their past relationships. They talked about their aspirations—how she tried to absorb as much as possible while sightseeing so she'd have lessons to share with her elementary school students, how he hoped for a life with more balance. The more time she spent with him, the more he reminded her of her father: good-mannered but playful, strong but gentle. And optimistic, even in the face of struggle.

"What's the worst that can happen?" Chris said at one point, trying to buck her up. "The good thing about being down is you can only go up." It was an expression her own father might have used.

On the drive home, they saw roadway signs for the Great New York State Fair, in Syracuse, and pulled off. When the boys ran ahead to examine a prizewinning cow, Chris slipped his hand into Tina's. It was the first time they'd really touched, and she recoiled. It was too tender, she thought. It was something people in a committed relationship did. She wasn't sure what was happening between them. But she was levelheaded enough now to face facts: Chris was going home to Germany, and Germany was three thousand miles away. Why sink your heart into something when you know—when you can see—it will wind up in pieces? Why bother? She was annoyed at him, and at herself. "What are you doing?" she snapped.

Chris raised their interlocked fingers to eye level, as if close study would convince Tina of the gesture's innocence. "I'm just holding your hand."

Tina lowered their hands, but didn't let go.

"Okay," Tina said after a few moments, as her breathing settled. "Just holding my hand. Okay."

Back in Newport News, she asked Chris to write his home address and phone number in her book. Then she drove him to Fredericksburg, where a bus was leaving for New York's JFK Airport. They gave each other a peck on the lips. Then the bus doors wheezed shut and he was gone.

At the house, Tina found herself short of breath. What had just happened? What had she done? Her emotions were roiling. Frantic, she ran to the counter by the back door. Where was her address book? It was the last thing he touched, and when she found it, under an old newspaper, she rippled through to the pages marked "H." Beneath "Chris Holter" and a street address, she saw now that he had also inscribed something else: "I love you." Then, a final notation: "I'll be back."

||

BACK HOME in Straubing, Chris buried himself in work, hoping to forget about the woman he'd met in America. "Back to the job," he kept telling himself. "Back to routine." But the routine seemed more and more like drudgery. He looked down at the conveyer belt and the never-ending parade of plastic circuit boards. Each time one came off on his end, another appeared at the other. His fingers had healed in America, but the copper wires scored them now as mercilessly as before.

"Just let it go," he told himself. "One day maybe you'll go back to America, and you can look her up. See if she remembers you. But for now, for a few years, just forget her. Forget. Forget."

Then, a couple of weeks later, a letter arrived. Chris's hand shook as he opened the envelope. Inside, beneath an amusing recap of their time together, Tina had written, "I love you, too."

Their phone bills got so expensive —$350 in one month— that they decided to mail each other cassette tapes instead. They filled entire forty-five-minute sides with stories from their lives and with songs they recorded off favorite albums. "I'm getting ready for work," one might begin. Or, "It's another snow day."

Her first trip to Germany, late that December, with Todd, had its share of cultural gaffes. Tina's informality shocked some of his relatives: she hugged everyone she met—handshakes were about as far as Chris's relatives typically went, even with family. And when there weren't enough chairs to go around during coffee and kuchen one afternoon, Tina just plopped down on the floor and took her food there.

"Get up, get up," Chris's mother said, aghast. "She'll catch cold down there."

His relatives tried to teach her German phrases. She tried to teach them the Mexican Hat Dance.

"My family likes you," Chris confided one night. "But I'm not sure they completely understand you."

American tourists weren't much seen in Straubing, and everywhere she went, people stopped to stare at the visitor and her son, who had become minor celebrities. "*Amerikaner*," kids shouted. "*Amerikaner*."

In February 1989, Chris returned to Virginia for a visit. By late that spring, he told his family he was moving to America to be with Tina. None of his siblings, all older, had left Straubing, and his mother, aggrieved, shook her head at the news. "Every generation has its crazy Holter," she said. "First Uncle Gerhard with his ideas about America. Now you. How will you survive? You don't know anything. All you have is this woman."

But Uncle Gerhard urged him to go. "The family ordered me back to Straubing, and for what? To sell shoes for the rest of my life.

"Go," Gerhard said. "Go for me."

Chris arrived in June and moved in with Tina and her son. He had no job prospects at first but soon enrolled in an apprentice program in brick masonry. In December, in the dining room of the nearby Chamberlin Hotel, with its sweeping view of Chesapeake Bay, Chris proposed.

They were married on Valentine's Day 1990, at the home of an elderly justice of the peace and his wife.

Depths

THE SUBWAY

During its construction, the New York subway
had few fans. The four years of excavation and engineering turned
Manhattan into a kind of war zone: dynamite booms, streets
blasted into ragged trenches, explosions that shattered glass and
terrorized horses and pedestrians, a string of grisly construction
deaths, and a gambling and prostitution racket to serve the influx
of miners. Some newspapers urged city leaders to call the whole
thing off. What price progress? they asked, according to one
history. But as soon as the Interborough Rapid Transit opened in
October 1904—"From City Hall to Harlem in 15 Seconds!"—the
subway would become inseparable from the city's identity and the
lives of its residents. By 1908, it was carrying some eight hundred
thousand riders a day, a third above its official capacity. But in a
city of great social stratification, the subway performed another
important function, one with no connection to transportation. As
M. L. Fried and V. J. DeFazio observed in 1974, in the journal
Psychiatry, "The subway is one of the few places in a large urban
center where all races and religions and most social classes are
confronted with one another and the same situation."

Chesa Sy had been traveling for nearly thirty hours when her plane landed at JFK. Sapped of any sense of time, she found a clock in the arrival area and realized that New York was precisely twelve hours behind Manila. Her home, in the Philippines, was literally halfway around the world.

It was August 2001, and nearing midnight. Her only thoughts, as she waited at the luggage carousel, were of the old high school friend she'd planned to stay with. Chesa had known Malaya since kindergarten in Dagupan City—both had Chinese fathers and Filipino mothers. They had been academic rivals in high school, dueling for the best grades. But Chesa had always cast herself as the more adventurous. So it was with some relish, Chesa thought, that Malaya announced a few years back that *she* was going to America, for a job as a nurse.

Chesa, thirty now, had a degree in accounting and a job as a bank teller in Manila. But in going to America—America!— Malaya had her beat. Malaya had even called Chesa back in May to bait her. "America is very different from the Philippines," she sniffed. "Much better. You'd see if you ever visit."

When the American Embassy finally sent Chesa a letter approving her visa, Chesa decided against giving Malaya the satisfaction of an advance warning. The best way to cut her friend down to size would be to show up at her door, unannounced. That would show her, all right.

But now that she was in this nearly windowless terminal, squinting at the airport map, she wondered whether she should have called Malaya first. The airport was labyrinthine and confusing. New York City, she suspected, would be even worse.

After collecting her bags, she followed a group of people she recognized from her flight. There was likely just one main route into New York, she thought, and this group seemed brisk and efficient in the way of people familiar with big cities. Outside a set of sliding glass doors, they all boarded a shuttle bus marked

"MTA/Subway." At the subway station, the other riders scattered so quickly that Chesa was left standing alone at the curb. A sign said "Howard Beach." But she had not heard of that part of New York. She feared that she was utterly lost.

||||

MILTON JENNINGS should have been in New York eight hours earlier. He was flying home from Reno, Nevada, after a weeklong hiking trip with his parents near their summer cabin in the California mountains. But there had been flight delays, and Milton, clean-cut and six feet tall, with a native New Englander's penchant for punctuality, was irritated at what he now saw would be less than a full night's sleep, He had moved to New York just seven months earlier for a job as a classical music reviewer at a big online retailer. He was expected at work first thing the next morning.

After a week of crisp mountain breezes, August in New York felt like a swamp, even at midnight. God knew how often the A train stopped at Howard Beach at this hour. He was eager to get back to his one-bedroom apartment in Brooklyn, unpack, and go to sleep.

"Excuse me?"

The woman's voice—accented and pleading—came from behind him in line at the token machine.

"Sir?"

He looked over his shoulder and saw a slender Asian woman with anxious eyes. Her dark hair, which glinted under the station lights, was tied in a loose ponytail that fell across the front of her shoulder. Milton raised his eyebrows to acknowledge her, but didn't speak.

"Excuse me," she said. "You know how I go to Chinatown?"

"Um, well, yeah," he said. "Let me just get a token first."

He led her to wall-mounted subway map and traced the blue line showing the A train's route.

"You'll come down here and across here," he said, sweeping his index finger across Brooklyn and the East River. "Then look out for Broadway-Nassau Street. That's your stop."

"Broadway? Broadway?" she said, with some dim note of recognition.

"Broadway-Nassau," he said. "It's the name of the stop in Chinatown. The subway stop. You should get off there."

"Tenk you."

From the worried look she gave him, he suspected she had only partly understood. Fresh off the boat, Milton thought, as he duck-walked his suitcases through the turnstile. Scattered along the faintly lit platform at almost equal intervals were four or five other riders, shadows, worn-looking and alone. The station, Milton saw, was undergoing remodeling for something called the AirTrain, a new tram that would link the subway system to the airport. That explained why the place was an obstacle course of plywood ramps, wire-mesh fencing, and bare, dangling light bulbs. What a mess, Milton thought, growing anxious for the sound of a train.

The Asian woman appeared along the platform. He smiled at her, more out of courtesy—and perhaps boredom—than anything else. She nodded. She stopped about six feet from him and set down her bags. They were the only two people at that end of the platform.

|||

CHESA WALKED in behind the gentle-looking man who had given her directions. He sat at one end of a long bench, and she, at the other. The train picked up speed. He had turned toward her and seemed to be saying something. But the train was shaking and rattling. She couldn't hear. She scooted down the bench until she was at arm's distance. The man, she saw now, had a very tidy haircut, precisely trimmed and brushed high across the forehead, the kind you saw on American presidents and little boys.

"I was asking if you know anything about New York."

He wore a pained look, as though discomfited, she thought, by the necessity of raising his voice.

"Oh, yes, tenk you," she said, pointing to her ears. "I know Brooklyn Bridge."

"Why are you here?"

"I see a friend from Philippines."

"Is that where you're from?"

"Manila."

"And you came by yourself to New York? That's pretty, well, brave." He looked at her kindly but gave his head a half shake. Did he maybe not approve of a woman traveling alone?

She shifted to what she hoped was a safer subject. "You like basketball?" she asked. She had played on her high school team and still watched NBA games on satellite TV. "Tim Duncan? San Antonio Spurs?"

He laughed. "Yeah, I don't know. If I watch any sport, it's baseball."

"I play guard in school," she said. "I make good free throws."

"Really?"

"In Philippines, they say I am tall."

He gave a shy laugh, looking at her sideways with a boyish smile. She pushed her hair over her ear, nodding enthusiastically. She was glad no one else was on their car. In her country, she would have felt self-conscious talking to a man alone in public.

|||

MILTON, THIRTY-FOUR years old, was not the chatty sort. He grew up in the Berkshires, in the rural northwestern corner of Massachusetts, and had been a reticent child, the son of art historians at the local college.

As a boy, he preferred the recordings of Mozart and Beethoven to the rough shouts of the schoolyard. His interest in music had blossomed so young that he had to ask his father to lower the phonograph needle onto the grooved vinyl—his own hands were too unsteady. He studied piano and trumpet and then shifted in college to obscure early music instruments like the harpsichord and cornetto. He was in the middle of a doctorate in ethnomusicology at Princeton in late 2000 when one day—he wasn't sure why then exactly—he suddenly lost heart. He had submerged so deeply in his studies that he had few friends and little life beyond the ivory tower. He hadn't dated a girl—not really—in five years. When a friend joked at a recent birthday that he was nearing middle age, it had stung. He was no longer sure he wanted the life of an academic, with its isolation and endlessly deferred gratification. When he saw a listing for the classical reviewing job in Manhattan, he glimpsed a way out. In New York, he knew, he'd live among some of the finest symphonies and opera companies in the world. He would inhabit music, not dissect it. He would share his discoveries not with some preening thesis adviser but with ordinary listeners as passionate as he.

In New York, music traveled with him everywhere. On the subway, to tune out the rush-hour clatter, he would load his portable CD player with some new album from work, shut his eyes, and lose himself in the wash of notes. Were more people on the train now, he would have done just that. Anonymity—the ability to be simultaneously surrounded by and withdrawn from other people—was one of the subway's chief pleasures. But tonight there was just one other rider in his car, and it would have felt awkward, particularly since they'd already spoken. The woman wore a lost look, and he felt a tinge of sympathy. Not that long ago, he had been a newcomer to the city. He still found the subway system mystifying enough to go nowhere without his pocket map.

The more they spoke, the sorrier he felt for her. The Brooklyn Bridge and the New York Knicks? If that's all she knew about the city, she was in trouble. At a minimum, Milton thought, her friend should have met her at the airport. "My stop is next," he told her, looking a little apologetic. His one-bedroom apartment, in Fort Greene, Brooklyn, was a few blocks from the Lafayette Avenue station. "You'll stay on this line for maybe fifteen more minutes. Look for signs on the wall that say 'Broadway-Nassau Street,' okay?"

"Tenk you," she said. "Please, sir, you can give me your phone number?" She said that because he had helped, she was obliged to return the favor.

"It's no problem, really."

"In my country, yes, it is necessary."

He took the fold-up subway map from his pocket and wrote his phone number in the margin. "This is a map—you may need it." Never expecting to hear from her again, he gripped his bags and disappeared into the night.

||||

AS SOON as Milton stepped off, a few drunk-looking teenagers piled in. They tumbled atop one other on one of the rear seats, snorting and laughing. Chesa hugged her bags and kept her face to the window, scanning the walls for station names. She hoped the man didn't misunderstand her request for his phone number. She wanted only to be proper. When she was a girl, her father sometimes reacted to ingratitude in his children with a Chinese expression: "If you do me one favor, I am honorable only if I return you ten." It wasn't enough, he told them, to reciprocate in kind. To restore *bao*, or balance, to a relationship, one had to repay a favor with a greater one. Her father had said it didn't matter when or how, so long as it was done eventually.

At the Broadway-Nassau Street station, Chesa doubled back through the underground passageways a few times before finding the stairs that led outside. She was hungry. But it was past 2 a.m. now, and stores nearby looked closed. Chesa did want to surprise Malaya, but a postmidnight knock on the door might be taking things too far. So she began searching for signs for hostels.

From the photos she'd seen on the Internet, she had imagined New York as a giant parking lot of yellow cabs. But the streets here, wherever she was, were a wasteland. She heard a tinkle of glass shattering behind her and shuddered as a trash truck rumbled past. It was fifteen minutes before a cab appeared.

"Please, hotel," she said, shoving her bags across the back seat.

"Any one in particular?" the man said.

"Hostel. For students."

He drove for what seemed like twenty-five minutes. She began to see familiar buildings, as if they'd been driving in circles. When he dropped her off, at a rundown rooming house on a street called Bowery, he asked for forty dollars.

Her sister had given her two thousand dollars in cash for the trip. It was supposed to stretch weeks, even a few months.

"Meter?" she asked.

She could see his eyes shift in the rearview mirror.

"It's broken."

She dug into her pocketbook for two twenty-dollar bills. At the hotel, she pushed another forty through the bars beneath a Plexiglas window. A Chinese man led her upstairs to a small room with paper-thin walls. She spent a sleepless night listening to the thuck-thuck of the ceiling fan and to the squabbling of a couple in the next room.

|||

AT SEVEN the next morning, jittery and frayed, Chesa left the hotel with all of her cash and found the nearest bank. She wired all but a few hundred dollars back to her sister. New York was not what she expected. She wasn't sure she could trust people here.

At a pay phone in Chinatown, she tried her friend's phone number. There was no answer. She walked to the Baxter Street address Malaya had given her months earlier, but no one came to the door. Was there more than one Baxter Street? Had she copied down the right numbers? She spent half a day knocking on neighbors' doors. Many of the people who answered spoke only Mandarin, and no one seemed to know the first thing about anyone named Malaya. What Chesa wouldn't find out until months later was that Malaya had left Manhattan weeks before for a job in a new city.

After a joyless lunch in a dimly lit restaurant, Chesa wove through the narrow streets, hoping to spot her friend among the sea of Asian faces. The neighborhood felt like a third-world bazaar, with stooped men in street stalls selling knockoff bags, costume jewelry, and stacks of exotic-looking fruit and vegetables. From the insides of small groceries came sharp odors of pork and fish.

She struggled to get her bearings. But with so many vendors selling the same products, she couldn't be sure she wasn't doubling back on herself. Then the sun scudded behind the buildings and shadows unfurled along the streets. At her wits' end, she reached into her pocket for the map with the phone number— mortified to be on the cusp of asking another favor.

||||

THE PHONE at Milton's apartment rang minutes after he entered. It had been a busy day at work, and he worried his boss was calling with yet another demand.

But the voice on the line was decidedly not his boss's.

"Hi, Milton."

"Yes?"

"It's Chesa. Girl from subway."

"Oh."

"I'm sorry to call."

"It's okay. What's up?"

"I look and look, but my friend, she is nowhere."

Milton brushed some newspapers off a chair in the kitchen and sat down, leaning his forehead against his hand. "I'm sorry to hear that, Chesa. Gosh, you sure you have no other information about this person?"

"Please, Milton, you're only person I know in America."

Milton felt a tightening in his stomach. "I'd like to help, Chesa, it's just, you know, I'm not sure I'd have any more luck."

"Luck, maybe for me," she said, her voice quavering. "You are only person I know."

This feels like a scam, Milton told himself. Befriend the trusting stranger on the subway, play the damsel in distress, then rob him blind. The perfect con.

"Milton?"

There was a long pause. Milton could hear her jagged breathing. "Where are you?" he said.

|||

OVER DINNER at a Bowery Street restaurant, he grilled her. What was her friend's name? Where exactly did she live? Why hadn't Chesa let her friend know she was coming? Where had she spent the night? What was she planning to do here besides visit her friend?

He kept his guard up, looking for holes in her story. But there was dread in her eyes, he saw, and a voice that sounded on the edge of breaking. She was worried, it seemed, not just for herself but for her friend. How is it, she asked, that someone disappears?

When the waiter set down their food, Milton could see tears pooling. He all of a sudden felt bad about his interrogation. This woman trusted him. Why, he wasn't sure. But she did. This intensity of feeling from another person was something he hadn't been around in a long time. The words came almost before his awareness of them. "I, you know, have a couch in my apartment," he said. "It's very uncomfortable. But you could sleep there for a night or two, if you needed to."

Outside, a cold rain was falling. He bought an umbrella from a sidewalk vendor, and she moved under it to keep dry as they carried her bags through the rain. They rode the Q train to his apartment. As it crossed the East River, an arc of lights smudged against rain-streaked windows. "See the Brooklyn Bridge?" Milton said. But when he turned toward the woman at his elbow, she was looking straight ahead. She was a total stranger. He raked his fingers across his beetled forehead and thought, I might just be the biggest sucker in the world.

|||

AS THE door to Milton's apartment clicked shut, Chesa felt unexpectedly vulnerable. She was no longer on a subway or in a restaurant—public places where people kept an eye on one another. She was in a man's apartment, behind a locked door. She had called him because she feared for her safety. But now she was in close quarters with a six-foot-tall man about whom she realized she knew nothing, no matter how trustworthy he seemed. Was she really better off here?

She studied his hands as he jimmied the futon away from the wall, unhooked its latches and laid it flat. He pulled neatly folded sheets from a closet and spread them across the mattress, then returned from another room with a pillow.

He shrugged, as if perturbed or embarrassed. "It's not the Hilton."

"It's okay."

"Chesa, you're welcome to sleep here for a few nights. But I just, well, I mean, I can't give you a key." When he left for work in the mornings, he told her, she'd have to clear out, too.

"Okay."

When she went into the tiny bathroom to change into her pajamas, she could hear rain pelting the window. She felt her pulse quicken. She turned the lock, then tested the door to make sure no one could get in.

In the morning, Milton drew Chesa maps to Manhattan landmarks—Central Park, the American Museum of Natural History, the Met. "You should get to know the city," he said. "And if you take another taxi, Chesa, make sure the meter's on. That cabdriver who charged you forty dollars—that should have been a six-dollar ride."

"Okay." She left her bags in Milton's apartment but took all her money, stuffing bills into the pockets of her coat and jeans. Most of those first few days, she ventured back to Chinatown, hoping to run into her friend. She stopped in laundries and groceries. She asked shopkeepers if they'd seen or heard of Malaya. New York was full of transients, a man selling international calling cards told her. It was hardly unusual for a new immigrant to be here one day, gone the next. A few shopkeepers thought Chesa was no more than another newcomer looking for work. A woman at a jewelry shop handed her a flyer for an agency that claimed to make immediate job placements, for a fee.

After a few days of fruitless searching, her money dwindling, Chesa went to the agency, a bunkerlike office beneath a butcher's shop. She handed over a few bills. The man behind the desk dispatched her the next day to a six-day-a-week, twelve-hour-a-day job as a cashier in a Korean deli.

When she crowed to Milton about her earnings—$350 a week—she was surprised to see him grimace. "For all those hours?" he said. "That's below minimum wage."

She told him that $350 was more than twice her monthly earnings in Manila. Then she handed him a wad of bills.

"For you," she said.

"For what?"

"My part of rent."

It was her first step, however small, toward restoring *bao* between them, she told herself. She wore the proud if somewhat nervous look of a girl bringing home an A on her math test.

After making tea for the two of them, Milton set something metallic in her hand.

"What's this?"

"The key. A copy for Chesa."

She folded her fingers over his, and the cold metal in her palm warmed. Milton didn't withdraw his hand, and they stood, touching, for a long moment. When Chesa looked up and their eyes met, they broke into nervous laughter. Their hands fell to their sides like scattering sparrows.

As the days passed, Milton came to admire her pluck. He doubted he'd have her courage—her ability to fend for herself—if he were deposited alone in a new country. She charged into the world with a self-assuredness that often eluded him. In his apartment in the evenings, he grew anxious for the sound of the front door unlatching. Even after twelve-hour shifts that Milton imagined as grueling, she came home with a cheerful look, as though the best part of her day were just beginning. In the dark, uncertain days after the September 11 attacks, she was one of the few things in his life that felt normal.

"Chesa?" he asked one morning in late September, after she'd cleared their cereal bowls. "Would you like to go to a movie? There's a matinee."

A first date, he told himself, then wondered if that's what you called it when two people already lived together. Others followed: walks through Prospect Park, a matinee of the New York City Opera. And soon, places Chesa chose: the Wonder Wheel at Coney Island; the beach, where Chesa dove in the water while Milton looked on, smiling, from the sand.

Milton held off telling friends and family about the woman in his apartment. In part, he was self-conscious: what would people think? But there was something else, too: For a guy who had always played by the rules, it was titillating to have a somewhat scandalous secret.

||||

THE THING Chesa liked most about Milton was how easy he was, how open. He took time to consider her ideas instead of automatically fighting them, the way her large family often did back in the Philippines. She had a decent childhood—her father owned a small candy company. But she was the third youngest of nine siblings and was accustomed to a noisy house full of brothers and sisters, each with their own opinion about her best interests. She and Milton disagreed sometimes, but he was always rational. He never yelled. And as she strolled with him through the city, looking up at him, her arm around his side, she felt protected, safe.

At the dinner table, when Chesa was a girl, her father drilled in his children what he saw as the essence of a successful romance: astrological affinity. He and his wife, he liked to say, had fallen in love because their Chinese zodiac signs were highly compatible. Whenever one of her brothers or sisters started dating someone new, her father would demand to know their birth year. In short order, after consulting the astrological charts, he would pronounce the relationship either fortuitous or foolish.

Chesa, who considered herself faultlessly modern, had always laughed off her father's superstitions. But in Milton's apartment one weekend that fall, she found herself clicking to a website on Chinese astrology.

"I found out something," she told Milton over breakfast.

"Oh?"

"You are a goat."

"Thanks a lot, Chesa," he said, putting down his cereal spoon. "What is that supposed to mean?"

"Chinese sign," she said. "Because you were born in 1967."

"And so what are you, some kind of sweet-smelling flower?"

"I'm a pig."

Her voice was so earnest that Milton couldn't resist laughing. "Okay, Pig," he said.

That evening, Chesa was back in front of the laptop. She discovered a website that measured the social compatibility of every zodiac pairing. Running her fingers over the grid to the spot where goat met pig, she grew short of breath. Such matches rated a nine out of ten.

"What *is* this?" Milton said, leaning over her shoulder.

"Goat and pig," she said. "Very good together. Read."

The website said that goats and pigs, along with cats, were in the same subgroup of signs. All three, it said, were "peace-loving and highly sensitive animals. They also have great ability to elicit and seek sympathy, hence they are considerate, love and sympathise with each other." What's more, "Pig requires Cat's crafty cunningness and Goat's civility and humility."

Milton gave her a skeptical look. Soon, though, her fascination with the zodiac became an inside joke. When he was feeling flirtatious, he would call her Pig.

"You want something, Goat?" she'd reply.

In late October, after a Sunday walk through streets raw with fall, they sat down on Milton's couch. Their hands found each other's faces and they kissed.

The next few weeks were a dream. Milton drove her to the Berkshires for Christmas to meet his parents. Chesa, who had never before seen snow, insisted on pulling onto the shoulder of the Taconic Parkway to sink her fingers into the white cold.

"Put on your gloves," Milton shouted from the car window.

"No," she said, lobbing a snowball at him. "I want to feel it with my hands."

When they returned to Brooklyn, they folded up the futon and Chesa moved into Milton's bedroom. They started saying, "I love you," and letting friends in on their relationship. New York was working out for Milton in ways he'd never expected.

With the new year upon them, however, they could no longer ignore a distressing reality: her six-month visa would expire in February. If she overstayed, Milton told her, she would be an illegal alien, subject to deportation.

"I don't care," Chesa said petulantly. Nothing mattered, she said, if they had each other.

"Well, I do care," Milton said. "You can't just break the law."

"Everybody does it," she pleaded.

"So that makes it right?"

Chesa wrinkled her brow, trying to hold back tears.

They started talking about other options. If they married, she said one night, trying to appeal to his rectitude, it would all be legal. It made some sense, Milton thought. They'd survived four months together in a small apartment. That boded well, didn't it? And marriage would make them—and her—legitimate.

"I guess we should really do it, right?" he said.

"Only if you are ready, Milton."

"I am, Chesa. I love you."

He knew the marriage would seem abrupt, particularly to friends who had just learned about Chesa. She agreed to his suggestion of a small, no-nonsense civil ceremony. They could hold it at Brooklyn Borough Hall. The sole requirement, some clerk told him, was a twenty-four-hour wait after submitting the application. He left work early one afternoon to buy an engagement ring—an aquamarine framed by two small diamonds. He handed her the black box over dinner at an Italian restaurant.

"What's this?" Chesa said.

"What do you think? It's an engagement ring."

She opened the box. "Why?"

"Oops. What I should have said first was, Will you marry me?"

"You don't already know the answer, Milton?" she said, shaking her head. "Didn't you remember what I said?" In Manila, rings weren't exchanged until the wedding day. She had told him that a while ago. "It's bad luck to do it before."

They picked at the rest of their meal in silence. What should have been one of their happiest nights together felt all of a sudden like a failure.

|||

HIS PARENTS had been skeptical before meeting Chesa. But when they saw how happy their son looked as he tore open gifts with her under the Christmas tree, they could no longer find good reasons to object. Now, though, when he told his parents about their plans, his mother said, "That's wonderful, Milton, but are you two really ready?"

"Of course, Mom," he said, with some pique. "Why wouldn't we be?"

The night he gave her the ring, he couldn't sleep. He loved Chesa. But he had always been deliberate before making big decisions. By any reasonable standard, what he was doing was rash. How well did he know Chesa? Was he doing it for the right reasons? Should a lifelong commitment to another person really be made under deadline pressure?

Two days before their wedding, at the kitchen table, Milton told Chesa he couldn't go through with it.

"You are cold, Milton," she said, weeping.

"I'm sorry, Chesa." He covered his eyelids with his fingertips and shook his head. "We probably should never have discussed it."

On an overcast day in February 2002, Milton and Chesa again rode the A train, but this time in the reverse direction. The terminal at JFK was thronged with travelers, many waiting in a long outdoor security line. It was five months after the September 11 attacks, and the airport was on high alert. Milton walked her to the back of the line. Saying he'd be late for work if he waited much longer, he waved goodbye. "I'll come visit this summer, okay?" he said.

|||

BACK IN the Philippines, Chesa moved in with her sister, who hired her to help work in a fish and produce store that her sister's family ran in the city of La Union. She told her sister that her fiancé would be visiting from America that summer. She spent evenings tidying up the guest room she had set aside for his stay. On lonely nights, she gazed at the pale blue stone on the ring he'd given her and thought about the places she'd take him when he visited.

The days passed. To keep herself busy, she started work on a gift for Milton: a needlepoint of four pigs sprawled atop one another in a grassy field. She spent hours carefully stitching, then brought it to a store for a matte and frame. She knew Milton would smile when he saw it. She tried for a moment to remember what his laugh sounded like.

But June passed, then July and August. Milton had called every week at first. But when she brought up his promise to visit, she could sense his discomfort. "I'm not sure yet, Chesa," he said. "If I can get the time, you know?" He called less often as the summer wore on, and then not at all.

It rained for several nights, and Chesa stayed up late in bed, crying. At first she blamed herself. Milton had taken her in off the streets, and she had repaid him with selfishness. But when weeks passed without a phone call, her heartache turned to anger. Milton was a fake. He was spineless. He had only pretended to love her. His quiet rationality—the thing she loved most about him—hid a cold heart.

In the fall of 2002, she flew back to New York on another six-month visa. She hoped never to see Milton again. She wanted only to work. Her father had passed away a while ago, and her mother was suffering from a serious kidney disease. Chesa wanted to help

that she was back in New York, she returned. She came on a Sunday because she knew that Milton, a creature of habit, always washed clothes on Saturdays. She told herself she did not want to bump into him. What she didn't know then was that Milton hadn't come the day before, because a work deadline had marooned him in the office. That Sunday afternoon, the laundry was jammed. Everyone on the block, Chesa thought, was cleaning their clothes before the Monday crush.

|||

MILTON WAS sitting in a metal folding chair, studying the dry skin on the back of his hands, when he heard the squeak of the front door. He looked up with a jolt. It was Chesa, struggling to shimmy a bulging bag of laundry through the door. Her jug of detergent was so heavy that she was having trouble balancing it all. The Chinese brothers behind the counter loped over to help her.

Milton felt his heart drop in his chest. "Chesa?" he said, standing up. He took a step toward her, trying to smile. But his muscles failed him. The expression came out lopsided.

"I got the pigs," he said, "the needlepoint, thank you."

She set her laundry bag on the lid of a washing machine but didn't move. "Okay."

"I wanted to talk to you."

"What happened?"

"I didn't know where to find you."

"You knew." She studied the doleful turn of his eyes, then shook her head. "But you never came."

"Work has been really busy," he said. "I wanted to, but I just couldn't. I don't know."

She narrowed her eyes and cocked her head to the side, shaking it again. "No vacation all that time?"

He took a step closer. "I cared for you, Chesa. I do still. But I was, I don't know, afraid."

She loosened the strings on her laundry bag and dropped a few blouses into the machine. "Pig, she pushed Goat too much?"

"Maybe a little," he said, with a small laugh of relief. "But I was an idiot. That's all."

When she saw his tears, she reached out with one hand. "Please, Milton."

He took her hand, and she laced her fingers between his. There was a short plastic bench across from a row of washing machines, and they sat down. For nearly two hours, they held each other, silently watching their clothes tumble and thinking hopefully about the next day, and the next.

Elevation

EMPIRE STATE BUILDING

The Empire State Building
was dreamt up by a former New York governor
in the Roaring Twenties and then built,
against all odds, during the doldrums of the
Great Depression. It opened in May 1931
as the tallest building in the world. Though
peerless as a symbol of Manhattan, its
singular art-deco façade was hewn from
material excavated from the very heartland
of America: the state of Indiana.

Claire was getting ready for bed when the phone rang. Even before she picked up, she felt sure it was Chuck. Typically, his voice betrayed no recognition of the late hour.

"Hey babe," it came, bright as morning. "I'm hopping over to New York this weekend. We gotta get together, paint the Big Apple red."

Claire rolled her eyes. "Oh, yeah?" she said, trying for enthusiasm as she slid beneath the covers. "That's great, but I don't live in the city."

"Where's Long Island?"

"It's near, but it's no Big Apple."

"Well, that's why they invented the train, sweetie, right?"

It was September 1969, and Claire Witten had started a year-long research fellowship at Brookhaven National Laboratory, more than an hour east by rail from Manhattan. She and Chuck had met that summer at a language program in Austria run by the College of Wooster, in Ohio. Claire and Chuck had been the only participants in their late twenties—everyone else was either in college or retired. So despite their differences—Chuck was loud, gregarious; Claire, quiet, reserved—they became friends and travel companions.

Socially fearless and outsized—both in personality and physical girth—Chuck could be winsome company as they drove through Switzerland, Italy, and Southern France. But the man didn't know when to stop. Often, just as she'd start yawning, Chuck would announce the onset of a second wind. Well past midnight sometimes, he would be driving them down a bumpy back road in search of some obscure historic site. Even more off-putting, especially considering his braggadocio, was a tendency, when low on money, to wire his father for cash.

Claire, twenty-nine, was the youngest of five kids raised on a small Missouri farm that didn't have so much as mechanical heat or running water. When the family was cold, her dad built a fire.

When she needed a new dress, she and her mother stitched one from the cotton sacks her dad gave them after emptying out the pig feed. She made high school valedictorian through hard work, and after graduate school she took a job teaching biology at Tougaloo College, a historically black school in Jackson, Mississippi. It wasn't a common career move for a white farm girl of her era. But because of her family's struggles, she often allied herself with underdogs.

That's partly why Chuck's sense of entitlement could be hard to take. He even talked to her sometimes as if she was his girlfriend, which was a bit ridiculous, since she never had anything more than platonic feelings for him.

"So what do you say, babe? We gonna get together?"

||

AS FAR as Tom Nisonger was concerned, Chuck couldn't have picked a worse weekend to visit.

Tom was working toward a PhD in political science at Columbia University and had already flunked his qualifying exams once. His next chance was just a few weeks away. If he failed again, Columbia would throw him out. He'd planned to spend every day till then buried in books. An exhausting weekend visit from his overcaffeinated college friend was exactly what he didn't need.

"I'd love to see you Chuck, but maybe—"

Chuck cut him off. "Hey, old pal, I've already bought the tickets. See ya Thursday night, all right? We'll have a helluva time."

"Well—"

"Relax, amigo. I'll introduce you to that chick I was telling you about, the tall, skinny one I met in Europe. Remember? She'll bring a friend for you. What do you think?"

Tom, who was twenty-five, had long ago learned the futility of resistance. The two had grown up together in the suburbs of Youngstown, Ohio—their dads were school superintendents in neighboring towns. Tom and Chuck both went to the College of Wooster, where they served as co-equipment managers for the basketball team. But that's where their similarities ended. Tom was introverted and intellectual. Chuck was a social creature with an outlandish sense of mischief. Tom contented himself with the quiet work of calculating the basketball team's statistics. Chuck appointed himself driver of the cheerleaders' van. And because the team was called the Fighting Scots, he took up the bagpipes and began sporting kilts. Students called him Pipes, but teachers were less amused. A professor who found the idea of men in kilts indecent took particular offense at Chuck's open-legged sitting position in class. "If you're going to dress like a woman," the teacher snapped one day, "you're going to need to sit like one."

As soon as he hung up, Tom realized that Chuck's visit to New York that weekend was a fait accompli. The formula for their relationship had always been that Chuck led and Tom followed.

|||

CLAIRE TOLD Chuck that they should meet on September 26, a Friday, at 1 p.m., on the eighty-sixth floor of the Empire State Building. It was an observation deck.

"I dig it," Chuck said. "Aerial view. Very groovy."

Not really, thought Claire. She had picked the city's tallest building for purely practical reasons: in a bewildering metropolis, the Empire State Building was the only building you couldn't miss. What's more, she thought, the observation deck was a kind of fine-grained filter: it could fit only so many people, thus reducing New York's swarming millions to a manageable group in which two people stood a good chance of finding each other.

She had reason for concern. On her only other visit to Manhattan, a couple of years earlier, a fellow Tougaloo professor who was a New York City native had tried to impress her with an insider's tour of the city. But the first day, he accidentally got on the wrong subway and they wound up in God-knows-where. Another day, looking out the window of his family's apartment, she watched a mother and daughter, maybe six years old, wade into some kind of street fair. A few minutes later, she saw the woman again, frantic. She was shouting, "Has anyone seen my girl?"

If New York confounded its natives, what chance did she and Chuck have? In the Empire State Building, Claire, her scientific mind always churning, saw a way to confound New York. By rising above the streets and away from the people, you could actually make the place half navigable.

"Or," Chuck said, "if you wanted to save on admission, I could just bring my bagpipes and belt out 'Scotland the Brave' in the middle of Times Square. In an hour, they'd have my name up in lights: *Pipes*, the new Broadway musical critics are raving about. You could meet me backstage—"

"Chuck, I have to go," Claire said.

"Look, doll, I'm not too worried about hooking up. My question's this: you find a nice girl for my friend yet?"

|||

TOM TOLD himself he'd draw a line with Chuck. The big exam was looming, and Tom couldn't let Chuck colonize the entire weekend. A short visit to the Empire State Building was fine.

Chuck turned up outside Tom's dormitory a little after noon that Friday, his sleeves rolled up, with the look of a man ready to take Manhattan by storm. Tom told him that they'd have to stop at the Barnard College library first.

"Girl's school?" Chuck said, grinning.

Tom nodded.

"You dog," Chuck said. "One date isn't enough for you? I'll bet the place is teeming with sweet young things."

"Actually just dropping off a book," Tom said.

"Oh, come on, brother, can't it wait?"

"It's already five days overdue, and with New York so expensive as it is, I can't really afford the fines."

"Tell you what, the extra day's on me," Chuck said. "We got girls waiting on a skyscraper."

"It'll take a second," Tom said. "It's not just the money. It's exam time. Someone else might need it."

The detour to Barnard took longer than expected. They got turned around on campus, and then there was a line at the circulation desk. It was nearly 1 p.m. when they boarded the subway, and while transferring to a second train, Tom patted his pants pocket: his wallet was missing. "I must have forgotten it at the library when I paid the fine," he said, looking down and shaking his head.

"You've got to be kidding me. Can't we get it tonight? I'll spot you."

"This is New York, Chuck. We better go back now."

|||

CLAIRE'S BOSS at Brookhaven knocked off early on Fridays to go sailing—the microorganisms in their lab had short life spans, and there was no point starting an experiment so close to the weekend. She slipped out just after he left and boarded the Long Island Rail Road to Penn Station. The city was much as she remembered it: big, overcrowded, impersonal. As she crossed Seventh Avenue, a taxi driver didn't so much as slow down as he whipped in front of her. Then, on West Thirty-third Street, a woman with bulging Macy's bags over each shoulder elbowed her way through a crush of pedestrians, jabbing Claire in the ribs. No apology. Not a word. People in the Midwest didn't behave this way. "So sorry," Claire said, as if willing the words into the other woman's mouth. But by then the woman was a good halfway down the block.

She was relieved at the sight of the Empire State Building. A few minutes in the city, and she was already eager to escape it—

even if only by means of altitude. With its setbacks, clean lines, and needle-tip mast, the building looked like some precision scientific instrument, a scalpel under operating room lights.

On the observation deck, assailed only by gusts of clean-smelling air, she commanded the city. To the north was Central Park, its lumpy green forms contrasting with the hard bright edges of the surrounding buildings. To the west, the glare of the Hudson River and the smokestacks of New Jersey. And the further south she gazed, the taller and more crowded the buildings, as if all the big boys in the school yard, in order to plot some mischief, had formed a huddle. Just try getting me up here, she thought, looking down at the taxis, yellow ants plying an unsolvable maze.

It was a glorious day—a thermometer she'd seen on her way said seventy degrees. The sun warmed her cheeks, and a northwest breeze lifted her hair. Nearly a thousand feet above the streets, everything was quiet. The trucks and cars were so distant that traffic sounded almost peaceful, like water rounding smooth stones in a stream. She glanced at her watch; it was now past 1:30. Where was Chuck? He was always early, sometimes comically so. If you invited him for dinner, he was liable to show up for lunch. She made a slow lap around the crowded observatory deck, scanning faces. There were mothers hoisting children, old men extending shaky fingers toward the Brooklyn Bridge. In one corner, a man in a rakish suit was pitching a woman backward for a kiss, as if in some classic movie still, while another man—"to the left, so I can fit the Chrysler Building"—took a photograph.

Feeling overwhelmed, Claire went inside the glass enclosure. She wanted to sit someplace where she could watch new arrivals from the elevators. But there were no seats. Even the radiators bore spikes. Management seemed to want you to fill up on views, then get out. Another fifteen minutes passed with no Chuck. Claire walked around the parapet again, then back through the glass enclosure. It was now two, a full hour after they'd planned to meet. Claire took a long breath. Chuck had swashbuckled his way through the back roads of Europe, she thought, but in New York City he may have finally met his match. She just prayed he wasn't in Times Square making good on his threat to regale tourists with his "Broadway musical."

With Chuck, though, anything was possible.

⫿

FROM THE subway stop at Herald Square, Tom and Chuck jogged the quarter mile to the Empire State Building. They were still breathing hard—Chuck, wheezing—when they stepped out of the elevator on the eighty-sixth floor. "Thank Jehoshaphat you're still here," Chuck said, striding toward a woman standing by the door to the observatory deck. "I'll let my oldest, best pal Tom here explain why we kept m'lady waiting."

Tom blushed when the woman turned toward him. She was pretty: tall and slim, with shoulder-length chestnut hair, long legs, and a floral-patterned miniskirt. Shoot, Tom thought, Chuck's a lucky guy. He even felt a little jealous. In college neither had been a lady's man. Chuck was overweight and at times overbearing. Tom had a friendly face, but was shy. When it came to girls, they both played in about the same league—or so Tom had thought.

On the observation deck, Tom, squinting into the sun, hemmed and hawed through an explanation and apology.

"You were returning a book to Barnard?" Claire asked, giving him a skeptical look. "You were at a girl's school?"

"Um, well, you see," Tom began, "Columbia, as big as it is, has only so many copies of even the most popular books."

"Right," Claire said, laughing, but letting her eyes linger. "Whatever you say."

"So where's his skirt?" Chuck said to Claire, stepping between them and taking each by the arm.

"Where's yours, Pipes?" Tom said, a little defensively. "You're the great Scot of Youngstown."

"Mellow out, cat, sheesh," Chuck said. "Slang. Skirt: chick, girl. Where's Tom's date?"

"I tried, Chuck," Claire said. "But I don't know many people in New York."

"What about the lab? Must be another eligible lady scientist or two there, right? Women's lib and all that."

"Just a middle-aged woman who I'm pretty sure is married."

"Tom would be okay with that," Chuck said, squeezing his friend's shoulder. "Right pal?"

"Hey, look at that horizon," Claire said. "I wonder how many states you can see from up here?"

Claire, Tom thought, sounded eager to change the subject, as if all this talk of dating had made her uncomfortable. He knew it made *him* uncomfortable.

"Actually," Tom said, walking to the railing beside her, "on a clear day you can see something like eighty miles. It's pretty neat. You can see New Jersey and Connecticut, and I think even Pennsylvania and Massachusetts."

"My goodness, how do you know that?" Claire said.

"Tom's a *New Yorker* now," Chuck interjected. "Columbia man. He's gotten too fancy for his old Ohio friends."

"At least he's polite," Claire said.

"What?" Chuck said, in mock exasperation.

"What do you mean, What?" Claire said.

Tom wasn't sure what was going on. But he sensed that Chuck may have misrepresented, or at least exaggerated, the nature of his relationship with Claire. It wouldn't be a first.

"Actually," Tom said, clearing his throat, "the reason I know about the visibility up here is that the last time I came here I was ten years old."

"Oh, yeah?" Claire said.

"With my mom and dad. And for weeks before leaving Youngstown, I read books about New York buildings."

"You must have been beside yourself when you finally got here."

"Actually," Tom said, "it was a little disappointing."

"Really, why?"

"I think the books did a number on my imagination. When they said skyscrapers, I thought they literally scraped the sky, even went up into space. My mom told me I turned to her while we were right about here and said, 'So it stops here? This is it?'"

"You see what books do to a perfectly good brain?" Chuck said. "Fills it with so much corn that the real world just has to let you down."

"Come on, Chuck. Leave the poor guy alone."

After dropping Claire at her hotel that night, Chuck turned to Tom and winked.

"Smoking girl, huh?"

"She seems very nice."

|||

THE NEXT three days were a whirlwind. The threesome ate dinner in Chinatown, walked through the Lower East Side, lunched at Reuben's, tried barbecue in Koreatown. They went to three museums.

Each day, Claire found herself more drawn to Tom, even if at first as a buffer against Chuck. Tom was unlike other men she knew in academia. At Tougaloo, with its lopsided male-to-female ratios among faculty, only the alpha males—loud, aggressive—managed to get her attention. And she admitted that she didn't mind feeling sought-after. But Tom was reticent. He gave her space to talk. He listened. "What is it like to be a white professor at a black college in the South?" he had asked.

When she told him that white supremacists had bombed the dean's house and the synagogue, he looked openly concerned. When she explained how conscience had driven her to take the job, he was self-effacing. He had convictions, but often felt too self-conscious to act on them, particularly if it meant rocking the boat. "I wish I had that kind of nerve," he told her.

"But didn't Columbia have a big student uprising last year?" she had asked, reminding him that his school wasn't exactly a bastion of conservatism. "I heard about all kinds of stuff: teach-ins, building occupations, class boycotts, a walkout at graduation."

"Yeah, I guess," Tom said. "Students were angry because Columbia wanted to build a new gym in Morningside Park."

"It was more than that, wasn't it?"

"Well, I guess some students saw it as an attempt to wall the university off from Harlem, with poor blacks on one side and privileged white students on the other."

"You didn't get swept up in all of that?"

"I sympathized, but I can't say I did a whole lot," he said. "The main thing I remember was that I didn't have to go to class for a few weeks."

It's refreshing, Claire thought, to be around a man who isn't always trying to impress you. Tom had been at Columbia for three years now, and was clearly more of an expert on the city than either she or Chuck. But he wasn't trying to pass himself off as some know-it-all. If anything, Claire thought, smiling to herself, he came off a little hokey.

"You can't trust that New York drivers will heed red lights," Tom had said at one point.

"Heed?" Chuck interjected.

"Yes," Tom said. "The signal may say to cross, but you still have to look both ways."

|||

ON SATURDAY afternoon, after a long walk through Midtown, Chuck whipped some kind of program from his coat pocket and flashed his friends a catlike grin.

"Broadway?" Claire asked.

"Better," Chuck said. "Playboy Club. I'm a Keyholder."

Inside the club, a seven-story building on East Fifty-ninth Street furnished in teak and leather, a bosomy woman in satin leotard, black bow tie, and three-inch heels walked over and perched provocatively on the back of a chair. Her hair, strawberry blond, was pulled back behind a pair of bunny ears.

"I'm your Bunny Evelyn, may I serve you?"

"Well, this is interesting," Tom said, casting a nervous glance at Claire, who was sitting opposite Chuck.

When Bunny Evelyn strutted back with a tray of drinks, Chuck looked at his companions and winked.

"Watch this," he said, nodding as she leaned back and dropped to her knee.

"That's called a Bunny Dip," Chuck said, winking at the waitress. "It's so, you know, their"—he cupped his hands in front of his chest—"don't fall out."

"Yeah, I know all about it," Claire said.

Chuck drained his martini and gave Claire a once over. "Oh, really?"

"Yeah, really," Claire said.

Tom raised his eyebrows and gave a crooked smile. "You've worked as a, um, Bunny?"

"Don't be ridiculous," she said. "But Gloria Steinem did. Went undercover and wrote a magazine piece about how awful the girls are treated."

"Here she goes with the women's lib," Chuck said.

Tom kneaded his hands. This was quite an awkward situation: Claire was a single woman with two men in a club where nearly every other woman was a sex object in a rabbit suit. But how unruffled she looked. She clearly didn't approve, but was somehow still enjoying herself. Tom felt both perplexity and a kind of admiration. "No, I'm interested," he said. "Is it really that terrible? With all these tips, it doesn't seem like a bad life."

"Um," Claire said, "Either of you ever tried a Bunny Dip in high heels?"

"Just a kilt," Chuck said. "Here, Tom." He handed his friend a dollar bill. "Some Bunny Money for our Bunny's troubles."

Tom looked at Claire, who nodded approvingly toward Bunny Evelyn as the young woman returned with another round. "Go ahead," Claire said, patting Tom on the hand.

Tom folded the dollar into quarters and then held it up between his thumb and forefinger. "Where shall I put it?" he asked Bunny Evelyn, looking her in the eye and grinning.

"Sir, it's always the tray."

|||

BY THE end of the next day, after a Circle Line boat tour around Manhattan, they were giddy from exhaustion.

Tom and Chuck walked Claire to Penn Station for her train back to Long Island. "So when are those exams you're so worked up about?" Claire asked Tom as they stood beneath the clicking departures board. Chuck had gone off to buy them cups of coffee.

"A few weeks," Tom said, taking off his tortoiseshell glasses and rubbing his eyes. "Thanks for reminding me."

"I promise I won't disturb you before then, but I do visit the city sometimes to see, you know, museums and the like," she said. "Do you have a phone number?"

"Um, well, sure." Tom hoped she didn't see his hand tremble as he put his glasses back on and fumbled in his coat pocket for a pen and scrap of paper.

"I'll give you mine, too," she said. She took his pen and put down the phone extensions to both her lab and her home.

The word "home" on the piece of paper seemed so personal, Tom thought. He wondered what a home at a government lab compound looked like, whether she had decorated it with her own feminine touches or left it spare, like a vacant college dorm room. He had never had a girl this pretty ask for his phone number, and he felt a little unsteady. If anyone deserved a chance with her, Tom thought, it was Chuck, who had seemed so smitten. Nothing will come of this phone number business, Tom told himself. Even if she and Chuck weren't really dating, she was probably just one of these women who flirted a bit with everybody.

||||

JUST THREE weeks remained until the exams that could make or break Tom's career. He had been fascinated by Stalin's purges of the Leningrad party and had already chosen it as the subject of his dissertation. But if he didn't first pass his qualifying exams, there would be no dissertation. The dense readings took every ounce of concentration.

"I'm glad you had a good time with Chuck," Tom's mother wrote in early October. "Hope it didn't interfere too much with your studying. . . . Be sure you get the right date for your test so you won't miss it."

She was right: he needed focus. But his thoughts kept detouring back to this unexpected weekend and his first sight of that woman atop the Empire State Building. What had happened with Claire, exactly? Should he call? Or maybe write? Would she? Was the "few weeks" he told her he needed to study so much time that she'd lose interest? Was she interested? Tom had liked the subtle but sassy way she sparred with Chuck—Tom had never quite figured out how to parry his friend's occasional inanities. Plus, she was a bona fide scientist, working at a national laboratory. How often—outside a James Bond movie—did you run across women who could wear a lab coat and a miniskirt with equal credibility?

The days crawled along, with autumn stealing sunlight and chilling the air. Many nights Tom would emerge from the library into darkness, his eyes throbbing and his brain putty. Back at his dorm, he took off his glasses and wool blazer and fell into bed, only to resume the drudgery the next morning.

|||

CLAIRE HAD little time to reflect on her weekend with Chuck and his friend. Her bosses at the lab conscripted her for a painstaking project to devise a new technique for DNA analysis. Her weekends, too, were full: trips to Woods Hole, Massachusetts, and Providence, Rhode Island, and sailing and dinner with her boss and his wife.

But the third weekend in October was distressingly free. The blank space in her otherwise chockablock calendar was so desolate that she felt compelled to fill it. "Autumn leaves," she wrote, looking out her apartment window.

Sunday dawned cloudy and cool, and her thoughts turned to the nice Columbia boy, the friend of Chuck's, she'd met a few weeks back. She wondered how his studies were coming. She recalled how anxious he was. She felt for him. He was the sort of guy, she thought, who'd loosen up a lot if he had the right kind of girlfriend. He had potential. She scolded herself for not trying harder to find him a date that weekend. It wasn't just that she didn't know many people in New York. It was also that you couldn't count on anything Chuck said. She might well go out of her way to rustle up a date, only to discover that Chuck's "friend" was a ruse meant to gin up additional female company—for Chuck. How could she have known Tom would be not just real but possibly a catch?

A high school friend of Claire's had just moved to New York from their hometown in Missouri for a job as a secretary to a bank executive. Myrna was smart, well-dressed, always abreast of the news. Tom might like her, Claire thought.

|||

TOM RECOGNIZED the voice and smiled. A cheerful sound, after all that library silence.

"I've got this friend who's new in town," Claire said. "I'm of half a mind to set you up."

"Oh. Um. I see."

"Are you okay?"

"Sorry, yes, everything's fine." He was sure she'd detected his disappointment.

"How are you feeling about the big test? It's this Thursday, right?"

"A little uneasy, to tell you the truth."

"Well, you're going to love Myrna. I'll be in the city this weekend, too. I'll chaperone, okay? Make sure you two don't get into any trouble."

"I mean, if you don't mind."

"We can all go out to celebrate your acing the exams."

Two days later, a letter arrived that only deepened his confusion.

"Dear Tom," Claire had written. "I'll arrive at Penn Station at 2:59 Friday afternoon. That will give us plenty of time to call Myrna—and I might even go to a very interesting seminar at the Columbia Medical School at 4 that afternoon. Make plans for the weekend however you like—I might suggest a bit of feminine logic tho'. Even if Myrna doesn't have plans for Friday she might prefer to wait until Saturday."

Tom scratched his head. He was no expert on women, but he was no dummy, either. If Claire wanted him to meet Myrna on Saturday, why was she arriving on Friday and hinting that he keep that evening free? What was this odd business of "feminine logic"? Was it Myrna's logic or Claire's? And why did Claire let drop that she would happen to be on the Columbia campus—a few minutes' walk from his dorm—within about an hour of arriving?

The whole situation made him feel a bit out of his depth. But there was more: "I am sure you can do well on your exams, Tom," her letter concluded. "Remember, even the New York Mets won the World Series!"

How wonderful: she was likening him to the "Miracle Mets," the come-from-behind team that had shed its "lovable losers" image the week before with its World Series upset over the Baltimore Orioles. He wasn't sure he wanted to be felt sorry for. Nor did he necessarily like that she set the bar so high. If he failed the exams, he worried, then he'd just be a loser. And not necessarily a lovable one.

|||

THE QUESTION came, as Tom had dreaded, the moment Claire spied him on the train platform.

"So?" she said, beaming, her voice climbing, as other passengers whooshed through and around them.

"So what?"

"The exams yesterday." She seemed almost to be shouting. "How'd they go?"

"I punted."

"What?"

"Here, let me carry your bag."

She handed him a small piece of luggage, and they began walking toward the station. "Punted? What does that mean?"

"I put off the exams till February. I was too nervous."

Claire narrowed her eyes and tilted her head. Tom couldn't tell whether she looked sympathetic or disappointed.

"It's normal to be nervous," she said. "But don't you think you'll be just as nervous in February?"

"Probably." He laughed, looking at her; then she shook her head and laughed, too.

"We're going to need to work on you, Columbia man," she said. "Teach you some study habits, as I do my own students."

"Good luck."

That night, at her suggestion, they went to see *Alice's Restaurant*. It was a film adaptation of the Arlo Guthrie song, about a man who parlays a trumped-up littering charge into a ticket out of the Vietnam War.

|||

WHEN TOM showed up at her hotel the next morning, Claire, who was wearing a batik miniskirt, thought she caught his eyes wandering for the briefest moment to her legs.

"Ready for your big date?" Claire chirped.

"Are you certain she'll like me?"

"I'm sure." But the truth was, she wasn't. Not now that Claire knew Tom better. Myrna was stiff, proper. She was every bit the banker's secretary, a woman whose conservative sensibility and fashions still mirrored the 1950s nearly a decade later. Tom, with his tortoiseshell glasses and short hair, was no hippy. Still, Claire was no longer sure how she felt about him and Myrna together.

They took the subway to the Barbizon Hotel for Women, on East Sixty-third Street. "You'll have to stay down here while I get her," Claire said in the lobby. "No men allowed above the ground floor."

Over the next eight hours, Claire watched with jumbled feelings as Tom and Myrna scrabbled for common ground. Myrna kept talking about how important it was that banks would soon be lowering the prime rate. Tom tried Soviet politics, the World Series, and one of his favorite topics of late: Republican New York Mayor John V. Lindsay, whom he admired for carrying on even after his own party refused to renominate him. Myrna nodded politely, and then shoved the conversation back to the only topic that seemed to interest her: the stalwart soldiers who were the nation's small banks.

"The prime rate, it affects everything, it really does," Myrna said over dinner.

"I don't doubt it," Tom replied, scratching his ear.

The date was a bust. Claire felt responsible. They dropped Myrna off at the Barbizon and headed to the subway. As they stepped down into the station, Tom looked at his wristwatch and yawned.

Claire looked at him. "It must be hard to have to pay for two girls on graduate student wages. But it was really nice of you."

Tom shrugged.

"I'm sorry if that was a waste of time. It's been so long since I've seen Myrna. I guess I didn't realize how much she'd changed."

"I should get back to my dorm," Tom said.

"On a Saturday night?"

"You were right about my study habits. If I'm going to make anything of myself, I've got to buckle down."

They exited the subway station silently.

"It was good to see you again," Tom said outside her hotel, smiling weakly. "Have a safe trip back."

As Tom turned to go, Claire said, "Well, wait, what are you doing tomorrow?"

Tom looked up at her cautiously. "I thought you said you had a morning train."

"Did I?" She leaned her head coyly over one shoulder so that her hair partly covered her eyes. "You know, I was thinking I didn't necessarily need to rush back."

||

THEY MET at a Japanese restaurant for a lunch of bean-thread noodles, then strolled under sunny skies for what seemed like miles.

In a coffeehouse window, they saw a poster for a rally at Lindsay campaign headquarters that evening. A little over a week was left before election day, and Lindsay, elected in 1965 as an anti-corruption crusader, was fighting for survival after a string of crises, including a botched response to a major blizzard. Even after losing the GOP primary to a little-known conservative state senator from Staten Island, Lindsay resurfaced as the candidate of the anemic New York Liberal Party.

He was now trying for a miracle with a new coalition of African Americans, Puerto Ricans, Jews, and wealthy liberals.

"He certainly is handsome," Claire said.

They got a table at the coffeehouse, and Tom handed her a newspaper opened to an article about Lindsay. They leaned in to read together. "I like his gumption," Tom said. "Did you see this? A big transit strike almost shut down the city his first day as mayor. Just two hours of sleep in his first couple of days in office, and that was just the start of the bad breaks. You've got to hand it to him for sticking with it."

"What kind of volunteering have you done?" Claire said.

"Excuse me?"

"Are you involved? In the campaign? You know—signs, knocking on doors, stuffing envelopes. You're the political science major."

"Oh, well, no, Claire," he said. "I've just been reading about him a lot."

"The world isn't going to change all by itself," she said. "If you spent five minutes at Tougaloo, you'd see the work it takes."

"Well, I mean, there is that rally tonight."

"And?"

"Would you go with me?"

By the time they arrived at the Lower East Side campaign office, a party was in full swing. Strobe lights pulsed from the ceiling, and Cream boomed from speakers someone had stood on a folding table. Young people—black, white, brown—in long hair and bell-bottoms gyrated on a makeshift dance floor. Tom felt like a bit of a square until Claire pulled him into the mass of swaying, sweaty bodies. They were pressed close, and Tom could feel her fingertips on his chest as she tried to repel the people crowding around them.

"Isn't this great?" Claire said as they danced.

"If Stalin had thrown parties like this, history might have been kinder to him."

"I don't know. I think this may be a sign Lindsay's going down. People are having too much fun."

Claire's train was set to leave Penn Station around 9 p.m. As they walked out, she stopped in front of a blown-up *New Yorker* cartoon propped beside the front door. It showed two pedestrians looking up as King Kong, astride the Empire State Building, crushed airplanes. The caption, apparently spoken by one of the bystanders, said, "Well that settles it, I'm voting for Procaccino."

"I don't get it," Claire said.

"That's because, as a Long Island resident, you're not as *hip* to New York news as I am," Tom said.

"So tell me."

"People blame Lindsay for everything, even if it's not his fault," he explained. That's why Mario Procaccino, the city comptroller, who was Lindsay's conservative Democratic rival for mayor, had such strong poll numbers, even though by everyone's lights he was a buffoon of a politician.

"You sound passionate," Claire said.

"I don't know I'd call it that."

Just outside the front door, they stopped at a table where a young man with long sideburns sat beneath a sign that said "Volunteers."

"Is there anything I can do?" Tom said, putting his hands on the table and looking defiantly at Claire.

"Sure, man," the young man said, "like, whatever moves you, you know? It takes all kinds."

"Something for beginners," Claire said, leaning in to look over the list of jobs.

"We need poll watchers," the young man said. "You'll be at the polling sites, keeping an eye on things, making sure everything's kosher. Can you dig that?"

"Do I need training?"

"Yeah, brother, we got orientation later this week. But mostly it's just common sense," the campaign worker said, winking at Claire. "What do you say, sweetie, he's got any?"

"More than enough to spare," she said, suddenly squeezing Tom's hand. With his other hand, Tom signed his name to the paper. He couldn't recall when he'd last felt this happy.

They stepped quickly down the sidewalk, as fast now as some of the natives, passing under the awnings of fancy restaurants and thrilling to the jazz of the night-drunk city. "Thanks," Tom said, taking Claire's hand.

"For what?"

|||

CLAIRE HAD billed the weekend as a chance for Tom to meet another girl. But as they approached Penn Station, she saw she'd fooled only herself. She had never before played pursuer. So she had made a show—not a particularly good one—of handing him off to someone else. She had told herself that a date with Myrna would be a sort of tryout. How would Tom behave? Was he such a loner that he would fall for just any girl? Or did he have manners, standards? She didn't like admitting it, even to herself, but she had felt a certain satisfaction at the date's demise, because of her own growing attraction. Tom was smart but understated. He had plenty of his own ideas but listened closely to other people, on the belief, it seemed, that every scintilla threw some new light on the world. Most of all, Claire liked the feeling of having insight into Tom's private battles: he wanted to make more of a mark in the world but was nearly oblivious about where to start. As a professor at Tougaloo at a time of social upheaval, she knew a thing or two about reform. In Tom, she felt, she had an eager pupil.

How to undo the weekend's false premise, however, eluded her. Tom responded to directness best. She feared the subtleties of the weekend—the way she looked at him Saturday evening, the way they'd danced—may have been lost on him. She cursed her imprecision.

They were on the platform now, waiting for her train to Long Island.

"Tom, I—I need to ask you something." She gave him an imploring look.

"Can it wait?" When he took her hand and drew her close, she cocked her head and gave him a small smile. They kissed as the train came in.

||

FROM EARLY November to Christmas, Claire and Tom spent every weekend together. Sometimes he took the train to Long Island, but mostly Claire came to New York. For two people who never quite got used to the city's sharp elbows, they looked to the world like any young couple whose love story was inseparable from the city. They visited the Aqueduct Race Track, the Brooklyn Museum, and the Bronx Zoo. They went to an exhibit on Pompeii in the East Village, a concert at the Cathedral Church of St. John the Divine, and a stage play of Lorraine Hansberry's "To Be Young, Gifted and Black." They walked the warrens of Wall Street, bought rice candy in Chinatown, and saw a Greenwich Village screening of the steamy Swedish avant-garde film *I Am Curious (Yellow)*. They traded copies of the *New York Times* and the *Village Voice*, and frequently consulted a book Claire had bought—*New York on $5 a Day*.

On Friday, November 7, at the Rainbow Room at Rockefeller Center, they raised rum sodas and toasted Mayor Lindsay, who had upset Procaccino at the polls three days before. The elegant bar, on the sixty-fifth floor, had a revolving dance floor whose glass tiles glowed with colored lights. Through the windows, as they swayed, Claire and Tom glimpsed the soaring lights of the Empire State Building.

||

AS THE days grew shorter, Tom wrestled with how much to tell his friend Chuck about his relationship with Claire. Chuck still lived with his parents, in Struthers, Ohio, and in one phone call, when Chuck asked, Tom said he'd seen her just a couple of times since Chuck's visit. But he didn't elaborate.

"Well, that's peachy, Tom, because I'm jetting out there in just a week or two," Chuck said. "We got to get together with Claire again. This time, we'll get her to swear on the Good Book that she's got another girl."

But Chuck, uncharacteristically, never followed through. Instead, he took to his typewriter and wrote Claire a single-spaced four-page letter full of stories about his life back home. He had found a teaching job, he told her, at Youngstown State University's department of speech. In November, he called to invite Claire to Thanksgiving with his family in Ohio.

Her heart sank: Chuck had no idea. What should she say? There was no time to think.

"Chuck, you know," she said finally, "I'll be in Ohio then."

"Gangbusters! You will?"

"Yes, to see Tom." She closed her eyes. "We'd love to see you."

For the first time in as long as Claire had known him—and it saddened her a little—Chuck was at a loss for words.

|||

THE DAY after Thanksgiving, Claire visited Tom at his childhood home in the Youngstown suburb of Boardman. His parents weren't quite sure what Tougaloo was, but they seemed impressed that their son's girlfriend was on a college faculty. "I hope some of this young lady's influence rubs off on you, Tom," his father said. "We'd like to see those three magic letters—P, H, and D—after his name," he said to Claire. "But we've seen a little more procrastination lately than his mother and I would like."

"I'm working on it," Claire said.

Chuck caught up with them that afternoon, and over the next three days the group visited the Butler Art Institute and the steel mills, and went to a party on the lake. Tom and Claire held hands and whispered into each other's ears.

If it hadn't been plain to Chuck before, it was now. After dropping Claire at the airport on Sunday, Tom drove to Chuck's to say goodbye. "You snatched her, pal," Chuck told his old friend. "Good for you."

"I'm not sure we would have met if it weren't for you, Chuck," he said. "We're grateful for that."

Chuck looked down, shook his head, and gave a halfhearted laugh. "If only I'd tried harder to get her to bring another girl. You ever see this?" He gestured to the wall above his desk. There was a framed photo of Claire, her hair fluttering by some seaside. "Our grand tour of Europe."

Tom didn't know what to say. Chuck lifted the photo off its hook and slid it, face down, into a desk drawer.

|||

BACK IN New York, the letters between Claire and Tom grew more amorous. In December, Tom signed a birthday card, "Love, Tom." In January, she signed a letter, "Love and kisses" and called him "My man." In February, to everyone's relief, Tom passed his qualifying exams, putting him on track to those three letters his father had harried him about.

Claire's fellowship at Brookhaven would be drawing to a close in late spring, and as the days grew warmer and longer, Tom grew anxious. In their weekdays apart he began sending her colorful greeting cards. One showed a pair of nuzzling porcupines under the caption, "As one porcupine said to another . . . I love you so much it hurts!!" Occasionally, he added a few words of his own: "Whenever we're apart, I want to be with you forever." Or: "P.S. I want to love you for always."

Constitutionally shy, Tom struggled to express his innermost feelings. He hoped that with the greeting cards and the hints he inscribed in the margins she would see he wanted to marry her. She was always picking up on social cues he missed; she'd have to glean his intentions.

Claire, it turned out, could see them perfectly. But if Tom wanted her, she decided, he would have to stand up and be counted.

The days closed in on Tom like wet concrete. Over dinner one night, Claire mentioned the date of her last paycheck from Brookhaven. She began talking about her fall schedule at Tougaloo and making notes for a new class she planned to teach. Tom awoke one morning after oversleeping and shook his head at his reflection in the bathroom mirror. His cheeks bore red lines from the creases in his pillow. His hair was getting too long.

On a Sunday in mid-March, Tom led Claire from Penn Station to his dorm room, pushing aside the books on his bed so she could sit—in case she needed to.

"Will you marry me, Claire?"

She gave him that small smile, the one he'd first seen moments before their first kiss. Then she closed her eyes and pressed her lips to his.

Crossroads

TIMES SQUARE

Times Square is a rebuke
to the logic of Manhattan's rectangular grid.
Broadway and Seventh Avenue intersect at
an acute angle and then slice the
surrounding blocks into an improbable
series of triangles and trapezoids. The effect
is a kind of parting of the seas. In a city
with few open vistas at street level, the
clearing makes Times Square an ideal
canvas for mass advertising. But it does
something else, too: it lays bare the artifice
of the grid and invests the square—with its
hundreds of thousands of daily visitors—
with a sense of raucous possibility.

Robin Miller had set aside the fourth day of her research trip to Manhattan for interviews with strangers on the street. How did the September 11 attacks affect you? she asked. What did the attacks mean for the city? If a memorial or museum were to be built on the site of the fallen towers, what should it look like?

But just ten months had passed since the attacks, and Robin, twenty-two, who grew up in small-town Minnesota, was getting a glimpse of how raw people's feelings still were. Some of the people she stopped obliged her questions. But the subject made a few—a young bicycle messenger, a middle-aged woman who worked near the site—so distraught that they excused themselves, brushing away tears.

Was it too soon? From the distance of her college campus, in Fargo, North Dakota, the question of how to design a 9/11 memorial had seemed like just a tougher version of the kinds of problems her fellow architecture students discussed all the time. It was solvable, she felt, with all the conventional tools of research: a list of good questions, a site survey, and persistence. But now that she was here in this heartbroken city of millions, Robin wondered whether conventional tools were enough.

||||

PATROLMAN MARCEL Sim drew the Times Square detail again tonight, and that suited him fine.

The swarms of tourists. The street peddlers. The barkers and scalpers. The hopheads and homeless. The panhandlers, pickpockets, and purse snatchers. And, inevitably, what the guys in blue called "holster sniffers." The men who buddied up to you with questions like, "Hey, what's it like to be a cop in New *York?*" or "What kind of heat you guys pack?" The women who asked, "Is your job dangerous?" and wanted to throw their arms around your shoulders and have pictures taken.

Times Square sometimes felt like the floodlit vortex for all of New York's explosive energy. To work foot patrol here, you had to have spring-loaded reflexes and eyes in the back of your head.

Marcel seemed to so revel in the whirlpool of humanity that his partners, laconic sorts, would sic tourists on him. If some family from Wisconsin wanted directions to the subway or the Olive Garden or *Aida*, the other cops would thrust their chins toward Marcel and say, "Ask him." Disoriented tourists were just one more blip in a gigantic video game. If Marcel could handle them along with all his other duties, that made him a better cop, not a softer one, no matter what the guys thought.

He had been an adrenaline junkie—"an envelope pusher," as he liked to put it—ever since he was a kid on Long Island. When those sirens at the Elmont firehouse would go off, Marcel, just ten years old, would fly out the front door and chase his neighbor—a volunteer fireman who'd been dating Marcel's older sister—as the man hoofed it to the station. Marcel would run and run, until the fireman lost him over the hill. Shuffling back home, gasping, Marcel dreamed about the day those sirens would call for him.

Marcel—thirty-six now—had been working twelve-hour shifts for months, and tonight was no exception. In the months since the attacks, the New York Police Department had a lot of the force working overtime, particularly at landmarks like Times Square. The city's Joint Terrorism Task Force wanted an "omnipresence" of uniforms in places seen as attractive terrorist targets. But as big as the NYPD was, it didn't have enough bodies to cover the city's every square inch. So the uniformed officers in Times Square kept on the move, shifting from one location to the next to foster an illusion of ubiquity.

|||

IT WAS just after 5 p.m. on a sweltering July day. Robin, wiped out after her day of man-on-the-street interviews, collapsed on the couch in the lobby of the Milford Plaza hotel, near Times

Square. Her professors in the architecture program at North Dakota State University had warned her she was taking on too much. A 9/11 memorial at Ground Zero was an ambitious thesis topic for a master's student to take on, at least in part because of her distance from Manhattan. They asked her to consider scaling back. One classmate, for instance, was designing a lakeside resort; others a concert hall or an ideal American home.

But Robin was insistent. She wanted to conceive of a monument at Ground Zero that would help bring closure. She wanted to design something that gave physical form to Kübler-Ross's five stages of grief and offered visitors a global look at the ravages of terrorism.

When the towers fell, Robin, who ran track in college, had been giving a client a fitness test at a gym in Fargo, where she worked part-time to help pay for school. Images of the burning buildings appeared on every TV screen, and the gym fell silent. She had never been to New York. She knew none of the victims. But the attacks felt intensely personal. She suspected that many other Americans, regardless of their proximity to the city, felt the same way.

Perhaps because of her athletic build, or maybe just some inborn temperament, she had often found herself in the role of protector. When someone picked on her twin sister or her brother with juvenile diabetes, she made a point of telling the person to back off. It wasn't long before she had a reputation. In second grade, she overheard a group of boys talking about beating up a girl in her class. When one of the boys said, "I think she's a friend of Robin's," the others suddenly lost their nerve. What gnawed at Robin about the perpetrators of 9/11 was that anyone could, for any reason, see the murder of innocents as justifiable.

"Are you okay, Robin?" someone asked, shaking her out of her torpor.

It was Charlotte, a fellow architecture student at North Dakota State. Charlotte, along with two other friends, Nancy and her brother Jim, had accompanied Robin on the seven-day trip to New York. Though they would split up during the day—Robin to work, the others to sightsee—they would regroup in the hotel in the evenings before dinner.

Robin smiled and got up off the couch. "Why, what's the matter? Do I look funny?"

"You look like you should drink something."

"A glass of water would be nice. It's so hot."

"I mean like a margarita," Charlotte said, and Robin laughed.

"New Yorkers are supernice, Charlotte. They're not the toughies people think they are."

"So what's the matter?"

"It's just super hard for some of them to talk about what happened. This one guy even started crying. I felt so bad."

"Well, when Jim and Nancy get here, let's go out and relax a little. Get something to eat and drink."

"You betcha, Charlotte. I guess that sounds good."

"You need a break, Robin. You work way too hard."

After showers and a change of clothes, the four friends walked north on Eighth Avenue, then east on West Forty-sixth Street, until they were inside the human pinball machine of Times Square. Giant video screens overhead splashed with ads for the World Wrestling Federation, Calvin Klein, and Destiny's Child.

"It's kind of like Christmas, ya know?" Robin said.

Jim rolled his eyes. "It's July, Robin."

"No, I get it," Nancy said.

"Right?" Robin said. "Like just after you wake up, before you go downstairs to unwrap presents. You know something great is inside, but you also have to wait to open it, ya know, so it stays a surprise."

"*Whatever*, you two," Jim said. "So, we gonna eat?"

They saw signs for McDonald's and Jamba Juice. "There's a T.G.I. Friday's over there," Nancy said, pointing up Broadway. "The one in Fargo's pretty good."

"I don't know, it seems like a lot of tourists would go there," Robin said. "I want real New York. Like a place locals go."

"And so you're just going to stop some random local and ask for a recommendation?" Nancy said. "That's not supersafe, ya know."

Robin turned and saw a group of police officers at the corner. "We'll ask them. They probably live here."

"Don't you think they might, like, be busy?" Charlotte said.

But Robin was already striding toward them, and her friends, shrugging, fell in line behind her.

"Hi, good evening, officers," Robin said brightly. She was surprised when the officers didn't immediately turn around.

"Oh, hi," she repeated, with a little wave this time, to get their attention. "We were wondering if you guys knew any good restaurants, ya know, like where the locals go."

There were four officers, and an older, craggy-looking one, pivoted on his heel and gave her a dubious once-over. "Sim," he growled out of the side of his mouth. Then, turning to Robin, he said, "He'll help ya."

A younger man stepped forward with a wry smile and tucked his cap under his arm. He had a buzz cut and a muscular build, with blue-gray eyes and a strong chin. "What are you, from Brooklyn?" He threw a look over his shoulder and winked at his partners, who erupted in low chuckles.

"No, actually, I'm from Moorhead," Robin said.

"That's near Greenpoint, right?" the officer said, to more laughter from the other cops.

"No. I don't know. I don't think so," Robin said earnestly. "It's in Minnesota. The state. Have you ever been?"

"Nah, I'm a New Yorkah," he said. "Closest to the Midwest I've been is Land O'Lakes."

"Oh, yeah? Where is that?"

"In my supermarket. Butter aisle. I enjoy it on my toast."

Robin wasn't sure of what to make of his style of conversation. She'd always thought of cops as Officer Friendly. Back in Moorhead, the police even ran a summer camp. Robin went for five summers, from ages eight to twelve; the nice policemen took the kids to picnics, movies, and swimming pools. This New York police officer had a different, well, attitude. Still, he was an officer. Out of respect for the law she decided to take his words at face value.

"I don't eat butter," she said matter-of-factly. "It's fattening. I eat margarine."

More guffaws from the other officers, who seemed to hear everything, even though they were almost facing the other way.

A store alarm sounded somewhere, and one of the cops was shouting at someone to back away from the store window.

"So what's it like being a cop in New York?" Nancy asked.

"Like anything else. Bad days. Worse days." He was ruggedly built, but there was a softness under his eyes Robin found disarming. She watched as he gave a guarded glance over his shoulder at a group of teenage boys in tank tops who had begun shadowboxing.

"So what was it you folks needed?"

Robin explained their search for real New York restaurants. The officer ticked off a short list: O'Lunney's Times Square Pub, The Pig 'n' Whistle, or, if they got on a subway, McSorley's.

There was a shirt pin above his badge—the letters "WTC" in white on a black background. World Trade Center, Robin thought. In newspaper stories she'd read in preparation for her trip, the cops came across as some of the day's biggest heroes. Were these police officers there? For a split second she thought of asking, of telling them about her thesis. But something about the moment wasn't right. After her experiences earlier in the day, she didn't know if she could take upsetting anyone else.

"Thanks a bunch for the recommendations, officer," she said, smiling.

"Enjoy," he said, smiling back and putting the cap back on his head. "Don't drink too much, all right?"

"Oh, we don't drink." Robin wanted him to know that they were responsible. "Not too much, anyways."

|||

AROUND THE corner, at a table at the Pig 'n' Whistle, Robin was radiant. The exhaustion from earlier in the day was gone. All she'd gotten were restaurant tips, but she felt as though talking to those police officers was a kind of baptism in the real New York. "You see what I mean, with those officers?" she said.

"They were nice, dontcha know," Nancy said. "At least the one guy was."

"Yeah, I can't believe he took all that time to talk to us. That was so nice."

"Don't you think they were laughing at us a little, too?" Charlotte asked.

"I don't think so," Robin said. "If only we'd taken a photo."

"I know."

After dinner, they went to a bar next door and talked about their plans for the trip's remaining three days. Charlotte wanted to see more museums. Jim and Nancy said they wanted to go to the top of the Empire State Building.

"Take a day off, Robin," Charlotte said.

Robin shook her head. "Too much work." She had been to the city zoning office to study setback restrictions, and had gotten a walking tour of Lower Manhattan from a North Dakota State architecture alumnus. But there was more to do: visiting the city's Department of Buildings, interviewing more New Yorkers in the street, videotaping other landmarks in Lower Manhattan.

"You gotta take a break," Nancy said.

Robin took a sip of beer. "Isn't that what we're doing now?"

By the time they left the bar, night had settled over the city.

"Now's when you really want to see Times Square," Jim said. "When the sky is totally dark like this, the lights jump right out at you. Talk about Christmas."

Robin was still aglow from talking to those NYPD officers earlier. "Jim, that's such a good idea."

‖|

AFTER SUNSET, Marcel's unit had moved from West Forty-fifth Street and Broadway to West Forty-seventh and Seventh Avenue, near the McDonald's. It was a busy night: they had to break up a couple of fistfights, call in tows of illegally parked cars. But, knock on wood, nothing serious. At around nine, Marcel studied the stream of pedestrians moving along Seventh Avenue and saw the girl with long hair who'd asked for restaurant advice a few hours earlier. The sight of her—purse over one shoulder, camera over the other—bobbing along with her friends was enough to make him chuckle. When she got within about five yards, Marcel grinned, winked at his partners, and called out, "Hey, Minnesota!"

She stopped for a second, and a group of camera-toting tourists behind her wavered before excusing their way past. Then her face flashed with recognition, and she waved and walked over. "Did you call me Minnesota?"

"That's where you're from, right?"

"My actual name is Robin."

"Robin, huh?" Marcel said.

"Yes, like the bird."

She was attractive, Marcel saw now, with long, dirty-blond hair, a moon-shaped face, and eyes that seemed by default to express both merriment and surprise. But she was a piece of work. Everything you said, she took at face value. Was she for real? Couldn't she see he was yanking her chain? Or was she just playing the straight man? Either way, Marcel thought, you couldn't resist razzing. "What's a robin bird?" he said, squinting. "I've never seen a robin bird."

She described its reddish orange breast and explained that they typically left northern regions during the winter because of the cold. She concluded by looking at the gold pin beside his badge and said, "I see your name is Officer Sim."

"Good. Good. You ever think about, you know, joining a detective squad?"

While her friends looked on silently smiling, she and Marcel made small talk: about museums worth visiting, about her college, about his job, about street smarts ("Any stranger that comes up to you that's not another tourist, keep walking," he counseled).

Charlotte looked at her watch and faked a yawn. "Robin, I think we should get going."

Marcel reached into his pocket for a card. "Here," he said, talking to the whole group but handing it to Robin. "If you guys need some security pointers or other ideas, whatever, give me a call."

"I'll take the number," Robin said, looking him in the eye. "But I would never call."

"Then give me your number. I'll check in after you see some of the museums, make sure you're behaving yourselves."

Robin looked at her friends. Charlotte shook her head. Jim shrugged. Then Nancy said, "Just give it to him."

"If you officers ever need a break," Robin said, "you should come to the Midwest."

"Sure," Marcel said, the sarcasm back now. "That would be my, like, number-one destination."

"I'm not kidding. I bet you'd love hot dish." Robin was referring to the ground beef and tater tot casserole that Minnesotans hold up as a kind of state dish. "Have you ever tried it?"

Marcel had no idea what she was talking about. A hot dish was what cops called a good-looking lady, but there was no way this girl would have known that.

"Oh, yeah," he said, jerking his head at the other officers. "These guys'll tell ya, I *love* a hot dish."

Before saying their goodbyes, Robin asked if the officers would pose for a photo. She handed Jim her camera and stepped between the younger officer and one of his partners. Nancy got on his other side and put her arm around a bored-looking third officer, on her left. Charlotte, having none of it, hung back with Jim.

"Is it okay if I put my arms around your shoulders?" Robin said. The officers chuckled.

"Yeah," Marcel said. "Just don't touch the gun belt."

Then Jim froze the image: Robin and Nancy beaming amid three stony-faced cops, and in the background a blaze of orange lights.

|||

BACK HOME on Long Island the next evening, Marcel opened his billfold and found the ATM receipt he'd written that girl's phone number on. Robin. *Like the bird.* He looked at the unfamiliar area code, smiled, and shook his head. It was amazing how innocent some people could be. The easy-breezy body language, the aw-shucks questions. Not a care in the world. The girl didn't even seem to realize that his remark about her being from Brooklyn was a joke; she answered as if he'd just made an honest mistake, one that she'd be happy to correct. Kumba *frickin'* ya. If she really were from Brooklyn, she would have instantly detected his sarcasm, and probably flipped him the bird.

Still, he had to admit: there was something nice about her happy-go-lucky shtick. Did everyone have to see the world as darkly as New Yorkers did?

|||

ROBIN WAS walking back to the hotel after another tough day of street interviews when her phone rang.

"Oh, hi there," Robin said. She was surprised but pleased.

How were they doing? Officer Sim wanted to know. Did they need any other recommendations?

This is the nicest cop, she thought. And who would have thought to find him in New York City, where people were supposed to be so cold?

He told her that Sunday was his day off. He had some errands to run near Times Square. He could meet her and her friends for coffee. He had some other ideas, he said, for good restaurants and places to see and whatnot.

"We're leaving the next day," she said. "But um, well, okay, I guess that would be fine."

They agreed to meet in her hotel's lobby two days later, at 5 p.m.

As soon as she hung up, though, she felt something amiss. In the heat of the phone call, she'd forgotten that Jim and Nancy were returning home on Saturday. And Charlotte was leaving Sunday morning. That would mean just her and this cop.

"What do you think, Nancy?" she asked over breakfast the next morning.

"He seemed supernice to me. Plus, he was a good-looker."

"I know," Robin said. "But he's a police officer, and from what you hear sometimes, a lot of them are players."

"Hear where? In the movies? I thought you said he wanted to meet all of us."

Two days later, after saying goodbye to her friends, she turned on the TV in her hotel room to catch up on the news. But she couldn't concentrate. Hearing an ambulance siren, she looked out her window and down at the swarms of anonymous New Yorkers striding, their bodies turned in on themselves, in the streets far below. That officer was due in the lobby in about a half hour.

She slipped his business card out of her pocketbook and reached for her cellphone. "Officer Sim?"

"Call me Marcel."

"It's Robin."

"Like I couldn't tell. Robin, like the bird, right?"

"I'm so sorry, Marcel," she said. "We're all kind of feeling run-down. I don't think we're going to be able to meet up."

There was a short silence before he spoke, and she thought she could hear him clearing his throat. "No sweat, Robin, of course," he said. "Safe travels home, all right? Be good."

|||

MARCEL, WHO lived with his father and stepmom in Nesconset, had been well into the hour-and-a-half drive to Manhattan when Robin called to cancel. It sounded like an excuse. But women were unpredictable like that. It was one of the reasons being a bachelor sometimes felt easier than being married: no expectations. At thirty-six, he'd seen enough of life to know that at the end of the day, you only had yourself. When he was a teenager, gangs moved into Elmont Memorial High and shot dead one of his best friends. That year, he learned to defend himself with his fists. By the time he joined the NYPD in 2000, he had already worked as a firefighter, EMT, and rescue diver. He had divorced two years earlier—he wanted kids, she didn't. He saw himself becoming one of those cops who was married to the job. From what he'd heard about the NYPD, you kind of needed to be. The biggest and most storied police force in America—there was no greater test of mettle. But just how soon that test would come was something he would never have predicted.

Not much changed in the weeks after that Minnesota girl blew him off. He kept up the twelve-hour shifts in Times Square, often now in plainclothes. His conversations weren't with tourists anymore but with the homeless who slept in building vestibules and brushed off referrals to shelters. He brought them leftover soup and bread from nearby food pantries and restaurants. Before long, they rewarded him with information about street criminals. Many were military vets who would have easily qualified for public services but refused. He admired their determination to wrestle demons alone.

As July turned to August, buzz on the force turned to the first anniversary of September 11. The talk of tributes, benefit concerts, and memorials stirred memories that Marcel had long tried to wall inside. The cellphones in the rubble that wouldn't stop ringing. The sight of severed arms and legs. The hats, the jackets. The wedding ring on someone's finger. The wallet-size photos of children float-ing in the flooded tunnels of the destroyed PATH station.

Marcel had been on a rare day off nearly a year earlier when his older sister called and told him to turn on the TV. One tower was al-ready on fire, and now, as he watched, a plane vaporized into the second one. His heart flailing against his chest, Marcel leaped into a car with a few cop neighbors and sped toward the city. When he arrived at the Midtown North Precinct, his captain, remembering Marcel's EMT training, ordered him to Ground Zero to help set up a forward triage center. No sooner had he arrived than the second tower fell, scattering clouds of debris through the streets and sowing pandemonium. Surrounded by screams and sobs, Marcel clawed through the whiteout and directed dazed pedestrians to safety.

Around noon, when some of the dust began to settle, he found his way to the Ten House fire station—so-called because it housed Engine 10 and Ladder 10, which had already lost several firefight-ers in the attack. In this grief-wracked setting, Marcel helped set up the South Forward Treatment and Triage Center, which was fast becoming a makeshift morgue. In between treating rescuers for injuries, respiratory problems, and exhaustion, he descended into the funereal quiet of the tunnels beneath the PATH station, bagging personal belongings and body parts.

A death that would haunt him for a long time was that of Of-ficer Moira Smith. She was guiding people out of the South Tower and trying to save a woman from an asthma attack when the building collapsed. She would be the only female NYPD of-ficer to die in the attacks. Marcel had met her a couple of times—she worked with one of his friends at a precinct attached to the police academy, where Marcel occasionally went for pro-fessional training. Smith was a thirteen-year veteran with a young daughter. Marcel had been impressed by her ability to balance motherhood with risky police work. No one had ordered her to Ground Zero—she went on her own, out of a sense of duty. And for her bravery, for doing her job, she lost her life.

Word had reached other officers that Smith's mother had refused to accept her daughter's death. She pleaded with rescuers to
find her—or some sign of her. When a police dog returned from
the debris one day with a gun belt that looked like Smith's, Marcel
put on a harness and dropped into the warren of voids the dog had
emerged from. But after forty feet, the rubble-choked voids grew
too narrow for passage. As he turned back, his heart sinking, he
thought about Officer Smith's mother and husband and daughter.
He saw how 9/11 would be unlike any other tragedy he'd seen in
his many years as an EMT and firefighter. He saw how its devas-
tation would ripple for decades across an untold number of lives.
The grief of survivors, he was sure, would soon give way to rage,
depression, guilt, substance abuse, domestic violence, psychosis.

He lived at Ten House for a week. Some days he worked so
hard and with so little self-awareness that he felt like an automa-
ton, a robocop. He shut out his darkest thoughts and focused on
the river of need streaming into the triage center. It is better not
to dwell, he told himself. It is better to make believe things will
be all right.

||

BACK AT North Dakota State, Robin plunged deeper into her
thesis. She organized the material she'd collected in New York
and prepared outlines, preliminary drawings, and a progress report for her professors.

She awoke on September 11, 2002, in a pensive mood. For
reasons she couldn't at first give voice to, her thoughts turned to
the police officer she'd met in Times Square. She pulled out a
binder where she'd stored keepsakes from the trip. Beneath a
crumpled map, subway tickets, and a brochure for the Guggenheim Museum, she found the photo of her and Nancy with the
three policemen. She looked at the dark patches beneath the one
officer's eyes, trying to divine what he had seen a year earlier. Di-
rectly or indirectly, she thought, the attacks had to have touched

every officer on that force. She felt a pang of regret, and shame, that she had stood him up. Even if he had been interested in her, what harm would there have been in a cup of coffee?

Inside her binder, she found the business card he had given her. She inhaled and haltingly dialed the phone number. "Marcel, this is Robin Miller."

"Who?"

"You gave me your card in Times Square a couple of months ago. You don't remember me, but I'm calling just to say that I appreciate whatever you did last September 11."

"Land O'Lakes! Of course I remember you. How's Minnesota?"

"I'm serious. I know it's the anniversary, and I wanted to see how you were doing."

"Peachy. How's the Midwest? You guys getting ready for your first ice storm yet?"

She laughed. "Don't be silly. Our fall isn't real different from New York."

They made small talk for a while. Then, for the first time, Robin told him about her architecture thesis. "I want to design something that helps people confront their grief. But, Marcel, I want it to be sensitive. I don't want to offend anyone."

"Yeah, Robin, that's probably a good idea," he said. "Your school's in, like, Fargo, right? They know a lot about Al Qaeda there?"

"Actually, that's why I may have to come back to New York."

She said that her professors had wanted her to gather more details about the buildings around Ground Zero.

"Well, hey, if you decide to come, give me a ring," he said. "I'll pick you up at the airport."

As she hung up the phone, she looked in the mirror and saw that she was smiling.

|||

HER PLANE landed at La Guardia a month later, and they met at the baggage claim. "So I was thinking that tomorrow night we could go out on that date we never had," he said on the drive to her hostel, near Central Park. "Remember?"

"Was that going to be a date?" she said, cocking her head flirtatiously. "I thought you were just going to tell us what other museums to see."

"So innocent," he cracked, shaking his head. "So naïve."

At an Italian restaurant the next evening, she told him more about her project. He nodded politely. At one point, he rolled up his shirt sleeve and showed her the tattoo on his upper arm: the numbers 9, 11, and 01 over a silhouetted Twin Towers, and as a backdrop an American flag in the shape of a public safety badge. "It's in memory of friends, police, firefighters," he said. The skin on his arm was softer, smoother than Robin would have guessed. There were freckles on his shoulder.

She wanted him to open up, to talk about his experiences. But nothing. Just a few sound bites about the heroism of men in uniform, the kind of truisms anyone who had watched TV coverage of the attacks might have come up with. Sitting across a restaurant booth from him, looking at the creases around his eyes, she was suddenly aware of their difference in age.

"Do you want to talk about something else?" she asked.

"Yeah, Robin. Maybe."

Grief, she was beginning to suspect, was something people had to come to on their own terms.

|||

MARCEL HAD never met someone who saw the world as brightly as Robin. She loved her family. She saw only goodness in people. Though the attacks hadn't touched her personally, she had a big enough heart to want to help people halfway across the country. And she saw hope and recovery as inevitable. To his ears, it sounded a little like a fairy tale. But it felt good sometimes to let go of his "New York defenses," as he called them, and look at the world through her eyes. He felt strangely protective of her, and not just because she was thirteen years younger. He didn't want his cynicism to rub off on her, to cloud her view of the world. Though he was physically attracted to her, he played cool. He saw how much she wanted to think well of people. He wanted to measure up to her expectations.

Over the next few days, he took her to a favorite Irish restaurant and to the American Museum of Natural History, where they sat in adjoining chairs in the darkened planetarium and listened to Harrison Ford narrate a new space show, *The Search for Life: Are We Alone?*

On Sunday, they walked the streets around Ground Zero. He showed her a Burger King that had served as a triage center and explained that the red X's still visible on buildings had been left by rescuers as a sign they'd been searched. Marcel treated her to everything. He pulled back chairs and held doors. But he never lingered after dropping her at the door of her hostel, where men and women were segregated on different floors.

Marcel had drifted from his Catholic faith after his parents' divorce. He was in fifth grade when they split, and after his mother moved to Arizona he watched his dad struggle to raise four kids on his own. If God was part of his life then, he felt, it was pretty hard to tell. Before long, the job was his only religion. This ambulance is my sanctuary, Marcel sometimes thought, as he raced the bleeding, broken, or breathless to some hospital, sirens bleating against the void. It is only here, in this box, that my life has meaning.

But after September 11, 2001, even that was gone. And in his searching, he had returned to church, first once every few weeks but now more regularly. At dinner with Robin that Friday, he asked, "Have you ever been to Saint Patrick's?"

|||

ROBIN WAS a practicing Catholic, seeing God's works in places big and small. She was surprised, though, when Marcel, who seemed so worldly and cynical, mentioned church. It wasn't a place she'd have guessed if someone had asked, Where do New York cops take dates on Saturdays? When he proposed they go the next day, she felt something bloom inside her. "No, I've never been," she said. "But I've heard of it. It's the famous one, right?"

In the sunlit pews, under Gothic ceilings of vaulted marble, they sat with knees touching. "Let us ask our Father," the priest said, "to forgive our sins and to bring us to forgive those who sin against us."

The worshipers stood up. "Our Father," they said, "who art in heaven, hallowed be thy name."

In Robin's church back home, it was custom during the Lord's Prayer to clasp hands with people beside you, stranger or friend. When she reached for Marcel's, though, he did something she had not expected: he lifted her hand and, with both of his, gently pressed her palm against his heart.

Was the East Coast custom different? She looked around. They were the only two people holding hands. There was no such custom here at all. Yet when the prayer ended—"the kingdom, the power, the glory . . . "—and Marcel was still gently holding her hand, she had never felt more grateful for being misunderstood.

Before saying goodbye at the airport the next day, they kissed for the first time.

|||

WITH ROBIN back in Fargo and Marcel back on the streets of New York, they talked nearly every night, sometimes for as many as four hours. In dribs and drabs, often in the wee hours of the night, Marcel let Robin in on his life in the attacks' aftermath. He told her about gruesome images he could not shake. He told her about friends who died: five police officers, four firemen, a paramedic. He told her about his aborted search for the remains of Officer Moira Smith. He told her about feeling powerless, as though he could not do enough to help. They were stories he hadn't told anyone else.

Robin just listened at first. She came to see that beneath his hard shell was a man who had known hurt as a kid—the divorce, the gunned-down friend—and now felt other people's suffering keenly. He had spent his life searching for ways to relieve some of that suffering. In big ways, like risking his own life to save someone else's, and small, like bringing soup to homeless vets in Times Square. But in his focus on others' suffering, she thought, he had perhaps neglected his own.

Robin's thesis offered cover for the asking and answering of difficult questions. In one phone call, she told Marcel she was thinking about a pair of shaftlike fountains that would fall each morning at the precise time—9:59 a.m., 10:28 a.m.—of the collapse of the South and North Towers. They would spring up again seconds later, she told him, a symbol of rebirth. But Marcel demurred. He told her it was too literal. He worried that seeing the fountains fall at exactly those times could cause survivors unnecessary anxiety. The more they talked, the more nuanced her designs became. The drawings she would eventually turn in featured shallow reflecting pools where the towers had stood. At a midpoint between the pools was an asymmetric cylindrical glass atrium where visitors would enter an underground museum and exhibit space. In her talks with Marcel, she came to see how the space would mean different things to the families and friends of the dead than it would to, say, tourists. In response, she designed a private, separate entrance for those who had lost loved ones in the attacks.

||||

WHEN OFFICER Sim told the guys at the precinct house that he was headed to Minnesota for a few days before Christmas, they were unsparing. "You're going where? Who's after you?"

"Nobody, except hopefully this girl I've been dating."

"Hold on a minute, there are five million women in this city," said one patrolman, an Italian American. "You can't just go down to Mulberry Street"—Manhattan's Little Italy, with its sidewalk cafés and bars—"and find yourself some hot dish?"

"Not like they have in Minnesota."

The razzing continued on the way to the airport. "Before you go, Sim, give me your tax number," a cop buddy who was driving said. Tax numbers were how the NYPD tracked officers' pensions.

"Why would I do that?"

"Because you might not come back. Like in that movie *Fargo*. Where that guy gets caught in the wood chipper. Somebody's gonna need to collect your pensh."

Marcel's first visit to Moorhead—in the days before Christmas 2002—was not without moments worthy of a Coen Brothers film. When Robin took Marcel to meet her twin sister at a campus bar, her sister showed up with a wanted poster she had ripped off the wall of a post office. It was for a white male with blue eyes and tattoos, a former paramedic and volunteer firefighter, who was wanted for a triple murder in Arizona, where Marcel had lived for a while in the 1990s.

"Robin, you better look at this." Her sister was dead serious. "Don't tell me this isn't a match."

Her sister had brought a friend, a six-foot-four brawler, in case the situation got out of hand. It took a few beers and even more reassurances—Robin had visited Marcel's station house, he had been back in New York for several years on the dates of the alleged murders—to convince Robin's sister and her burly friend that not everyone from New York was a serial killer.

Caught up in the holiday spirit, Robin's mother, for her part, gave Marcel an early Christmas present: a glass tree ornament shaped like a pickle, a German tradition. Marcel was not the blushing type. But he came close when he opened the card from Robin's mother: "Hope you and your pickle make it home in one piece."

When Robin led him on a snowmobiling expedition across a frozen lake, Marcel clung to his seat in fear. Afterward, he scratched his head at the camouflage every other person on the lake seemed to be wearing. "Where's the Army base?" asked Marcel, who was partial to Guess jeans, black sports coats, and Doc Martins.

"They're not soldiers," Robin said. "Camos are just casual wear up here."

The only thing that seemed to make sense that first visit was that this was Robin's home. People left their doors unlocked. They held doors for strangers. Motorists stopped for pedestrians and drove cars you'd never know had horns. Where a New Yorker might have dismissively said, "Fugheddaboudit," Minnesotans were always ready with a "You betcha." In the trust and warmth locals felt toward one another, Marcel saw that he had in some sense misjudged Robin. Her values were as much a product of her hometown as his values were of his.

|||

IN JULY 2003, two months after graduation, Robin moved to New York to be with Marcel. They slept in separate bedrooms in the house on Long Island where Marcel had been living with his father and stepmom. Robin worked as a sales clerk at a clothing store while applying to architecture firms in the city. As fall approached, Marcel secretly shopped for a ring in the antique styles he knew Robin liked.

On a visit to Moorhead that October, Marcel told Robin's father, Mike Miller, that he wanted a moment alone with him. Mr. Miller, a former meat cutter who now hosted a local radio show on fishing, invited Marcel to a tournament he was taking part in on Waubay Lake, in South Dakota. Mr. Miller was still in his bath towel, having stepped out of the shower after a long day of angling, when Marcel unburdened himself. "Mr. Miller, I love your daughter," he said. "In every possible way, she is my better half. With your permission, sir, I'd like to ask her to marry me."

"Sheez, Marcel," he said testily, "you could have at least waited until I had my pants on." Then a smile leaped across his face, he laughed, and he thumped Marcel on the back. "Go get her."

That night, at Untitled, a restaurant in downtown Fargo, Marcel proposed.

|||

THEY WANTED to marry near Robin's home. But they would be planning the wedding from some 1,200 miles away, in New York, and they suspected they would need a full year. As they looked over the calendar for 2004, one weekend date kept leaping out at them: Saturday, September 11.

Not everyone understood at first. But they would, the couple felt, once they heard their story. Out of the darkness of that day came a few specks of light—and their love story was one of them.

September 11 had sent tidal waves across the world, but as the days passed, the waves broke into a million ripples and flowed in rivulets to the least likely reaches of the country, before washing back in some inevitable way to New York. As Marcel continued to work through his anguish, he saw a September 11 wedding as a chance to surround his most painful memories with better ones, so that one day the good might outnumber the bad. That year, at Robin's urging, he sought help for the first time. He enrolled in the World Trade Center Medical Monitoring and Treatment Program, a government-funded program of free medical care and psychological counseling for survivors of the attacks.

|||

IN THE months after their wedding, life in New York seemed possible. Robin, after a grueling battery of interviews, landed a job with a firm that remodeled Manhattan restaurants and built homes in the Hamptons. Marcel won a prestigious "Finest of the Finest" award from the police union for climbing onto a ledge at the Time Warner Center to stop a suicidal twenty-two-year-old man from leaping to his death. The brass promoted him to a plainclothes unit, and he was getting good vibes about his chances for a dream job in the Emergency Service Unit, an elite squad whose members perform rescue, SWAT, and other high-level tactical operations. (The unit lost more members on September 11 than any other in the NYPD.) But the pressures of city life began to wear on Robin. She was commuting two hours each way to her job. She returned so late that she and her new husband would scarcely finish packing lunch and laying out clothes for the next day before it was time to go to bed. Adding to her stress was that Marcel, never thinking for his own safety, had some distressing close calls. He cut open his hand taking a knife from a robber who had begun stabbing people in a bodega; he wrestled with a coked-up street peddler who managed to unholster Marcel's gun; and he was struck by a van that blew through a red light.

Robin admired Marcel's fearlessness, but she grew increasingly worried about him. Especially unsettling were the vague reports he'd bring home some nights of possible plots to blow up buildings or subways. Marcel could see his wife's unhappiness. They were starting to talk about having children, and even he conceded the difficulty of being good parents in their current circumstances.

The NYPD let officers retire with partial pensions after as few as five years of service. For Marcel, that would be 2005. He began making inquiries, telling superiors about his plans for a family, and worrying about the flak he'd get from the other guys in the precinct. This time, though, none came. "It's just a job, buddy," his commander said. "You stay here too long, you forget that."

In April 2005, Marcel walked into One Police Plaza and filed his retirement papers. First he said goodbye to friends. Then he said goodbye to the city.

By the summer, he and Robin were in a pickup truck bound for Minnesota.

Renovations

THE METROPOLITAN
MUSEUM OF ART

Viewed from the steps along
Fifth Avenue, the Metropolitan Museum of
Art broadcasts permanence: its façade,
spanning four city blocks, is a masterwork
of classical columns, caryatids, and
medallion reliefs. But the museum's current
form is actually an amalgam of more than a
century of redesigns, encapsulations, and
additions. In 1882, not long after the
museum opened to the public, one art
critic called it "a forcible example of
architectural ugliness, out of harmony and
keeping with its avowed purpose . . .
fit only for a winter garden or railway
depot." The Met would earn a reputation
as one of the city's finest public buildings
only after round and round of revision.

When Mara Gailitis awoke, the tiny apartment above the drugstore on Lexington Avenue still smelled like a spice bazaar. The night before had been her Christmas party, an annual rite now well-known among her acquaintances for the elaborate and sometimes eccentric dishes she prepared.

At age thirty-three, Mara had yet to outgrow her introversion. Her parents were old-world Latvian aristocrats who believed that the highest virtue in children was silence. She had hated that part of her childhood, though its aftereffects were still with her. Her party—her only one each year—had always been strategic. With this one social nicety, she hoped to discharge an entire year's social debts. She invited everyone who had asked her to anything. Her guest list was a bricolage of the disparate worlds she straddled: a student from ballet class, a friend from her days as a substitute teacher in Harlem, a German from the office.

This year, 1975, Mara made *rijstaffel*, a traditional Dutch Indonesian feast. It meant "rice table." But it was actually a vast smorgasbord of appetizers and pungent sauces, or *sambals*, set out in small dishes and served with a variety of cooked grains. Mara had spent a week gathering ingredients for chili pastes, chutneys, banana fritters, coconut-dusted peanuts, and tofu omelets. What she may have lacked in social effusion, she sought to make up for in the assertiveness of her food. (The year before, she had made the Brazilian national dish, *feijoada*.)

The party fell on a Saturday. And for a shimmering moment, when the apartment was full and there was laughter and music and people were eating and talking and playing records, she felt she belonged. But then, one by one, her guests went home, as they always did, and the apartment was again, as so often, still. When she crawled out of bed at three the next afternoon, the room was cold and the sky was already streaked violet and gray. She glanced up at the ceiling. In a flight of whimsy not long ago, she had painted it with a trompe l'oeil of a bright blue sky dabbed with puffs of cloud. But it didn't help. It was December 21—the winter solstice—and the gloom outside her window made her feel even more alone.

||

FOR BOB Koppel, Sundays brought a sense of exhausted possibility. Sundays were the stern-faced schoolmarm standing, arms crossed, at the end of each week, reminding us of life's relentless repetition, and of the futility of escape. For much of this cold, gray day, he knocked about the apartment, pacing the parquet floors and thinking that his psychoanalytic session the next morning could not come too soon.

His mother, a French teacher, had died of a brain tumor when he was twenty, and when she left the world something of himself went with her. The lessons of tradition and purpose the rabbis had taught at the yeshiva in Queens seemed suddenly hollow. What did they know of the real world, of its cruel exactions? It was shameful for a grandson and nephew of great rabbis to think this way. Yet it was he how he felt.

Looked at in a certain light, the eight years since his mother's death had been a search for a replacement. If not for her, exactly, then for meaning. After graduating from Yeshiva University, he signed up with the Vista program and taught school in Harlem for a year. When his tour was over, he enrolled in a doctoral program in philosophy at Columbia, finding intellectual solace in the writings of the existentialists and phenomenologists. For four years Bob worked, if without much conviction, toward a PhD. But then, around the time of a breakup with a longtime girlfriend, he dropped out. All that remained now was psychoanalysis. Its focus on dreams and symbols and on enigmas of mind and self was about the only thing in his life that felt real.

Lying on the couch, still in his underwear, he ran his fingers over the stubble on his face. He wondered, mostly as an intellectual exercise, how long it had been since his last shave. Then, studying the runic shapes of clouds lolling past the window of his East Eighty-fifth Street apartment, he fell asleep. He awoke in a fog. He looked at his watch—3:05 p.m.—and then at the front door. A scornful pile of unopened mail filled a stand by the doorway, and for a moment he considered opening a few letters. Leafing the pile in search of a safe place to start, he found the square-shaped program from his visit the week before to the Metropolitan Museum of Art. When he was a boy, the Met was one of the few places besides synagogues, Shabbat dinners, and bar mitzvahs where his mother and father took him on weekends. He came to see it as a kind of secular temple. It was in some ways the last tether to his past.

Under the listings for December 21 was a lecture on "The Christmas Story in Painting" and a film, *A Child's Christmas in Wales*. Great, he thought, shaking his head and understanding why his parents often skipped the museum in late December. Deeper in the program, though, he noticed a few exhibits he hadn't had time for.

Just an hour or so was left before closing. He put on a ragged pair of Levi's, a wool sweater, and a red hunting coat. Then he headed out of his building into the frostbit air.

|||

MARA WANTED the sight and sound of other people. That is, she wanted not so much to talk to people as to move among them. It was what people did at Christmastime, wasn't it? Why should she putter around the apartment and mope?

She swallowed a few spoonfuls of leftover *rijstaffel* and then wrestled herself into bluejeans, Brazilian leather boots, and a blue sweater she had knitted for herself. She combed her hair, letting a few blond locks rest on the high cheekbones that were another part of her inheritance. From her apartment, it was three blocks to the Metropolitan Museum of Art. If she hurried, she'd have an hour before it closed.

She leaned, shivering, into the arctic wind blasting up East Eighty-fourth Street. Everyone there will be with someone, she thought. Everyone but me.

At 3:15, a tour group was leaving the museum and coming down the steps to Fifth Avenue. Couples were huddling for warmth, their words turning to steam. Mara hustled past them and into the warmth of the Great Hall. Behind the stairs—in the Medieval Sculpture Hall—was the Christmas tree, a twenty-foot-tall blue spruce. It was bedizened with eighteenth-century Neapolitan figurines of censer-toting cherubs in undulating robes. At the base was an exquisitely detailed baroque Nativity scene, with crèche shepherds and sheep, a group of curious peasants, and the three Magi with a menagerie that included a camel, goats, and an elephant.

Mara examined the faces of children as they entered the room: first the open mouths and wide eyes, then the slow smile and giddy questions. "Look, Mommy, look, do you see?" "Can we get one, please, Daddy?" "How do they put the angels up so high?" A father in a dark suit knelt down, draped his arm around his young daughter, and told the story of the Nativity. Something welled inside Mara. She turned away, toward the escalators, but a tapestry she hadn't noticed before stopped her cold.

|||

BOB NOTICED the woman as he entered the Medieval Sculpture Hall. He felt immediately sorry—faintly heartbroken even—that she seemed to be leaving. Her hair, the color of wheat, fell simply, like some milkmaid's, down her back. Her cheekbones looked Nordic and her jeans, so snug they might have been lacquered on. Not every object of beauty here, he thought, was in the catalog. He glanced up at the glimmering tree for only a moment before turning his head again. She hadn't left. She was there, somewhat distant now, near the entrance to the hall, her arms on her hips and her right leg forward a little bit. She looked as though she were taking notes on a painting.

Then something else: farther along the same wall, perhaps twenty feet away, another man was stealing glances at her while his wife, or girlfriend, was looking in the other direction. Others see it too, Bob thought. It was a kind of validation. When he turned back a second later, though, the woman was gone. Again, a pang akin to heartbreak. What had so absorbed her seemed like the most pressing question in the world. What kind of art drew women like her?

He approached the wall where she had stood and was surprised. It was not a painting at all but a somewhat faded tapestry. There was a sea of anxious faces, kings with scepters, bent men with canes. There was a young woman with hands clasped at her navel, a naked baby. It was a difficult image, not even particularly colorful. The heavy-handed religious imagery was even a bit of a downer. It didn't make sense. Was this woman in graduate school? A student of art history, perhaps? What in Heaven's name was this thing? Bob squinted at the plaque: the tapestry, it said, was an allegory of man's fall and eventual salvation. Brussels. Early 1500s. When he saw the title, Bob shook his head and smiled. The tapestry was called "Episode from the Story of the Redemption of Man."

|||

ON THE second floor, at the entrance to the special exhibition galleries, there was a sign for a new exhibit: "Patterns of Collecting." Yes, Mara had read something about it in the *Times*. The Met's swashbuckling young director, Thomas Hoving, had wanted to both show off the encyclopedic scope of the museum's collections and explain its policies and procedures for acquiring works of art. Some five hundred of the twenty thousand objects collected between 1965 and 1975 would be on display, ranging from Egyptian sphinxes to Roman bronzes, from a French fountain and Tibetan robes to a New England highboy and photographs by Man Ray.

The exhibit required the cooperation of all eighteen of the Met's curatorial departments and had prompted Hoving to commission a companion paperback, an anthology of the Met's curatorial war stories called *The Chase, the Capture.* What had the critic said? The exhibit, true, was a paean to the breadth and quality of the Met's collection. But it was also an act of defensiveness on the part of Hoving, who had been criticized for his ravenous pursuit of new treasures, with price no object. In 1962, while still an associate curator, he had traced a twelfth-century Bury St. Edmunds Cross, carved in walrus ivory, to a bank vault in Zurich and openly pleaded with the dealer. "I am being devoured by this cross," he said. "I want it, I need it." He got it. In 1970, as director, Hoving authorized the Met to pay a record-setting $5.5 million at auction for Diego Velázquez's *Juan de Pareja.*

Mara had discovered painting and writing as a girl, her imagination an escape from her parents' austerity and the upheavals of her early years. Latvia had been whipsawed by successive Soviet and Nazi occupations by the time she was born, in Riga, in 1942. Her family—her father was an esteemed physician; her mother, a nurse—became refugees in wartime Germany. With the help of a Rhode Island doctor and the Unitarian Church, the family immigrated to the United States in 1950, settling in Newport. Looking around this city of seaside mansions and patrician country clubs, seven-year-old Mara knew almost from the moment she arrived that she would never feel at home. Her father would build a successful medical practice in the city— treating the city's upper crust—because the people in those mansions liked his high European bearing, the very thing that made him so cold at home.

Until the birth of two siblings when she was twelve and thirteen, she had been an only child. In her isolation, she would amble along Thames Street, making up stories about the people inside the old bars and musty houses. She wrote elaborate poems. She painted pictures of lonely boats on the seashore. In high school, she won the poetry award and high praise from teachers. But none of that mattered to her parents. When they saw her hunched over her sketch pad or writing journal, they sputtered disapproval. "Waste of time," her mother said. "Who needs words? Especially yours."

College, at Brown, wasn't the escape she'd hoped for. When her parents saw creative writing and art courses on her report card, they threatened to cut off tuition. They wanted her to switch to more practical subjects, like science or German. Only now, after graduating and moving to New York, did she have the freedom to indulge her passions. She had day jobs—as a substitute teacher, a receptionist at a film-editing firm, an assistant to the head of a company that shipped American films to Germany. But her real life, as she saw it, unfolded after work. In ballet class. In front of the easel. In the hour before bed, when she filled her journals with free associations on art, literature, and life.

|||

UP THE escalator and past the European painting rooms, Bob entered the new exhibit, searching. He had somehow missed this in the program. But what an idea: the Met had lowered its drawbridge. It was letting people inside the castle. It had given in to the urge to tell its own story, to make sense of the past ten years of its life. The museum, Bob thought appreciatively, was in psychoanalysis.

The museum had even made public the examination list curators used to size up possible acquisitions. Bob studied the dozen or so stages of evaluation. Immediate impression. Description. Condition, wear, and age. Style. History. Outside expert advice. Scientific analysis. Doubts list. Then, "Conclusion: Does the work stack up to the original impression?"

He walked past a Renaissance bed, a terra-cotta relief by Thor-valdsen, and some carvings from pre-Columbian Mexico before finding himself in a room of Egyptian antiquities: a quartz lion god from 3100 BC; a limestone bust of a king; the head of Amenhotep III, carved in black stone. The room was half lit, and Bob had thought it empty. But then he heard a footstep at the other end and froze: Her. Behind the cascades of blond hair was an intelligent, al-most philosophical face. With her fingers laced behind her back, she was studying the plaque beside some ruin. A *vision*. That was the word that came to him: *vision*. With his arms clasped behind his back, he moved toward her, keeping his eyes on the display cases.

"It's funny," he began, looking at her for a second, then back at the display. "This term 'dynasty' they've got on all the panels. Weren't the historical periods in Egypt called kingdoms?"

He was blessed—or cursed, he sometimes thought—with an almost perfect recall of trivia from the classes he'd taken in col-lege as breadth requirements. At parties with other graduate stu-dents, he found that these morsels, when strategically dispensed, gave him a worldly air. But the woman turned and stepped to the next case without so much as a glance. Did she think he was talking to someone else? Maybe she didn't hear?

Bob caught up to her and said, "Did you have a chance to see any of the Cycladic figurines in the other room? I don't think it occurred to me until today just how much influence they must have had on Brancusi's work from the '30s. Have you seen his figures at the Guggenheim?"

She tilted her head only far enough for him to see her roll her eyes. Then she stalked away.

Just behind him, now, a voice: stentorian, effulgent. It hooked him like a gaff to the neck. "Why, young man," it said, "I could not agree more with what you just said."

His first impression, after turning around, was not a pleasant one. Just five inches away, with a smile that seemed to express gratitude, was a strong-shouldered matron in her early sixties, white curls festooning a red face and bifocals, her girth magnified by a lumpy black coat. The absurdity of the situation settled around him like the walls of a padded cell. "With what *I* just said?" Bob said.

"Who else, silly?" she said. "Brancusi. Of *course* Brancusi. Never in this museum have I heard anything so incisive. And from Mrs. Silverman, you should know, that's a high compliment."

God save me, Bob thought.

|||

MARA HAD perfected the art of escape. Her long blond hair, slim physique, and Scandinavian-looking features drew constant stares from men, some of whom apparently felt it reasonable to simply start following her. Her life was in this way a paradox: she was a loner with too much would-be company, most of it male. Mara wasn't like those of her friends who, for fear of being alone, strung one boyfriend along until a better one came along. Men, with their persistence, their need to control, made her easily claustrophobic. Mara had made peace with loneliness as a girl. She had learned compensations. And so the moment a boyfriend fell short, she was gone.

She was a distaff Houdini, particularly when some stranger was in pursuit, as there appeared to be now. She considered the options: duck through a side door to the women's restroom, flee to another wing of the museum, or just leave. She had been enjoying the exhibit; she didn't want to leave. But there was his voice again, with another pretentious observation. She could feel that he was close. She knew that if she so much as glanced his way, he would take encouragement. So she turned away, dropping her gaze to the floor and taking in, to her left, no more than a pair of saddle shoes.

Then, divine intervention. Another voice—an older woman's, bracing, proud—answered the man's question, the one Mara was sure had been posed to her. Mara skipped ahead, then looked over her shoulder. Saddle Shoes was at a safe remove. He was tall. His back was toward her. He was nearly nose-to-nose with this implausible, larger-than-life interloper.

The predator turned prey. Mara smiled to herself and made her getaway.

|||

BOB COULD hardly remember the last time someone found him so interesting. This Mrs. Silverman seemed so tickled by his every observation that at any moment he half expected her to take his arm and invite him to a home-cooked meal. Her full name was Iris Silverman, she confided. She was a retired school-teacher from the Upper West Side and a sucker for people who loved art like she loved art.

Bob played along, mixing half-remembered details from one of his art history classes with tidbits from a television program on the ancients he'd recently seen on PBS. "That's delightful," Mrs. Silverman said, chortling. And Bob had to admit: her contributions to the conversation were reasonably well informed. They sauntered from case to case, passing a tomb door and a statue of the jackal-headed Egyptian god Anubis. Mrs. Silverman laughed at his jokes and patted him sympathetically on the arm. All the while, the woman Bob really wanted was slipping further and further away.

|||

THERE WAS no harm in looking now. Mara was far enough away, and Saddle Shoes so engrossed with his new companion, that she would escape notice. He was interesting-looking, this man. Jeans, a bright red jacket, and a crewneck sweater over a T-shirt. Intelligent eyes. And young. Well, younger than she. He and whoever this woman was were speaking with enough brio for Mara—and really everyone—to hear. He was a little full of himself maybe, but there was more in his head than just one lucky pickup line. His face—that heavy brow—looked a little pained. Yet he *was* listening to this odd lady, at least twice his age, and was even making a kind of effort to amuse her.

Without knowing why precisely, Mara stopped. She stood in front of a 3,400-year-old Egyptian object the wall label called a "mirror." It was a battered bronze disk now far too worn for reflection. She waited there, kneeling slightly, studying its details, as Saddle Shoes and big coat lady inched nearer. In a minute, they were beside her. Despite herself, Mara turned, straightened, and threaded a strand of hair behind her ear. Then she looked at him.

"When you look in that mirror," she asked casually, "what do you see?"

"I see a civilization that set great store by appearances."

Mara was surprised by his tone. He was responding not like a man twice blown off, but as though Mara had been part of the conversation all along. She saw now that he had clear blue eyes, a dimpled chin, a head of wavy chestnut brown hair. Big coat lady was at his other elbow, looking at Mara cautiously, as if it were occurring to her that she had perhaps unfairly wrested this young man from his date.

"Yes, precisely," Mara said. "The pharaohs and their mummies. If they wore that much makeup in death, you might imagine the fuss they made in life."

"Egyptians pioneered cosmetics, didn't they?" said Saddle Shoes. "All that eyeliner, Cleopatra's baths in milk and honey."

Mara stepped to the next display case. "Yes, and they fetishized youth and certain arrangements of facial bones. I don't know if in that sense their culture was much different from our own. You've seen Nefertiti?"

"Haven't met her. But I've seen photos of the bust in magazines."

"A cover girl. By my lights she'd have as many admirers on Madison Avenue today as she did as the wife of Akhenaten."

They entered a series of rooms of modern photographs—Man Ray, Walker Evans. Mara looked over her shoulder. Big coat lady was nowhere to be found.

||||

THIS WOMAN wasn't what Bob had expected. He had picked up stunners before. But even when he got to know them, their looks continued, for him, to be their winningest asset. This curious woman, however, had managed a bait and switch. No sooner had she started talking than her physical beauty receded. Something else held him: the way her words, voice, and hand movements worked together, with a ballerina's grace, to give shape to some idea. The turning up of a palm, the raising of a shoulder. Her almost slow-motion delivery of words, so that each syllable received its due. And a way of connecting the least congruous of ideas, so that what seemed to defy logic one second made perfect sense the next.

Another thing that struck him was that her speech had none of the fashionable intonations—were they borrowed from Mary Tyler Moore?—that made so many women he knew, regardless of intelligence, sound the same. This woman's words, if anything, were literary, a little eccentric even. He couldn't place it.

After they exchanged names, he asked, "Are you Dutch?"

She laughed. They had left the exhibit and were padding along the balcony overlooking the Great Hall.

"No, I was born in Riga."

An embarrassing gap in his knowledge. "That's in, right, some-where, what, Baltic—"

"Latvia. And you?" She stopped by the railing. Below, a man was pushing a broom across the vast marble floor.

"I was raised Jewish, by way of Jamaica Estates, but I'm not sure what I believe in anymore," he said. "What about you? What do you believe in?"

"Photosynthesis," she said.

||

MANY OF Mara's would-be suitors had started in with flattery or personal questions, and they typically got nowhere. This guy, this Bob, was different. As they moved through the exhibit, he focused not on her but on the art. He gave her room to speak, to observe. He gave her a safe distance from which to size up his intelligence, his way of seeing. They walked down the grand staircase into the Great Hall, where a guard was making a sweeping motion toward the front door. "Closing time, folks," he said. "Exit here, please."

Outside, a light snow was falling.

"Would you like some coffee?" he said.

"Oh, well, no. No, thank you."

"It's gotten cold these last few days."

"Yes."

They walked in an awkward silence down the steps, the sounds of the city muffled under thickening snow. On Fifth Avenue, they gazed up at the museum, its columns and arches looking in the failing light like some ancient cathedral.

"These snowflakes are big enough to crawl under," Mara said, feeling suddenly self-conscious. She had rebuffed his invitation. Yet here she was still talking to him. Why?

Bob looked up, smiling. Mara watched a dime-sized flake make a soft landing on his eyelash. He blinked it away, with a slapstick expression that somehow reminded her of Harpo Marx.

"Yes," she said.

"Yes to what?"

"To beating the cold. Coffee would be nice."

|||

AT THE L&H Bakery, a café on Second Avenue that resembled some old babushka's kitchen, they found a corner table.

"What do you think?" Bob said, gesturing at the Eastern European matrons at the counter kibitzing over bowls of goulash.

"Intimations of Edward Hopper," Mara said.

"A cross between *Nighthawks* and, let's say, Isaac Bashevis Singer. It's why I love it."

Mara told Bob that she'd studied at Brown with John Hawkes, the postmodern novelist, and had written for magazines but that her parents had never encouraged her. When she went to San Francisco for a couple of years after graduation, they sent her articles about rapes and murders. They warned that she would turn into a hippie and wind up in a ditch. "Mara's run away," they told their friends, as if they'd washed their hands of her. She had come to New York nine years ago, in 1966, in hopes of finding herself.

"I would have liked to run away," Bob said, "but never got farther than the Upper East Side. Do you still talk to them?"

"My mom calls sometimes, but only to offer what she sees as solutions," Mara said.

"To what?"

"To the chagrin my unmarried state causes her."

"Well, my goodness, what did she propose?"

"More lipstick, of course. And a permanent. The last time we spoke, there was even, as I recall, a quite generous offer to buy me a wig."

Bob shook his head. "How mothers suffer for their children."

"How children suffer for their mothers."

"Maybe, but I think there's a certain elegance to your mother's *Weltanschauung*. We waste all this money and time searching our souls. But what if the answer to loneliness really *were* a new tube of lipstick?"

"And yet it's not anyone's loneliness that bothers her." Mara, who had been gazing into her empty coffee cup, looked up, blinking, as if shaken from a dream. This talk of her parents had lasted too long. She reached behind her neck and drew her tresses over her shoulder and down one side of her chest, as if this new alignment were a kind of set change. "Bob, how do you know so much about art? Are you a graduate student?"

"Is it the stubble or the clothes?"

"I ask seriously, Mr. Funny."

He told her he had been studying philosophy at Columbia, but had lost his conviction. He wanted to leave more of a mark in the world. He had done some acting off Broadway. He was working on a play. He had interviewed writers and artists as the host of a local-access TV show. His dream, though, was to write fiction. It was one of the reasons he was in psychoanalysis; to write about the human condition, he felt, he had to first understand his own psyche.

"That's interesting," Mara said. "Because you seem to me like a man of action."

"I feel lost in a sea of indecision."

On the street, the snow was coming down in droopy pinwheels. Bob helped her into her coat and wanted more than anything to kiss her. He wanted to sanctify their chance meeting, to seal it. But something restrained him. When she spun around, her arms now fully through her sleeves, he reached only for her hands. She had not yet put on her gloves, and when their fingertips touched, he could feel a slight roughness. Her fingers, he sensed, had not spent the day on a manicure table or in a pot of cold cream.

"I like your hands," he said.

"You do?" She turned up her palms as if searching for something she hadn't noticed before. "Why?"

"They're the hands of someone who makes things."

They parted in opposite directions, toward apartments five blocks apart. The snow was falling harder now, hooding the streetlamps in white lace.

|||

BOB HAD recently started work at an education institute at Columbia, but with just three days until Christmas, nobody felt like working. While his co-workers bantered about their holiday plans, Bob brooded. He was shuffling papers on his desk one moment, pacing the back hall the next.

"Stop working so hard, Bob," one of his office mates said. "You'll make the rest of us look bad."

"Just trying to solve a puzzle."

"Right on, brother. Feel like talking about it?"

"No."

He had to see Mara again. She was a rare thing: brainy, eccentric, beautiful. He knew how easy it would be to lose her. He had won her over for a few hours. But women like her weren't wanting for charming men. One false step, he feared, and she'd vanish, just as she had after he'd first spoken to her, perhaps a little too abruptly, at the Met. He bent his head into his hands, and plowed his fingers through his hair.

On the subway ride home, he read a review of a new French film—*Where There's Smoke*—playing at the Cinema Studio. It was directed by André Cayatte, a New Wave filmmaker who had made a splash a decade earlier with a pair of films—told from the dueling viewpoints of a husband and wife—called *Anatomy of a Marriage*.

The Cinema Studio had a reputation for arty, intellectual films. Bob tore out the review and smiled.

|||

MARA WAS in her apartment that afternoon, waiting for her clothes at the Laundromat across the street to dry, when the phone rang. It was Bob. A new film was playing, across from Lincoln Center, in about a half hour. He knew it was ridiculously late notice. Would she join him?

Mara was on the sidewalk outside her building a minute later, hailing a cab. She found him at the entrance. Gone were the ratty jeans, saddle shoes, and crewneck sweater. Today he was in a tweed blazer, corduroy pants, a scarf, and polished boots. His hair was combed back in a debonair wave. And he had shaved.

She stood with her hands on her hips and gave him a once-over. "You're reborn."

"Frye boots. Just picked them up."

"I wouldn't have guessed you were a clothes horse."

"My outfit yesterday wasn't, well, representative."

"But what if I liked yesterday's representation?"

"Then you're welcome to pluck it, at your own risk, from the laundry." Which reminded Mara that in her rush to meet him, she'd forgotten all about hers.

||

A HALF hour after the opening credits, Bob's heart sank. The film was a dud. An overcooked police procedural about a corrupt mayor's race in a Paris suburb. With bad subtitles. He dreaded the moment the lights came up. His face would betray his sense of failure. Then, in the film's second hour, something happened. A suspect named Jacques hurled himself out a window. There was a quick cut to one of his frustrated pursuers. The subtitle that flashed on the screen said, "Jacques defenestrated!"

Bob found himself quaking with laughter. At almost the same time, he heard a squeal from Mara: she was almost doubled over in her seat. They made eye contact, and that made them laugh more. It was a moment of knowing—and seeing—that each would remember for a long time.

||

THEY MADE plans to meet again two nights later, at the Whitney Museum of American Art, which had mounted a solo exhibit of works by the modernist sculptor Mark di Suvero. Bob was there at exactly 5:30. He didn't want to pass up so much as a minute with her. But there was no Mara. Ten minutes passed, then thirty. Bob wandered distractedly through abstract figures of wood and steel. The Met had worked such magic. He was hoping to find even more here. But without Mara, the art seemed empty, lifeless. Was she okay? She was street-smart. But New York City, on the brink of bankruptcy, had made head- lines of late for its soaring violent crime rate. He should have met her outside her office. That would have been the gentle- manly thing to do.

Shaking his head at his stupidity, he left the exhibit and en- tered a dark side room. Inside, the Whitney appeared to be screening something from its collection of experimental films. Bob pawed his way through the gloom, finding a seat atop a row of bleacher-style benches. On the screen was an out-of-focus shot of a hand opening and closing a bread box. Again. And again. He watched the hand, and the bread-box door, opening and closing, for a half hour.

Pressing his fingers against his temples, he just felt sorry. For himself. For his situation. For whatever it was that was keeping Mara.

|||

EVEN WHEN she was falling for someone, *especially* when she was, Mara hewed to routine. She had learned in her twenties how easy it was to lose perspective, to give up the everyday things that made you happy because of a man. She had rashly accepted two marriage proposals in the past, only to break them after her senses returned. She was older now and, yes, wiser. *The Venera- ble Mara*, she sometimes called herself.

Bob was perceptive, a cultural savant, a good talker. When they were the only two people in that theater to wonder why the subtitle writers couldn't have just said "tossed himself out a win- dow," she knew he shared not just her vocabulary but an eye for the absurd. In her family, nobody laughed. And yet, here was this man—"The One," as she wrote in her diary—who laughed.

But this date at the Whitney would be their third in the four days since meeting. Some pacing, she felt, was prudent. She had ballet after work, and would stay for the whole class, even it meant running a little late. If Bob didn't understand, well, that was something better to know now than later. After changing back into street clothes and looking at her watch, though, she realized she had lost track of time: she was nearly an hour late. When her cab got stuck behind a line of cars at a red light, she nearly panicked. She bit her nails, then dug them into the edge of the vinyl seat. "Please, is there any other way?"

"It's New York at seven on a weeknight, lady, whaddaya want?"

She dashed upstairs to the di Suvero exhibit, brushed a loose strand of hair from her face, and circled through the rooms full of oddly joined wood planks and mangled machine-age steel. She was on her third lap when she noticed something: a shadowy room branching off one of the halls. She entered, her heart flopping against her chest, and was struck blind by the darkness.

|||

THE FILM reel clicked, and the bread box opened and closed, and opened again. Bob was in a kind of stupor when he registered someone entering the room. A woman's figure, wading through the murk, then turning and surveying the seats. Bob couldn't see the woman's face. But he knew. From her height. From her figure. From the way the light from the projector frosted the outlines of her hair, like some illuminated saint.

He padded down the steps beside the seats. "Mara?"

She turned. With her palms on his chest, she pushed him backwards until his boot heels struck the rear wall. She looked up, and their lips touched. "I had to find you," she whispered fervently. "I had to."

|||

IN THE spring, they moved in together. Bob juggled oranges by the kitchen counter in the mornings to make her laugh. He served her omelets and ice cream and Portuguese wine. His face was so expressive that Mara could read in its arrangement of creases how happy she made him. He was some magical redress, it sometimes felt, for all her childhood privations.

They went to movies and museums. They held hands through performances of the New York City Ballet and the New York City Opera. When he played pickup basketball by the East River on weekends, she'd bring him iced coffee. Then she'd sit on a bench, by turns studying him and reading a book, until he was ready to go home.

One afternoon, as they returned home in locked hands after a summer walk through the city—beads of sweat at their temples, bliss etched on their faces—an old woman stepped out of an apartment building and cried, "It's Romeo and Juliet."

The analogy was truer than the woman could know. Bob's family, Orthodox Jews descended from a long line of rabbis, would never consent to his marrying a gentile. Her family, aristocratic Lutherans, bore old-world prejudices toward Jews.

"Maybe we just tell people what they want to hear," Bob had said one Saturday morning, in a bout of exasperation.

"No," Mara said.

She could live with disapproval but not dishonesty, not in a relationship she felt had been born of candor. Mara completed her conversion to Judaism a few weeks before their wedding. She did it neither for God nor to spite her parents, but so that she and Bob would not have to lie to his family. Bob and his widowed father had grown estranged after he married a woman Bob never took to. He knew that if his father had doubts about Mara's faith, he'd keep them to himself. But Bob was close to his mother's parents—they had grown closer since his mother's death—and he worried they'd demand assurances of Mara's Jewish identity, and that of their great-grandchildren. In the end, despite her high Nordic features, his grandparents never asked.

Bob Koppel and Mara Gailitis were married in late 1976, in two separate ceremonies. The first, on Thanksgiving Day, at a Newport courthouse, was for her family. The second, a couple of weeks later, at Temple Emanu-El, on Manhattan's Upper East Side, was for his. Their families would never meet.

After Mara had moved her last box of clothes into Bob's apartment, he asked if there was anything she wanted to change.

"You're making me queen?" she asked, relieved.

"To a degree."

She was less than fond of the bizarre Symbolist posters on his walls and the giant black "King Kong couch" he'd had since forever. Their destinies lay elsewhere, she told him, and like a teenager realizing he'd outgrown his GI Joes, Bob relented.

When the trash men had hauled it all away, Bob asked Mara to make something new. "Anything so we don't have to look at these blank walls."

She set to work on a painting of the two of them nuzzling at their favorite park by the East River. The city's fiscal woes had left little money for park upkeep; lawns had browned and trees withered. In the painting, however, Mara depicted the park as a scrupulously landscaped British estate.

Sightlines

WASHINGTON SQUARE PARK

Over more than forty years in government,
Robert Moses, New York's "Master Builder," tattooed
the city with hundreds of miles of expressways and many of
its bridges and tunnels. Longtime residents were forced
from homes, and old neighborhoods razed, in the name of
a scorched earth brand of urban renewal. Though never
elected to office, Moses inspired dread in mayors and
governors alike. At one point, he held twelve job titles,
including city parks commissioner, simultaneously; he was
a modern day emperor. Then, in the smallest of places,
he met his match: Washington Square Park, a 9.75-acre
Greenwich Village gathering spot beloved of artists,
intellectuals and every kind of dissident. Moses had fought
to carve a depressed four-lane highway though its very
center. But the park's defenders were so impassioned that
for one of the first times in his life, he had to back down.
They not only scuttled his plan but persuaded the city,
in the spring of 1959, to keep cars out for good.
Revelers at the victory party called it a "grand closing."

Daniel Letourneau stepped out of the car he'd borrowed and into the bedlam of Broadway at noon. Eddies of tourists carried him through the narrows of Times Square before dispersing into the glittery light of a nearly cloudless sky.

The air was spiked with spring and motor exhaust and scents reeling off warm bodies. Daniel walked and walked, like some lion on the loose, turning down one street, then another, feeling his way across the city with his senses. But after an hour, he found he could no longer ignore the torn envelope in his pocket, the one where he'd written the addresses from his mother.

Daniel, who was twenty-four, had told people back home, in France, that he was going to New York to learn English. A Paris business school he'd applied to had said that without near fluency, he could not be admitted. The school, he had hoped, would give him the kind of direction he'd failed to find either in college or afterward as a chef.

But it was June 2000, a month into his trip, and his English was as shaky as ever. The trouble was that even in America, he was surrounded by French speakers. He waited tables at a French bistro in New Jersey. The owner was Bernard, a temperamental older Frenchman whose French-speaking children Daniel babysat in exchange for room and board. When Daniel went out, it was with a Frenchman named Pierre, an old friend from culinary school who was the bistro's sous-chef. Adding to Daniel's claustrophobia were Bernard's increasingly frequent tongue-lashings. "Because you cooked at a three-star restaurant in Paris makes you better than me?" Bernard had said, resentful of Daniel's popularity with the kitchen staff. "Here, I am boss, you understand?"

Instead of a crash course in English, the summer was turning into a dispiriting study in the insularity of French expatriate life in America.

With just two and a half weeks until his return flight to Paris, Daniel called his mother. Though she was the owner of a small Spanish-French translation agency in Paris, she had a pragmatic streak from an earlier career as a nurse. On the phone a few days earlier, she had told Daniel to look for a short-term job at a translation agency in New York. "Put on a nice shirt and tell them you're my son." She read off a few Manhattan addresses where she had contacts. "Maybe one them will let you be a fly on the wall for the next two weeks."

"But what would I do, exactly?" Daniel asked.

"Observe. Listen. Make coffee. Whatever they ask. It will be good for you."

Daniel, who grew up in the working-class suburbs of Paris, didn't have much in the way of business attire. He had packed for a summer of restaurant work and baby-sitting, not cold-call office interviews in one of America's most cutthroat cities. At the bottom of his suitcase, he found a passable navy-blue shirt and his one pair of gray slacks without scuffed hems. Then he borrowed a car from a friend at the restaurant and pointed it toward Midtown Manhattan.

|||

RETURNING TO New York University after a stroll through Greenwich Village, Sarah Cross felt more excited about the out-of-town visitor she was expecting that evening. Alejandro was from a chapter in her life that now seemed far away, when critics from the newspapers raved about her dancing (a body that was "boneless, weightless," arms that moved "as if caressing long delicate strands of sea moss" or "swimming through honey"), when she performed at places like the Kennedy Center and toured Europe and South America. Alejandro, a fellow dancer, had introduced himself after a performance in Venezuela, and they had become lovers. Sequestered now in this more ordinary life, Sarah looked forward to a night's escape. She had enrolled at NYU that summer to do what she had never managed before: sink roots. Over a professional dance career that began when she was fifteen, she had started—and stopped—college a half dozen times. Now, at twenty-two, she was trying again. She hoped that NYU, her mother's alma mater, would somehow be different. But would it? She had been in town just a few weeks, and though school was fine, Manhattan seemed altogether too much.

A daughter of the Washington, D.C., suburbs, she struggled to be herself here. Say something friendly to strangers on the street, and they looked at you as if you were either a scam artist or a candidate for a one-night stand.

She couldn't hide behind that battle-hardened gaze so many New Yorkers wore. Maybe it was because of her sensibilities as a dancer, but she couldn't deaden herself to the physical energy of people around her. And in Greenwich Village, as she walked along streets like Broadway and Lafayette—robins wheeling overhead, sunshine washing around her like a warm bath—the energy was nearly overwhelming.

||||

DANIEL TOUCHED a handkerchief to his brow and ran his palm over his shirtfront to smooth creases. He paced outside the front door of the first address on his mother's list, rehearsing an introduction. "Hi, my name is Daniel. I am a chef, but I am learning English. My mom says she knows you. Can you give me a job for two weeks, so I can practice the international language of business?"

It sounded so inane that a laugh escaped his throat. Ridiculous. No doubt New York had a million foreigners like him, all angling for a break. Why should anyone care about his problems? In the lobby, a wary-looking guard behind a semicircular desk asked, "May I help you?" Daniel took off his sunglasses and began to say something, but he was drowned out by a thunderclap of hip-hop from a passing car and then a burst of laughter from a group of young women in business suits who were waving key cards to summon an elevator.

"I'm sorry?" the guard said to Daniel, scrunching his face into a mask of incomprehension. "Couldn't hear a word."

"Please," Daniel said, backing away. "It's no problem."

He left the building, balled up the list of addresses, and flung it in the first trash bin outside.

|||

SARAH WAS sure Alejandro knew even less Manhattan geography than she did, and she had debated where they might meet without his getting lost. The only conspicuous place near NYU—an easy-to-spot green rectangle on her pocket map—was Washington Square Park.

But Sarah knew from having passed that it was big. It had statues, a fountain, and a set of interlacing paths the length of several city blocks. She had yet to finish her paper for her afternoon Spanish class. But glancing at her watch, she saw she could spare a minute to survey the park; she would settle on a meeting spot, then head to the library to write her paper.

Sarah entered from the north, walking under the white marble arch and glimpsing a carnival of flesh. The greens were so thick with sunbathers that people had to wobble on tiptoe between the bodies to find their towels. Nearby, at the foot of a monument, a shirtless man was strumming a guitar while a contortionist twisted herself into a pretzel. Teenagers on skates flew by so fast that Sarah shuddered. Down a side path, Sarah saw older men bent over tables of chess and young women in bathing suits slathering lotion on one another's backs. She heard a shriek and wheeled around: a couple on a bench—NYU students?—were tangled up in a kiss.

Sarah reached into her bag for a tube of sunscreen. The energy here was overwhelming, too. But it was different from the kind on the street.

|||

WITH HIS dress shirt untucked, Daniel walked and walked. Down Fifth Avenue. Onto Broadway. Through Union Square. He felt himself in a fever, as though the city and its people were spirits joined in some primeval rite of rebirth. The women, especially. Whenever a lovely one let her eyes linger, he felt electricity streak from his temples to his feet. For just one day, I won't think about jobs, about school, about the future, he told himself. In sun like this, on streets like this, how could you not live for the moment?

A little after three, his throat dry and his calves pulsing with a pleasant exhaustion, he entered a small grocery. He set a bottle of beer and a couple of crumpled up bills on the counter. The cashier dropped the bottle into a brown bag and handed it back. He took a long sip. He had tried to blot Elena from his mind these past few days, but now thoughts of her returned. They had met when he was thirteen, during a year he'd spent at a high school in Madrid. They fell in love and stayed together for the next decade. But the past couple of years had been unhappy. Growing up had cast a harsher light on their differences. The physical part of their relationship was gone. And with both working long hours to get a leg up in the restaurant industry— Elena worked as an assistant cook—they rarely had time for each other. It felt sometimes like work was just an excuse, a convenient way to avoid confronting their problems. They had quarreled just before Daniel left, and their e-mails during his visit to America were strained. With the beer inside him now, he wondered how she was doing. He wanted to know whether all this craziness was in his head or if their relationship had simply run its course.

He found a pay phone, and with the calling card in his wallet, he dialed France. The walk, the heat, had infused him with a kind of serenity. The phone rang and rang. Then her voice, faint, foreign, on an answering machine. He left a message that sounded, even to him, distant. Across the street was a park, and at one end a giant marble arch. It reminded Daniel of another arch, and he walked toward it, drinking from his brown bag. The sight of sunbathers and street performers made him feel like an investment banker who had somehow parachuted onto a beach. He was wearing a button-down shirt, slacks, and oxfords in a sea of tank tops, sandals, and swimwear. His untucked shirt made it even worse: people would probably think he'd had too much wine with lunch.

He wanted badly to change. This shirt, these pants—they were not who he was. Passing a hot dog vendor and a sketch artist, he found a seat on a ledge under a tree along the periphery of the central plaza. People wouldn't notice him here. After the day's exertion, the beer was making him a little light-headed. He anguished for a moment over what to tell his mother about his aborted job search. Then he reminded himself: not today.

About thirty feet to his right, something caught his eye: a slender woman with a pen and notebook. She was sitting in a lotus position, her back a perfect line. She had a pixie haircut and a tomboyish dusting of freckles. But what struck Daniel was her impeccable posture. Just sitting there, in an act as everyday as reading a book, she had arranged her limbs—effortlessly, it seemed—into a pose worthy of sculpture.

Daniel rose, dodging an in-line skater as he walked to another ledge, just ten feet from the woman. Up close, she seemed both twice as beautiful and twice as unreachable. He was glad now for one part of his wardrobe: his sunglasses. He could admire her undetected.

|||

A FEW steps down one of the curving walks, Sarah sized up the granite likeness of George Washington, robed and serious. Could she meet Alejandro here? Down another path, she considered the bronze of Gen. Giuseppe Garibaldi, bearded, with flowing hair, cast in the act of unsheathing a sword. But then she noticed a woman about her age spread a picnic blanket on the grass. Sarah inhaled deeply and then released the air, slowly, through her mouth. Her search, and the library, could wait. She walked to the periphery of the central plaza and sat down on a concrete ledge in the shade of a tree. It was the perfect place— close in, but protected—to watch this manic samba of color and flesh and sound.

Sarah had been writing in her Spanish notebook for about fifteen minutes when she got the feeling that someone was looking at her. Turning to her left, she noticed a man in a dress shirt and dark glasses. He was sitting about ten feet away, under the shade of the same tree but on a ledge slightly higher than hers. He was definitely looking in her direction. But because of his dark sunglasses, she couldn't tell whether he had been specifically looking at her.

She turned back to her notebook for a few minutes. But that feeling of being watched—a fixity at the edge of her vision— didn't go away. When she turned to her side this time, she was sure. The man's sunglasses were now resting on top of his head, and he was, yes, looking right at her. He was handsome, about her age. Something about his willowy posture and brushed-back dark hair—she had seen his type before on her overseas travels— suggested that he was not American. It was not the hard stare she was accustomed to from American men. No, it was open, earnest, something like a boy's.

With his nice shirt and slacks, he must be some kind of businessman, she told herself. One of these guys who gins up his lunch break with aimless flirting. Whoever he was, he'd soon be back at some soulless job in a corporate office.

Her cellphone jangled, and she quickly turned away, reaching into her bag. She had gotten the phone a few days before, but the technology still bedeviled her. When she went to answer, she pressed what turned out to be the off button and found herself speaking into a dead line. The phone rang twice more, and again, each time, she accidentally hung up on the caller. "Hello?" she said. "Hello? Is anyone there? Can you hear me?" She looked to her left again and saw that the man was still there. And he was laughing. At her.

Now an older Puerto Rican man staggered toward her from the plaza. He was singing a Spanish song and spinning, as if dancing with an imaginary partner. He teetered toward her and stopped. "Me gusta tu pelo," he said to her. *I like your hair.* Sarah had learned Spanish on a semester of language school in Barcelona three years before. Her grandmother was Puerto Rican, and Sarah had wanted to better communicate with her. "Vale," she told the man now, smiling. *Okay.* The man made a little bow. Sarah winced at the smell of alcohol. Washington Square Park, she decided, wasn't working out too well as a study hall. She tacked a rushed ending onto her Spanish paper and stuffed her folders into her bag. Glancing over her shoulder again, she saw that the businessman was still there. He was still looking at her.

Okay, she told herself. Enough's enough.

She turned to face him, defiantly crossed her arms, and stared back.

|||

WHEN DANIEL had laughed at her slapstick with the cellphone, he knew she'd noticed. The next step would be to say something. But what? Daniel had been in the same relationship since he was thirteen. He had no idea what a man was supposed to say to a woman in a park in New York. With his halting English, he worried that in any case he wouldn't be understood. So he fell back on what he recognized was adolescent: he looked at her with an open, innocent expression. The mood in the park was so sublime that he felt certain she would take it for what it was—not the unblinking stare of some predator, but a harmless gesture of admiration.

Then something strange: when he next looked over, she was speaking with some drunk in Spanish. From his year of high school in Madrid, where his mother had grown up, he recognized the woman's accent as a Spaniard's. Daniel looked more closely at the cover of one of her books, which she held against her chest, and made out Spanish words. If she were from Spain, then maybe he was agonizing over nothing. If neither was a native English speaker, then she would perhaps forgive—or even appreciate—a fumble.

But before he had time to work out an opening line, she did something that shocked him. She aimed her body—and that perfect posture—straight at him.

|||

LATER, IT would be hard to explain. It would sound implausible or just weird. Even to them. But for the next half hour, on that warm June day in Washington Square Park, Daniel and Sarah just looked at each other. For a full thirty minutes, they wordlessly studied each other's faces. The silent exchange of expressions—yearning, fear, pleasure, doubt—made Daniel feel like a mime re-enacting some universal story about the phases of love. By the end, because he was already in a relationship, Daniel was prepared to walk away. He was ready to let those thirty minutes stand as lived poetry—an instance of beauty he'd remember forever, precisely because words never had a chance to muck it up.

When she first returned his gaze, Sarah had in mind only a game. Who would blink first? Who would be chicken? Then, after a moment, something gave. The man's face, she saw, was as expressive as a dancer's and as unguarded as a child's. She felt she could read in its lines his every feeling. This is who I am, he seemed to be saying. I am absolutely ready to fall in love. When

Sarah's face broadcast fear, he responded by looking down, sub-missively, and then up, with a puppy's drooping eyes. She nodded slowly. I trust you, she told him with her eyes. I won't be afraid.

Sarah had thrown herself into fast-burning romances before. She had seen so much change in her short life that love had come to seem ephemeral, a seed better devoured on sight than tended into uncertain maturity. Her parents had divorced when she was a toddler. She was just eight when her mother—a professional ballerina in New York before becoming a child psychiatrist—was diagnosed with a rare intestinal cancer. Sarah had been the youngest member of her dance company by at least five years. With so much time on the road, her relationships with men had seldom been more than flings. So much of life was unpre-dictable that it was sometimes safest to keep moving. The dance critics who called her "weightless" had no way of know-ing the depth of their insight. There in the park, Sarah felt weightless again, and drawn by the familiar gravity of someone else's desire.

|||

THEN REALITY intervened. Looking at her watch, Sarah saw that little time remained before Spanish class. She hadn't eaten lunch and felt suddenly hungry. She picked up her bags and walked toward the man. He looked startled by her approach. "I'm sorry," she said. "I need to eat something. I have to go."

"Oh," Daniel said. "Um, eres Española?" he added hopefully.

"No. Why do you think that?"

The man she'd spoken to, and her book, Daniel explained.

Sarah laughed. His English was so-so, but she could under-stand him. "So you're Spanish?"

"No," he said. "French. Should we eat something?"

Across the street, at a small deli swarming with students, they bought a quiche and unwrapped it on the steps of a nearby NYU building.

"This quiche is pretty bad," Sarah said.

"Yes, I think I can taste the plastic." Daniel rewrapped it and set it between them on the step.

"So how do you know Spanish?"

"My mom is from Madrid," he said, brushing some of the crumbs off his sleeve.

"Great, so you can check my Spanish paper."

"Por supuesto."

He ran the fingers of his left hand across the pages of her notebook, and on one, the important one, was a ring. "You're married?"

"No," he said. "My girlfriend and I bought them for each other. But not because we are married."

"That's really nice." She let her eyes linger on his hands, so he would not see her disappointment, and then noticed something else: the scars. His wrists bore a crosshatch of what looked like half-healed cuts or burns. "Your hands."

"I'm a chef," he said, a little self-consciously. "Here." He pointed out a minor error of grammar in the paper and handed it back to her, smiling.

The eyes, voracious and dark, that had held her in the park seemed less assured at this closer distance. "I should be getting to class," she said.

"Later we can meet?"

"Actually," she said, "I'm meeting a friend. A guy."

"Entiendo," Daniel said, looking down. There was long pause. Then he looked back up, catching her eyes again.

"I have a cellphone—"

"I don't know," he said abruptly. "Maybe it's better to go."

Daniel kneaded his hands. Sarah played with a strap on her bag, looking at him and then back at the park. Neither seemed able to pull away.

"Here," she began, reaching into her bag for a pen.

"No, please," he said, shaking his head. "At 3 p.m. tomorrow, I will be sitting under the same tree." If she were still interested then, she could find him there. If not, he said, the day's beauty would stand, undiminished.

|||

THE NEXT morning, Daniel was consumed with the question of clothes. That stiff dress shirt and those slacks were not him. Sarah had said she was a dancer—an artist. When she showed up the next day—*if* she showed—he wanted her to see that he, too, was an adventurer, a bon vivant. He decided on his most striking outfit: a blue cotton kimono with a white jacket that he'd bought recently in Paris's Chinatown.

After parting with Sarah the afternoon before, Daniel had been gripped by a kind of delirium. He wove back into the park, and then out again. He flitted in and out of record stores on Eighth Street and Sixth Avenue, trying in vain to remember which American hip-hop albums he had always wanted on vinyl.

On the train to Manhattan now, his heart galloped. He was no longer a tourist drifting aimlessly through a new city. He was a suitor with a destination. Serendipity had given way to intention, lightness to weight. He entered the park a few minutes before three. It was another warm day, but a Friday, and the throngs of sun worshipers and musicians seemed even a little thicker than the day before.

He found their tree, the one beside the walkway to Washington Square South. But the only sign of life on their ledge, besides some students bent over books, was a pigeon pecking at the concrete. Daniel circled the central plaza. All the ledges looked the same. Did he have the right spot? Was he turned around? Toward the fountain at the center, pigeons chased one another in circles, wings aflutter. They leaped awkwardly, toes scrabbling, in some ancient mating dance. Five minutes passed. Then another five. He had a feeling of falling. New York was a city of eight million people. He didn't even know this woman's last name.

All this buildup, he told himself, shaking his head. For what? She's with the friend, the guy, whoever he was—she said so herself. Of course she's not coming. It was 3:25. He decided to make one more pass, then leave. This time, though, she was there. She had brought two bottles of peach-flavored iced tea.

||||

THE EVENING before, Sarah had met the Venezuelan dancer. She spent the night with him, but her body had felt borrowed rather than given. Here it was different: Stretched out beside Daniel under this tree, sunlight trickling like warm honey through the branches, Sarah felt whole. She told him a little about the mother who raised her, and the father she seldom saw. He told her about his childhood among working-class Arabs and Algerians in the Paris suburb of Argenteuil. As a teenager, he had formed a hip-hop band with some of his immigrant neighbors.

"I was the lyricist."

"You mean you rapped?"

He blushed. "A little."

"I'm supposed to have dinner at my aunt's place in Brooklyn," Sarah said eventually.

"Brooklyn is I think cool," Daniel said, sitting up and looking excited. "Jay-Z, Biggie Smalls, no?"

"My aunt's not a rapper, but she and my uncle cook awesome food."

"Yeah?"

"I could probably get you a dinner invite. Just wait a sec."

Over her cell phone, Sarah told Aunt Rita a story about "this lonely French exchange student in my dorm."

"Oh?"

"Poor guy, he knows no one in the city, and he's really homesick. I realize it's last-minute. Is there room?"

With the phone still pressed to her ear, she looked at Daniel, who was shaking his head at the ruse.

At Aunt Rita's apartment, Daniel, with a kind of old-world courtesy, took turns shaking hands with everyone in the room. Aunt Rita had been a social activist in the 1960s—her first husband was a Black Panther—and Daniel charmed her with his literacy in modern protest movements, a subject he'd studied in college. Later, Daniel and Sarah's Puerto Rican–born uncle, who loved to cook, had a long, animated discussion about food. Daniel conversed with him in fluent Spanish.

Sarah and Daniel traded lingering looks over the dinner table. Aunt Rita, apparently catching one, winked at her niece, who turned crimson. *Lonely French exchange student*, my derrière, the wink said.

At the top of the subway steps on their way back, Sarah tugged Daniel's sleeve and made a sultry pout. Daniel bent down to kiss her.

Sarah knew how it went from here—a tryst that blazed for a night or two and then flamed out like a meteorite hitting desert. But back in her dorm room, as her hands moved over him, Daniel asked if they could slow down. He didn't want to cheapen whatever was happening between them. They stretched out on her bed, their bodies stippled by the streetlight outside the window. She noticed a triangle of smooth, discolored skin on his chest and traced it with her forefinger. "This doesn't look like a cooking injury."

"I was born with a problem in my heart." As a newborn, he told her, he had been diagnosed with interventricular communication—a hole that let blood seep between the left and right passageways of his heart. Right after his birth, doctors were so worried that they kept him in isolation. For thirty days, he had no physical contact with his parents. The scar on his chest was from surgery he'd undergone as a toddler.

"I'm so sorry, Daniel."

That night, they did nothing but hold each other.

||||

WHEN DANIEL showed up at the bistro the next evening, a Saturday, his boss was red-faced. Daniel hadn't called to say he would be staying in the city. He hadn't been scheduled to work that Friday, but still, Bernard said, he needed to know his whereabouts. Bernard told Daniel he was demoted. Rather than cooking or even busing tables, Daniel would be washing dishes. Daniel made little money as it was, but as a dishwasher he wouldn't even qualify for a share of the tips. Daniel could tell from Bernard's twisted features that his boss wanted nothing more than to humiliate him in front of the staff.

But it didn't work. Daniel was in such a mood from his night with Sarah that, even while elbow deep in dish soap, he couldn't stop reeling off jokes. Everyone in the kitchen was in hysterics. Except Bernard, who was doing a slow burn. After desserts went out to the last diners, Bernard lit into Daniel. "You know what I think?" he said, cornering Daniel in the kitchen. "I think you are trying to steal from me."

"What?" Daniel said. "How?"

"I don't how exactly, but I will find out. I think you are trying to sabotage my business, and when I get to the bottom of it, believe me, you will be sorry."

Daniel could feel heat rise in his temples. He had toiled long hours for scant pay, and, now, to be accused of sabotage? Just because he refused to kowtow to another of Bernard's perennially sour moods? "You know what, Bernard," he said, shrugging as he untied his apron. "I don't need this job. Find someone else."

Daniel returned to Bernard's basement, where he had been living, and opened his suitcase. Just two days earlier, he had been searching for a second job. Now he had quit the only one he had. As he shoved in clothes and toiletries, he wondered whether he would have been so rash without Sarah.

The next morning, he remembered the name of a budget hotel he'd stayed at on a family visit to Manhattan as a teenager: The Carlton Arms. Yes, there it was in a phone book. He found it the next day, on Third Avenue and East Twenty-fifth Street, and booked a room at a discounted weekly rate.

|||

WAITING THAT evening by their tree, Daniel looked out over a park that bore little resemblance to the one where he'd met Sarah a few days before. Rain fell from clouds the color of wet wool, and a raw wind raked the concrete walkways. There were no crowds, no pretzel carts, no musicians. Even the drunks had sought shelter. Daniel turned his face to the sky, letting the rain fall on his cheeks. He felt a tap on his shoulder. Turning around, he saw Sarah in a puffy red jacket. He had called her just minutes earlier, and already she was here. She moved toward him, leaning her cheek against his sweater, damp with rain.

"Aren't you cold?" she said.

"My room is warmer," Daniel said.

The only time they left his hotel room over the next ten days was when hunger drove them to the deli across the street, often around 3 a.m.

|||

ON THE flight home to Paris, Daniel composed a tortured letter to Elena, his girlfriend of more than a decade. "I spent the last ten days with someone I met in New York," he wrote, "and the way I feel now, I can't say I won't see her again." That evening, back in his Paris apartment, he read it to her aloud. Elena, weeping, confessed that for the past five months, she, too, had been having an affair.

Three weeks later, Daniel was on a jetliner back to New York. He moved into a closet-sized hundred-dollar-a-week room in a flophouse and spent every free moment with Sarah. In August, when her mother needed emergency hip surgery for radiation damage caused by her earlier cancer treatments, Sarah dropped out of summer school. "Will you come with me, Daniel?" she asked, her face rippled with anguish.

"Won't I be in your way?"

"My mother will love you, Daniel. Please."

Back in Sarah's childhood home, in Rockville, Maryland, Daniel mowed the lawn and cooked. He added bright touches— including a painting—to the living room where Sarah's mother would spend her recovery. He read her mother French poetry and took part in a goofy skit involving a vacuum cleaner that Sarah and her sister put on to lift their mother's spirits.

Every day, speaking with Sarah, her relatives, or the cashier at the coffee shop, Daniel could hear his English grow stronger. As her mother's condition stabilized, Sarah rejoined her dance company in Washington. Daniel came to rehearsals, taking a seat in one of the darkened back rows. He hadn't tired of watching her. A stage, he thought, was the perfect platform for her physical grace. Each time she moved across it—or above it, it sometimes seemed—he felt like he was discovering her anew.

And so passed the perfect summer.

Then, in September, a letter from Paris. It was from the business school that had turned Daniel away the year before. He had passed the school's English test, it said. A spot was waiting for him in that fall's entering class.

"Are you really going to go?" Sarah asked one night, tenderly, as he lay beside her in her darkened childhood bedroom.

"It's why I came."

"But haven't things changed?"

|||

FOR A short while, after Daniel left, they pretended things would remain the same. Sarah came to Paris for a semester of French. Daniel came to Washington for a summer business internship. But otherwise, for nearly two and a half years, they lived apart. Soon their relationship started to unravel.

The time difference magnified the physical distance: Sarah would be starting her day as Daniel was ending his, and when they spoke on the phone, their emotional states seldom synced. Business school had brought out an aggressively ambitious side of Daniel that Sarah hadn't seen before, and she began to question how thoroughly she knew him. Daniel, for his part, saw his admission to an elite business school as an almost impossibly lucky break. His earlier academic record wasn't exemplary, and his adventure in New York—career-wise, anyway—had been a disaster. He saw a new start and feared he wouldn't get a better one. When he and Sarah met, he saw now, they had few responsibilities and all the time in the world. But with Sarah's anxiety over her mother's illness and Daniel's growing preoccupation with his career, those things were gone. Over the phone one evening, the tensions exploded. They quarreled bitterly, and the hurt they inflicted on each other felt irreparable. Months passed in silence.

||

DANIEL GRADUATED from business school, but decided to further his education rather than leap into an uncertain job market. Cornell University, in upstate New York, accepted him into a PhD program in finance. In the fall of 2002, his father and brother flew to America to help him move in. Daniel sent a short e-mail to Sarah around that time, mentioning with few specifics that he planned to take his father and brother to Manhattan for a weekend before their return to France.

It was not an invitation—even Sarah could see that. Still, she got into her car one morning in Maryland and drove to New York. Pulling to the curb on some Midtown street, taxis bleating as they careened past, she picked up her cellphone and dialed The Carlton Arms. If he had decided to stay there, she told herself, it would mean something. Wouldn't it? "Daniel Letourneau, please," she told the operator.

And then there was his voice, at once alien and familiar.

"Sarah?"

"I'm here."

"Where?"

"Here."

She found him in their old room—the one whose closet they'd etched their names in two years before—and tumbled with him onto the bed. But by the morning after the second night, the chill had returned. Their rituals felt like words repeated too many times.

The next winter, Sarah's mother fell ill again. Sarah was still grieving over Daniel when the news came, and it plunged her into a paralyzing depression. She was a semester away from a bachelor's degree at the University of Maryland, where she'd transferred from NYU, but couldn't summon the will to go to class. More worryingly, she was losing interest in the one thing that had never failed her: dance. She was technically in peak form. Her company was embarking on a daring new work. But dancing no longer brought any satisfaction. She lost so much weight that her mother and sister began to fear for her health.

Where once she was weightless, boneless, now she was all stone. Doubts bore down on her like a murderous mob. Can I abandon my mother, even as her condition worsens? Should I quit school, again, when I'm closer than ever to graduating? Can I leave the dance company I love and start again in a new place? Some evenings, after turning off the reading light in her bedroom, she cried inconsolably. Her family could see her heartache. Her Great Aunt Sule, from Puerto Rico, looked at her one day and said, "Tienes tristeza saliendo por los ojos." *You have sadness pouring out of your eyes.*

Then, from her sick bed one morning, Sarah's mother looked up and squeezed her daughter's hand. "Go to Ithaca," her mother said. She had grown fond of Daniel during his summer visit a couple of years earlier. "But go as an explorer. Give yourself permission to fail. Talk to him. See if you can untangle things. If not, your whole life is in front of you."

"What about you, Mom?"

"Your sister and I will manage fine."

Later that same day, Sarah answered the phone and heard a long-absent voice: her father's. Since leaving Milwaukee, where her parents had lived before the divorce, Sarah had seen him perhaps once or twice a year. He rarely called the house now, mostly because he worried that his former wife would answer.

"Hey, sweetie, it's your dad, I have a quick question for your sister," he said, with that Wisconsin accent. "But hey, it's been a while, how ya' doin'?"

Sarah burst into tears. They hadn't spoken in months. She had never before confided in him. But her misery over the breakup with Daniel was so consuming that she told her father everything.

"Oh, sweetie," he said with a tenderness she hadn't heard before. "Well, what are you going to do about it?"

"I think I should go to Ithaca. To be with him."

She felt sure her father would respond with his hallmark pragmatism, saying he didn't think she should give up school or dance for a crapshoot. But then he spoke, and she felt a little breathless. His advice was a mirror of her mother's. He even used the same metaphor about going "as an explorer." Up to that point, she had never understood how her parents were ever together. Now, for the first time in her life, they seemed to agree on something.

She drove to Ithaca on a cold and cloudy day in February 2003 and carried her bags into Daniel's two-bedroom apartment, which overlooked an icy Cayuga Lake. He helped her unpack, and for dinner he made *cocido*, a hearty Spanish stew of meat, garbanzo beans, carrots, and potatoes. He had cooked it before, on days he knew Sarah needed bucking up.

"Did I ask you to make this?" Sarah asked, holding back tears. "I knew."

|||

AT FIRST, nothing came easy. They had sprinted, but never walked, and the slow-and-steady tested them, as did the long road. But there was comfort in nearness. You could make mistakes when you lived together because you knew you'd wake up the next morning with another chance. Nearness. It was the sole, unaccountable reason for their ever meeting. Without nearness, she and Daniel would have nothing.

As the days turned to weeks, they found a precarious footing. He cleaned and cooked. She shopped for groceries and washed the clothes. While Daniel worked on his PhD, Sarah took classes in massage and began making friends. Over the next few months, little by little, they built a foundation that no number of steamy nights in a hotel room could equal.

Sarah had long ago told herself that she would never fall in love, let alone marry. Such was the fate of weightless children. But slowly, as fall turned to winter and winter to spring, something was growing inside her—and between her and Daniel—that felt unfamiliar but powerful and good.

Epilogue

New York City demands engagement with strangers. The sidewalks and subways are so crowded that we have no choice but to overhear private conversations and see faces at distances normally reserved for intimates. We are often close enough to see the crow's feet taking hold on a young face, smell the kimchi wafting from the paper bag, spot the flask in the back pocket. We are privy to strangers' ambitions, fears, and preoccupations in an almost unnatural way. When we accidentally knock into someone, we know, whether or not we apologize, to expect at least partial forgiveness.

The people who live in New York City share these bonds deeply. The rigors of daily life in a place with twenty-eight thousand residents per square mile—seventy-one thousand per square mile in Manhattan—make New Yorkers family, even if they have not yet spoken to the neighbor across the hall. But the city leaves no less of an imprint on visitors, for whose necks it reserves its hottest breath. The tourists emerging from the subway in Times Square freeze, like startled animals, for only a moment, before surrendering themselves—and a measure of privacy—to the will of the crowd.

As I walked through Manhattan on a recent April day, I wondered how much of all this played into the love stories I'd been writing. The conventional wisdom is that enforced physical proximity prompts us to raise our guard. We walk fast and avoid eye contact to protect the only privacy left us in a place where so much of who we are, what we eat, and where we shop is out there for all to see. As true as that may be most of the time, I wonder if it neglects something crucial. When someone attractive enters our orbit in New York, that same enforced proximity offers opportunity. A man on the subway is already close enough to that interesting-looking woman to casually strike up a conversation. If she rejects him, he doesn't lose face. He hadn't ventured anything, he can tell himself. He hadn't walked across the bar to hit on her; he hadn't just bought her a drink. He was there anyway, and, well, to make small talk was only friendly. The woman, for her part, needs make no explanation or apology to excuse herself. This is her stop; no one stays on a train forever. But if the woman finds the man attractive—and hadn't already started the conversation herself—you have the start of a New York love story.

I couldn't help think of Tina Wagenbrenner asking Chris Holter about his accent on the crowded upper deck of the Statue of Liberty ferry, or Jean Westrum letting that good-looking sailor Danny Lynch sit next to her on that jammed midnight train out of Grand Central. Chris found Tina simply because there was no other place to sit. Were that train to New England any less full, Danny, who was shy, would have lacked an innocent excuse to ask Jean for the seat beside her. He might have simply deposited her bag, bid goodnight, and retreated to an empty row somewhere to sleep. Crowded places give us more chances—and better cover—to reach out to the person next to us.

In the introduction, I wrote about research on the role of adrenaline and dopamine in stirring feelings of attraction between strangers. Psychologists have found that when people are excited, afraid, or worked up by physical exercise or some novel situation, they are more likely to feel attraction. As I looked back over the stories, it was hard not to see just these sorts of precursors. Daniel Letourneau had abandoned a job search and had just finished a three-hour stroll through springtime Manhattan when he entered Washington Square Park and set eyes on Sarah

Cross. Sofia Feldman was walking through an unfamiliar part of Midtown at night when she tripped and bumped into Matt Fitzgerald, himself reeling from a failed engagement. Claire Witten, a small-town Missouri girl, was atop the Empire State Building, worried about her missing friend, when she met Tom Nisonger. Chesa Sy had arrived in America at midnight, anxious and alone, when she asked Milton Jennings directions to Chinatown. Officer Marcel Sim was working a demanding nighttime detail when he was approached by Robin Miller, a young Minnesota woman both rattled by a tough workday and enraptured by the spectacle of Times Square. And Joey Filip was hungry and heartbroken on that gusty afternoon in Central Park when Quartermaster Third Class Willis Langford sauntered up with advice on lighting a cigarette.

But what of the other couple? Neither crowds nor adrenaline appear to tell us much about Bob Koppel and Mara Gailitis. Both were New York City residents and regulars at the Metropolitan Museum of Art. The museum was close to their apartments on the Upper East Side. It wasn't crowded, and nothing particularly dramatic happened before their meeting. But a few facts stand out. The Met is in many ways the ultimate "beautiful room," an aesthetic showplace where the psychologists Abraham Maslow and Norbett Mintz might well have expected visitors to rate others' appearances highly. What's more, few places in New York gave Bob or Mara more emotional satisfaction. Both were well-read intellectuals with a studied appreciation of art. The museum was for them a kind of playground. In the 1960s, the psychologists Albert Mehrabian and James A. Russell, whose research I cite in the introduction, identified "pleasure" as the best predictor of "affiliation among strangers." When people are in a place that makes them feel good, they are more apt to feel friendly toward nearby strangers. For Bob and Mara—and perhaps also for the inimitable Mrs. Silverman—the Met was such a place. But there was another factor, too: what the urbanist William Whyte called "triangulation." The Met is a giant showcase of triangulating objects, or conversation pieces, that permit strangers to trade observations while keeping the focus off themselves.

None of this is to suggest the inevitability of any of these unions. Nearly all of the men and women I interviewed seemed achingly aware of the improbability of their meeting, let alone marrying. Several at first lied to relatives about how they met, fearful of how it might look. Some returned to the places they met, reenacting their movements like accident investigators at the scene of a crash. Others found ways to sanctify chance, to ritualize the randomness, as if by giving it a familiar stamp they might wrest back control from the unknowable forces that shape our lives. The Holters married on Valentine's Day, the Sims on September 11. The Langfords married on Thanksgiving, as did the Koppels. The Letourneaus named their daughter Valentina. Jean Lynch wrote up her how-we-met story for the local newspaper as a fiftieth-anniversary present to her dying husband. The Fitzgeralds devoted a page of their wedding program to a fairy-tale retelling of the night they met, as if the unlikeliness of their love story were as ancient as time.

|||

I'M NOT blind to the dark side of public spaces. Parks and squares have also seen plenty of thefts, drug deals, and worse. The anonymity of crowds can invite predators. Ethnic tensions can explode in violence. But urban pathology is not the subject of this book. Nor do I think it reflects most of what goes on in public spaces, certainly not the best-designed ones. I suspect that the "broken windows" theory—that poorly maintained places invite crime—is as applicable to public spaces as it is to private ones. If a space is designed well and looks cared for and loved, troublemakers will think twice before entering. William Whyte proved as much in the 1980s with his work on the redesign of Bryant Park, an eight-acre green behind the New York Public Library. By the 1970s, Bryant Park had been dubbed "Needle Park," a nest of drugs and prostitution so dangerous that police patrolled it in pairs. In came Whyte. His recommendations led designers to widen its narrow entrances, install food kiosks, and take down a perimeter of hedges that had made the park invisible from the sidewalk. Today it is one of the most successful urban parks in America, a Midtown oasis that in warm months draws some twenty thousand visitors a day.

Most of the couples in this book told me they would not have met but for place. The landmarks and public spaces where they spoke their first words were not mere backdrops. They were villages—a small place within a larger one—that slowed time just long enough for two busy people to catch each other's eye. In rereading their stories recently, though, I noticed something that mattered at least as much: the couples were open, and ready, to fall in love.

Postscripts

GREEN: Joey and Willis

I found the tale of the "Park Cinderella" and her "Sailor Prince Charming" in a newspaper database at the Library of Congress. I was entering search terms that I hoped would pull up stories about couples who'd met in Central Park. News articles were appearing in reverse chronological order, and toward the end of a very long list were pages of stories about this one couple: a Texas sailor who had met a runaway in Central Park. The story was charming, and heartbreaking. There was just one problem: they were all published in 1941. Neither Joey nor Willis appeared in a single story since. Was there any chance either were still alive?

Enter Google. My search for "Willis Langford" turned up a web page for a salesman of nutritional supplements in California. In the upper-right corner was a photo of a gray-haired man with a familiar-looking dimpled chin. In his bio, he said he had turned eighty-nine in September 2008. The age fit. I e-mailed, and two days later I got a reply. "I am indeed the same party," Mr. Langford wrote.

We agreed to meet at an International House of Pancakes—his suggestion—near his home in Oceanside, a short drive north of San Diego. "My granddaughter is a waitress there, and they serve good common food," he explained. "We can occupy a booth as long as we desire."

The man with ruler-straight posture who greeted me on the bench outside looked at least two decades younger than his ninety years. He was tall, wiry, and slim, and wore a striped dress shirt, a gray goatee, and dark pants with a cowboy-sized belt buckle. He had a clear voice and a quick mind. Over lunch—he ordered ham with waffles—he told me he attributed his health to a "positive attitude" and nutritional supplements. He had brought a folder stuffed with newspaper clippings and family letters from the early 1940s, and photographs of his great-grandchildren.

Mr. Langford told me that he and Joey (she later went by Paula) had been married nearly sixty-four years when she died, at eighty-two, some four years earlier. They had four children, eight grandchildren, and sixteen great-grandchildren. Our waitress, Nikki, was one of those grandkids. When she heard us talking about her grandparents' love story, she sat down on her grandpa's side of the booth and wiped away tears.

"I miss Grandma, I really do," she said. Nikki said that her grandmother had never told her the story of how she'd met her grandfather but, toward the end of her life, had shared it with Nikki's own daughter.

Willis and Joey left Seattle after the Allied victory in World War II and moved to Long Beach, California, where Willis rose to the command of the landing tank ship USS *Tioga County*. He was released from active duty in the late 1950s and retired from the Navy in 1979. He then became a salesman and entrepreneur, selling everything from encyclopedias to aluminum pots and, most recently, vitamins.

The day after their wedding, Willis swore that Joey would never work again. Joey poured all of her energies into her children, and throughout her life she remained quiet and introspective. She never again heard from her mother or sisters.

Willis said I was the first writer to ask about their love story in sixty-eight years. It was a story that made him proud. In 1994, he committed his recollections to paper in a short personal account he titled "A Tale of Prince Charming." The nickname—which a Philadelphia headline writer had used in 1941—drew some ribbing from his shipmates back then. But it didn't seem to bother him anymore.

Joey, however, had shared little of his nostalgia. Her years in New Jersey and New York—with her father's death, her mother's abandonment, her life on the streets—had been so painful that she never spoke about them, even with her husband. Despite the hoopla surrounding their fairy-tale meeting and marriage, most of her children didn't learn the story until her death.

COLLISION: Sofia and Matt

Matt Fitzgerald and Sofia Feldman (pseudonyms) were married on August 15, 2009, at a restored nineteenth-century steel foundry in Long Island City.

Their religious differences had loomed large during their engagement. Neither was particularly observant. But Matt had gone to Catholic school in Rochester and had gone with his family to church every Sunday. Both of his older siblings had married Catholics. But in faith, as in other parts of his life, he had cut his own path, resenting the way the Catholic tradition seemed to "force-feed" worshipers its doctrine. Sofia had gone to a Jewish Sunday school and was bat mitzvahed, though outside the High Holidays her parents rarely went to synagogue.

Matt's parents liked Sofia right away—his dad took her out for a milkshake on her first visit to Rochester. But they had a lot of questions about Judaism: What's a seder? What are the rituals? What is the structure of the family? Sofia's parents were more guarded, and Matt wondered how they felt about him. In October 2008, about a week after Yom Kippur, Matt asked to speak with her father. During a walk together, Matt asked for his daughter's hand in marriage. "It was the most nerve-racking moment in my life," Matt told me when I met the couple for brunch at Rue 57, a restaurant near the spot where they met.

Mr. Feldman gave his blessing and then launched into a speech that made him sound like a real estate agent congratulating a buyer on his new home. "She's really a great girl, Matt," he said. "She's funny. She's cute. You made a great choice."

Their wedding ceremony was a showcase of religious amity, with both a rabbi and a priest officiating. Matt smashed the glass, a Jewish custom said to ward off evil spirits, and drank from the rabbi's wine cup. The priest spoke a little Hebrew, then read from the New Testament. Their chuppah—the Jewish bridal canopy symbolizing the couple's future home—consisted of a giant wreath hung from the rafters. The hora, however, was not without its rough spots. "It was the most chaotic hora I've ever seen," Sofia told me.

"Once the music started," said Matt, "some people got into the circle and started doing the concentric circle thing. Other people were standing still and clapping, and they didn't know what to do, and it just turned into a mosh pit."

Less than a month had passed since their wedding, and after brunch I followed the couple as they retraced the steps of their first encounter some five years earlier. We walked to the crosstown bus stop where Matt first spotted Sofia, then across the street to the length of sidewalk—under the marquee for Carnegie Hall's Weill Recital Hall—where Sofia, with her big viola, fell into him. "It's like hallowed ground for us in some ways," Matt said, part of the mythology of their relationship. "If two people worked together, how they first met doesn't really matter. It doesn't matter if they met on Monday or Tuesday, or in this conference room or that conference room."

But this was different. In their wedding program, Sofia retold the story of their meeting as a fairy tale. *Once upon a time, a knight was strolling down a lane and looked upon a fair maiden conversing with some friends . . .*

As the relationship deepened, it wasn't so much the randomness of their meeting that they marveled at. Plenty of people meet in the streets of big cities only to discover they have nothing in common. What struck them was the improbability of such an encounter ever leading to marriage—and the realization, however paradoxical, that they could have met almost no other way. "We've often thought that these dating websites would never put us together," Sofia said. "Catholic, Jewish—the algorithm would definitely bypass us."

"In that first year of medical school," Matt added, "even when times were a little difficult, we both had a certain sense of, 'Maybe there's something bigger than us at work here.'"

Neither is converting to the other's faith, and they recognize the choices they will face when they have children. But Sofia says that their chance meeting has deepened her sense of spirituality. "Whenever we would hit a rough patch, I would always think, This is not just about me and Matt, It's about me and Matt and whoever brought us together. I actually became a little more religious."

It was late afternoon on a clear September day in Midtown, and the sun was dipping through the spaces between the buildings. We were standing outside the Duane Reade pharmacy on the corner of Sixth Avenue and Fifty-seventh Street, where five years earlier a lost boy had first asked a wary girl if she wanted to keep talking and she'd said okay. Before we said our goodbyes, Sofia looked at the corner, and at Matt, then slid her arm around his waist. She said, "It's a private miracle that makes you believe in something."

NAVIGATION: Jean and Danny

A decade ago, as the fiftieth anniversary of their meeting neared, Jean wanted to surprise Danny. Without telling him, she decided to write a short account for their local newspaper of the day they met. She wanted her husband to "discover" it. But Danny was diagnosed with cancer in 2000, and Jean felt she couldn't wait any longer. She wrote it a year early and turned it in to *Newsday*. The paper published it in a regular column written by readers called "Love Story." The headline: "A Long, Happy Journey for Strangers on a Train."

I came across the story while searching electronic newspaper archives for couples who met in Grand Central Terminal. A moment later, however, I discovered that *Newsday* had published another story about Danny nearly five years later: his obituary. He died, of cancer, on July 11, 2005, at seventy-three. When I called Jean in the summer of 2009, I wasn't sure what to expect. Their son, Dan Jr., picked up the phone and told me his mother wasn't feeling so well anymore. He had moved from San Diego to help take care of her. I told him about the book and asked whether his mother might be inclined—and well enough—to share her love story.

"I think she would like that very much," he said.

When he put his mother on the phone, I understood almost right away what he'd meant. Jean Lynch was by turns high-spirited and wistful as she told the story; Danny had been the center of her life for a half century. In the weeks after that first conversation, she sent me e-mails rich with illuminating details. "You have made me feel good in so many ways, as I am enjoying looking back through my life with different eyes," she said in one. "I thank you for this, even if Dan's and my story doesn't end up in your book."

On a brisk morning in late November 2009, I visited her and Dan Jr. in her cozy house, on a leafy street in Hauppauge, New York. She was as tall as she had advertised, and was warm, down-to-earth, and even something of a cutup. She and her son seemed to enjoy teasing each other. I could see why a shy, introspective man might have taken an immediate liking to her.

We spoke at a kitchen table piled with photo albums and neat stacks of letters she and Danny had exchanged during their courtship. Beside her at the head of the table was the birdcage basket, only a little tarnished, that she had been carrying when she and Danny met. Over coffee and homemade nut cake, she told the story in greater detail, veering between laughter and tears. Afterward, Jean and her son drove me to a Long Island Rail Road stop, and as I got out, she said, "Thanks for making an old lady happy."

She and Danny (as an older man, he preferred Dan) married on December 27, 1952, at Hancock Congregational Church in Lexington, Massachusetts. Their first child, Dan Jr., was born in January 1954, and two girls would come later. Dan was honorably discharged from the Navy in July 1955, a torpedoman first class. But his transition to civilian life was anything but easy. He had contracted tuberculosis and was hospitalized for a year and a half. When he was released, doctors told him to avoid strenuous work. He drove a cab around Lexington for a year.

His confinement deepened his longing for the outdoors. When he was well enough, he enrolled at the University of Massachusetts, Amherst, on the G.I. bill and studied wildlife biology and conservation. He got a job at the Massachusetts Department of Fish and Game, releasing pheasants and stocking fish ponds, before moving with his family to New York, where he worked his way up through parks and wildlife jobs with the state. He retired in 1993 as general parks manager for the entire Long Island region, where he was credited with developing nature centers, improving streams, and building woodland trails and fish hatchery ponds.

"It was pretty much his dream job," Dan Jr. told me. "He was always outside, going to all the different parks on Long Island. You could walk through the park with him, and he'd see things no one else saw."

Jean worked as a teacher's aide for a few years and made oil paintings while raising the children. She has five grandchildren. Despite a few health problems, she seems as open to new experiences now as she was as a nineteen-year-old at Grand Central.

On our way to the Long Island Rail Road station, she confided that she'd recently attended a concert of a heavy metal band a grandson played in. Did she like it? "I had to wear earplugs," she said. "But yes!"

In 2005, Danny spent about ten days in the hospital before slipping into a terminal coma. One day, toward the end, while Jean was at his bedside holding his hand, he opened his eyes and looked at his wife. Before closing them again and drifting off to some faraway place, he said, "I'm glad I met you."

FREESTANDING: Tina and Chris

I found the Holters through a search of online newspaper archives. Mike Holtzclaw, an arts critic at the *Daily Press* of Newport News, had written a Valentine's Day piece in 1998 about local couples' favorite romance movies. Toward the bottom was a paragraph about the Holters.

"Tina was vacationing in New York City, and Chris was visiting the U.S. from his native Germany when they met at the Statue of Liberty," Holtzclaw had written. "It is only natural then, that they share an affinity for 'Sleepless in Seattle,' a movie in which the ultimate long-distance romance is finally brought face-to-face at another New York landmark, the Empire State Building."

I called Holtzclaw, who had played tennis with the couple in what he called his "prechildren days," and he graciously tracked them down. "I think you'll like them," he wrote in an e-mail.

When I first called Tina, she was ebullient. Some two decades later, it was clear that she still relished the story of how she and "Schwartzie" had met. In our first, brief phone conversation, I picked up on a strong sentimental streak. "I'm a person who believes in things happening for a reason," she said. "If you put something out to the universe, the universe adapts to meet your needs. Not that our lives have been that easy. We've had many obstacles. But the universe always seems to provide."

A month later, driving down to Newport News to meet the couple on a steamy July weekend, I wrestled with some of same questions Tina's friends had: What about the big age difference? What was Chris really after? Hadn't Tina rushed into things?

When I called on the way to offer to treat them to dinner at any restaurant in town, Tina picked Smokey Bones, a chain restaurant at the edge of a strip mall. Its motto was "Good food, good drinks and good times." Tina had brought coupons for half-off burgers, and when the waitress came by for drink orders, she and Chris suggested a "Bucket of Beer" for the table. An ice-filled pail of Coors and Miller Lite bottles arrived a few minutes later. Within about a half hour of meeting, my skepticism had given way. This was a couple who lived in the moment, who didn't take themselves particularly seriously, who took time to celebrate the small blessings that make life bearable. Chris is less effusive than his wife, but an abashed smile—like that of a teenager caught with a racy magazine—crossed his face when I asked what first drew him to Tina. "She was an 'American woman'"—you could hear the quotation marks as he spoke—"and I thought she was hot." Then he shrugged good-naturedly, as if embarrassed that the story was no more complicated than that.

Tina, for her part, is the sort of woman who sees small miracles everywhere. She was quick with affection—she hugged me as soon we met. And she was free with tears; at various points in our interview, we stopped to give her time to collect herself. Though in wedding photos the age gap seems pronounced, two decades later it would draw no special notice. They are both of a certain age, well tanned, with a few wrinkles. Chris's swoop of blond hair is gone—he wears his head bald. Tina, still slim, favors tank tops and spaghetti straps that lop a decade off her age.

Despite its story-book beginning, their life together has seen its share of struggles. Chris works long hours as a brick mason, spending days on the road building and remodeling homes across Virginia. Tina retired in 2002 after thirty-two years as an elementary school teacher. To help make ends meet, she still works part-time, delivering pizzas for a local Papa John's. In 1997, at age seventeen, her son Todd had his own son. Tina and Chris are helping to raise the boy in their own home.

More than two decades after they met, the Statue of Liberty remains a personal totem. They returned three years after their wedding to re-enact the day they met. And when the Statue of Liberty's crown reopened on July 4, 2009, for the first time since 9/11, she and Schwartzie celebrated at home with a champagne brunch. If visitors ask nicely, Tina is happy display her Statue of Liberty beer stein and muffin tin.

In ways big and small, they see the statue—and New York—as their matchmaker.

"I'd never been to a big city," Chris reflected when I visited the couple at their lived-in-looking home near a river in Newport News. "When you get there the first time, it's hard to describe. You feel so small when you walk through the skyscrapers and see all these people. You are open to anything. Everything is new."

They visit Liz and Ron on Long Island nearly every Thanksgiving and make a point of taking the upper deck of the Verrazano Bridge so they can catch a glimpse of the statue. "It takes our eyes off the road," Tina jokes, "which you don't want to do for too long on that bridge."

"We say, 'Oh, look,'" Chris says, "and sometimes talk about, 'What are the odds of people meeting there and being together all these years?'"

"We look out at her," says Tina, "and say, 'There's our Lady.'"

DEPTHS: Chesa and Milton

In late January 2003, four months after her return from the Philippines, Chesa Sy married Milton Jennings (pseudonyms) at Brooklyn Borough Hall. Chesa wore a long-sleeved red dress; Milton, a navy suit with a red tie. The only guests were Milton's parents and brother, the apartment building superintendent, and a couple of Milton's friends. Chesa's family could not afford the trip. Back at his apartment afterward, Milton handed Chesa a ring—a new one, given at the proper time.

Milton remains a classical music reviewer and editor. Chesa took college classes in accounting, worked for five years as a cashier at a bookstore, and is making plans to open her own business. In September 2009, at the federal courthouse in Brooklyn, she became a U.S. citizen. The couple now live together in an only slightly bigger apartment, in Jackson Heights, Queens.

The day before her citizenship interview in 2009, Chesa and Milton revisited the places where their lives together began: the streets of Chinatown, the rundown hotel where she spent her first night, the restaurant in the Bowery where they met after she called and said he was the only person she knew in America. It was a last homage to the improbable places that drew them closer. They saw no need to re-ride the A train. Its riddles, they felt, were far easier to fathom: on a train car, particularly an empty one, people have little choice but to notice one another. The couple joked that they were grateful for the train's noisy wheels. If the train were quieter, they might not have needed to sit so close to hear each other.

All the same, Chesa credits their union to the mysteries of the zodiac. "Fate," she said, when I met the couple at a coffee shop near their apartment in March 2009.

Milton is more earthbound. "I think about it a lot." He touched the side of his coffee cup and flashed Chesa a smile. "You look at it in hindsight, and it all seems remarkable. But at the time, it was just one disjointed thing after another."

ELEVATION: Claire and Tom

Finding couples who married atop the Empire State Building is easy: the building's marketing team and brides.com host an annual essay contest for couples who wish to wed hundreds of feet above the street. (The couples are married in back-to-back half-hour ceremonies that begin at 7 a.m. on Valentine's Day.) But how to find couples who actually met there? I started plugging different combinations of search terms—"met," "married," "wedding," "Empire State Building"—into Google. Deep in the search results was a link to a November 2008 speech that one Tom Nisonger gave to Indiana University's chapter of Beta Phi Mu, an honor society for librarians. While warming up the audience with a few information science jokes, he mentioned that he and his wife, Claire, had "met at the Empire State Building, but I was an hour late because I left my wallet in a library. She says it was a portent of things to come."

Bingo. I found Nisonger's e-mail address on the university website, and he wrote back a few days later. "I will share with you the more detailed description that I used to tell my students in class, as well as some additional information," he wrote. "As you will notice, there are amusing as well as romantic aspects to the story."

There was a nebbishy earnestness that immediately charmed me. I soon made plans to visit their home, near the campus of Indiana University, where Tom worked for two decades as a professor of library sciences and where Claire still teaches molecular biology.

When we met in the summer of 2009, Tom, sixty-six, looked every bit the professor emeritus. Crystal blue eyes gazed through thick glasses, and a wiry white beard looked trimmed perhaps less assiduously than it had been during his working days. Claire, at seventy, is still slim, tall, and quick-witted. They live at the edge of Bloomington, in a leafy subdivision down the street from the city's visitor's center. Their home is decorated with bric-a-brac from their world travels—tapestries, masks, figurines—and surrounded by dogwood and ash trees. Two cats, Tesla (after the scientist) and Tressel (after the Ohio State football coach), roam the house.

Within minutes of arriving, Tom handed me a timeline of their courtship that he'd prepared in anticipation of my visit. It included precise dates, names of shows and restaurants, and selected quotes from their love letters. He had also printed out the weather page from the September 27, 1969, *New York Times*, so I could accurately describe conditions on the day they met. Before heading to my hotel after dinner, Tom gave me yet more homework: a stack of letters from their courtship, a 1969 calendar in which Claire had recorded their first dates, and the scrap of paper (Tom had kept it) on which Claire first wrote her phone number and address the weekend they met.

"Can you tell he's a librarian?" Claire asked.

The story of their meeting, he told me, was part of his campus persona. Each semester, on the first day of class, he told it to students as an icebreaker. The library angle was a plus. "When I went back to the circulation desk at the Barnard Library, my wallet was still there and the money was still in it," he'd say, setting up the punch line. "This tells you something about the integrity of librarians. In many places in New York City it would have been, Bye-bye wallet."

Claire's take on the lost-wallet story has less to do with librarians than with her husband's generally unhurried pace. "It was a portent of things to come," she says, "because I've been waiting on him ever since."

Tom and Claire were married on July 5, 1970, at the Wesley United Methodist Church in Claire's hometown of Trenton, Missouri. A wedding notice in the newspaper noted that "the bride wore a gown she made herself of white silk organza over satin peau de soie." (Chuck, who served as an usher, married an accountant and taught at community colleges around Washington, D.C. He lost his wife to ovarian cancer in 1983 and died of diabetes in 2001, at the age of fifty-eight. Myrna, for her part, married her boss, the bank executive.)

Soon after their engagement, Claire quit her position at Tougaloo and got a job at a Columbia research lab while Tom finished his dissertation. With the academic job market for political scientists tight, Tom moved with Claire to Pittsburgh to pursue a master's in library science. He got his first job at the University of Manitoba in Canada, where they adopted two young children.

He worked for eight years as the head of library acquisitions at the University of Texas, Dallas, before landing a tenure-track job, in 1988, at Indiana University. He wrote three books and scores of articles and won several teaching awards before retiring in 2008 as director of the campus's Master of Library Science program. He now spends his days traveling with Claire, studying genealogy, and working on a sprawling family tree. In addition to teaching, Claire mentors underprivileged students and helps administer a summer program that brings minority high school students to campus to study science.

The couple still thrill to the idea that their relationship—with all its small private moments—took root in one of the world's most illustrious buildings. Their pride in the Empire State Building is palpable, as if its fate were entwined with their own.

"We have always considered the Empire State Building 'our building,'" Tom wrote to me an e-mail, "and humorously thought that while some couples have a 'song' we have a 'building.'"

They returned to the observation deck on July 4, 1970, the day before their first anniversary, to watch fireworks crackle over New York. On later anniversaries, they rented movies that exalted the building: *King Kong, An Affair to Remember, Sleepless in Seattle*. An anniversary in the mid-1990s was a little less romantic. They had heard that the Empire State Quarry, the source of the building's exquisite limestone façade, was just a half hour from their home in North Bloomington. The quarry was private and did not give tours, nor was its precise location noted on maps. With the help of reference librarians at Indiana University, however, Tom and Claire were able to determine its rough coordinates.

If the Empire State Building was the birthplace of their relationship, Tom thought, wouldn't it be nice to visit the building's birthplace? Not so much, they discovered. They scrabbled up a small hillside in the woods and soon found themselves looking out across a ragged landscape of exposed rock. Then they heard gunshots. "Some rednecks nearby were doing target practice with rifles," Claire recalled. They turned back to their car a few minutes later.

"The people shooting guns took away something," Tom said, dryly. "Still, I thought we had a sense of accomplishment just having seen it."

"It's a big deserted hole in the ground," Claire said, demurring.

"Let's put it this way," Tom added, "the quarry is not nearly as romantic as the building."

CROSSROADS: Robin and Marcel

After leaving New York, Robin and Marcel Sim bought a half acre of land in Moorhead, Minnesota, a ten-minute walk from her parents. Robin drafted blueprints for her first freestanding residential structure: their own house. It was a custom two-story craftsman-style home with a large front porch and flower boxes in the windows. The couple tiled the floors, painted the interiors, and finished the basement with their own hands.

Robin got a job with an architecture firm in Fargo, where she helped build and remodel courthouses, hotels, and offices. By 2009, she had made enough of an impression to be named "Intern Architect of the Year" by North Dakota's chapter of the American Institute of Architects. In January 2010, after completing the last of nine exams, she became a fully licensed registered architect.

Marcel was hired by a local ambulance company and rose quickly to a supervisory position. He continues to work in the public safety field.

In March 2008, their first child, a daughter named Sarah, was born. In May 2010 came Sophia.

Marcel has come around to the gentler rhythms of his adopted home but has yet to fully abandon his "New York defenses." When motorists flash their headlights at him, he says only half-jokingly, it still takes him a moment to realize they aren't gangsters looking for a fight but friendly neighbors saying hello.

In their living room, the bookshelves by the fireplace are lined with the photos of Times Square that Robin had taken the night they met. Robin has tried in other ways to ease her husband's occasional homesickness. She hung up a shower curtain emblazoned with a map of Manhattan and sewed the circular symbols of the A, C, and E subway lines into a set of bathroom towels.

When I asked whether Times Square had played any role in their coming together, she said it had "opened her senses."

"I compare it to waking up at Christmas, before opening presents," she told me. "The excitement of not knowing, of being like a child, when even little things excite you. The neon lights in Times Square were like wrapping paper, and the feeling you get inside is just of happiness and discovery. You don't know what's going to be around the corner."

It was a feeling she found nowhere else in city. "Even though I'd never been there, Times Square felt very comfortable, very safe. It was so well lit, and everyone around you, they're all in similar frames of mind: it's all about fun and relaxation and having a good time. There's that famous kiss from World War II, and you can understand it: there's this energy that goes through your body."

Had the setting been different, she told me, she wasn't sure she would have felt comfortable buttonholing a big-city police officer—certainly not to ask for restaurant advice. "In Times Square, when I started talking to Marcel for the first time, I felt in some ways like I already knew him."

It was Marcel's job to talk to strangers, all kinds. On a typical shift in Times Square, he fielded dozens of questions from tourists. The crowds and chaos of Times Square kept him in a hyper-alert state, but the clincher for him was less the place than the person. "I used to tell Robin that she's from the 'Land of Make Believe,' where everything is cheery and everyone's on the same level and everyone's good." But then he saw her more clearly, as a person who discounted material things, loved her family, and felt connected to the world through faith. "What you see on her outside was what I had kept inside," Marcel told me on the phone one day. "She is who I was, or wanted to be, before I was tainted and desensitized by my occupation. I can be like that now, with her."

RENOVATIONS: Mara and Bob

When the Koppels first told me the name of the exhibit where they met—"Patterns of Collecting"—I was struck by its resonance with their love story. Bob, after all, had been wandering through a collection of the world's most beautiful objects when he spotted yet another one, and had to have her. Mara, however, would be no one's collectible, which only heightened Bob's desire.

What none of us knew then was that the exhibit's creator had invited just such comparisons. In November 2009 I took an elevator down to the library on the Met's ground floor and asked for the files on "Patterns of Collecting," which had long ago been taken down. The files led me to a 1975 book, *The Chase, the Capture: Collecting at the Metropolitan*, that the Met's then-director, Thomas Hoving, co-wrote as a companion to the exhibit. "The chase and the capture of a great work of art," Hoving begins, "is one of the most exciting endeavors in life—as dramatic, emotional, and fulfilling as a love affair. And love affairs, at least some of them, should be told about." Could Hoving have imagined that one such affair would begin right there in his exhibit?

Bob and Mara left New York less than a year after marrying, moving briefly to the Berkshires, in Massachusetts, and then, in

1978, to Chicago, where Bob's brother worked in finance. Bob learned the trade and joined the Chicago Mercantile Exchange, becoming a successful commodities trader and writing a half dozen books on the psychology of trading and investing. (His latest is *Investing and the Irrational Mind.*) He also raises money for nonprofit groups.

Mara helped establish an after-school program at the University of Chicago Laboratory Schools. She paints out of a home studio and works in the gift shop at the Museum of Contemporary Art, Chicago. In 1998, she published a book called *Women of the Pits*, a collection of stories about the then-small sorority of women who had broken into the male-dominated world of trading.

Their two children, Lily and Niko, live in New York City. Both are writers.

One of Mara's favorite paintings hangs above a desk in Lily's Manhattan apartment: it is oil and ink, on unstretched canvas, and depicts the Great Hall of the Metropolitan Museum of Art. On its face, it is a straightforward, if slightly whimsical, rendering of the museum's majestic marble entrance hall. But look closer— in the center of a rosette, on the side of an urn, at the base of a column—and you'll find the names "Bob," "Lily," and "Niko" hidden, like some runic code, in the architectural details.

"It was a birthday present for Bob," Mara, still lithe and lovely at sixty-eight, told me when I visited the couple in May 2010 in Chicago's historic Old Town. The walls of their condo, on the second floor of a late nineteenth-century former parish house, are covered with Mara's art: a painting of a trio of wild-eyed New Guinea Mudmen, a man in a leopard-print leotard fighting off a lion, a disembodied eye floating in a sea of tears. At first glance, a pen-and-ink in Bob's office looks like a tree in full bloom. But if you come in closer, you see that every leaf and branch is made up of tiny repetitions of her husband's first name.

"I really believe life is very accidental," Mara said as we settled onto couches in the living room with dessert after a lunch of home-cooked softshell crabs, heirloom tomatoes, and white wine. "If you wait a second one way or another, your entire life is different. The fact that Bob and I met in this place, that our paths just intersected, made all the difference. When I saw him, it was a moment of recognition. It was like everything in life was revealed in this one moment."

Bob, who still wears his hair, white now, in rakish waves, was dressed in a zip-up cardigan sweater, a striped dress shirt, and a loosely knotted green tie printed with images of a stork. His vocal cadences bear a striking resemblance to those of Woody Allen. "Was it Robert Pirsig, in *Zen and the Art of Motorcycle Maintenance*, who said something like, 'Truth knocks at the door, and you act as if no one is home'? It's strange how a lot of people just live their lives that way. We've commodified every aspect of American life. People believe if they have something more expensive, bigger, life will be better. We're not geared to think, 'Wow, I found this truth or this person who is really amazing.' We can't be satisfied with that. To be in love, contrary to what is generally thought in this society, is to find someone who you really are happy with and to just allow the both of you the freedom to let that love reveal itself over time."

SIGHTLINES: Sarah and Daniel

Sarah Cross and Daniel Letourneau (pseudonyms) were married on July 18, 2004, at a white-clapboard eighteenth-century inn overlooking Cayuta Lake, just outside Ithaca.

The end of their courtship—and the start of something more—had none of the drama of its chance start in Washington Square Park some four years earlier. Every few weeks, over breakfast in Ithaca, they would take the relationship's measure with a simple question. "So, do you think we should get married?" one would ask the other.

"I'm not sure. What do you think?"

The banter became a kind of inside joke, a way of expressing confidence in their progress while still waiting for all the pieces to fall into place. Then, on a bright Sunday morning, in the fall of 2003, they awoke and gazed out their bedroom window onto a campus strewn with brightly hued fallen leaves.

"So, do you think we should get married?" he said.

"Yes."

"Okay."

"Can we call our parents?"

"Yes."

"Now?"

"Yes."

The celebration spanned three days, with some sixty of Daniel's relatives and friends flying in from France to join one hundred of Sarah's. Daniel's cousins sang a French choral song they had written in honor of the couple. Sarah took his relatives into town for real American cheeseburgers. Wary of American cooking standards, the French ordered their burgers "extra, extra rare."

Cornell awarded Daniel a PhD in the spring of 2008 and soon hired him. He is now an assistant professor of real estate finance at the university's School of Hotel Administration. Sarah worked as a massage therapist for three years, until their first child, a daughter they named Valentina, was born, in February 2007. She now takes care of her daughter full-time.

Sarah can recall the sensory details of that day in June 2000 when she and Daniel met, but mainly in impressions. "I felt like there were bright colors," she said when I interviewed her in the spring of 2009 at a café in Washington, D.C., where she was visiting her sister. "It felt bright and vibrant. People looked beautiful."

A friend lives a block from Washington Square Park, and when Sarah and Daniel visit, they often stroll through, looking for the tree they were under when they first locked eyes. As the years pass, though, the setting has felt less a part of her story than the city's. "It's never had the same kind of vibe as it did that day," she told me. "I visit this place where this huge thing happened to us, and there's no sign of it. Millions of people have been through since and have been sitting in those same spots. It captures something about the feel of New York City. The multitudes of people and the stories that happen every day that are anonymous. Many moments are come-and-go, but some completely change the course of a person's life. Now, when I'm there, I think, How many stories have happened in this park? How many people have had their lives change course in this place?"

Daniel's memory of the day they met is more vivid. When I visited the couple in Ithaca in October 2009, I brought a map of the park. Daniel zeroed in instantly on the tree they had been sitting under, then traced his movements around the fountain and along the walks. For him, Washington Square Park remains nothing more or less than the birthplace of their relationship. The thirty minutes they'd spent studying each other's faces, before exchanging a single word, remains for him a moment of silent poetry.

"There was an entire wordless conversation between two strangers," he told me. "I was not tempted at all to talk. It felt like we *were* talking. We were probably a little too far apart for a conversation to take place naturally, and it would have been very awkward to break the intimacy of the moment with words. So one of us would smile, and the other would smile back. It felt like it was an entire life. After thirty minutes, we'd said everything. I was left with the feeling that maybe there was nothing else to say."

Sarah told me she had returned his gaze only to challenge him. "First it was kind of me being, Okay, who are you and what are you doing?" she told me. "Then it very quickly changed, and I would say it was the look on Daniel's face that made it change. He was completely exposing himself emotionally. He was, 'This is who I am.'"

We were sitting at their dining room table, and Valentina came running in from the next room, where she'd been watching a children's movie. She clutched at her father's knee, and he hoisted her into his lap. "My life was set on a very different path," Daniel said, looking across the table at Sarah. "I don't think we had any reason to meet, except for randomness. Except for just luck. The way we met has given me certainty that I know nothing. I'd been for eleven years in a relationship with Elena, and I was sure I was going to marry her. Then, in twenty minutes, my life was just upside down."

Acknowledgments

My first book, *My Father's Paradise*, a family saga published in 2008, was a labor of love. It recounted my father's immigrant journey from the back roads of Kurdish Iraq to the freeways of Los Angeles, and took readers across three continents and three thousand years of history. This book is admittedly a lighter undertaking, but one with no less heartfelt a purpose.

I am indebted to the following people for helping shape my thinking on the interplay of environment and behavior. Fred Kent, the founder and president of Project for Public Spaces, took time out of his frantic schedule to sit for an interview at his Manhattan offices. Helen Fisher, a research professor at Rutgers University, gave me a crash course on the neurochemistry of love. Andrew Stuck, an urban designer in London, shared fascinating reports from the "Romantic Walkshops" he has led through cities around the globe. Arthur Aron, a prominent social psychologist now at Stony Brook University, sharpened my understanding of his seminal work on the link between arousal and attraction. Los Angeles architect Steven Lopez, a family friend, cast light on why some public spaces rouse while others alienate. Beatrice Wright, a retired psychology professor at the University of Kansas, shared memories about her late colleague and friend professor Roger Barker.

Though I never met them, I am thankful for urban visionaries like William H. Whyte, Jane Jacobs, and Ray Oldenburg. They have written with greater eloquence than I could ever muster about why Americans must care about the life of cities. I learned a great deal about the environmental preconditions for attraction from the writings of social psychologists like Albert Mehrabian, James Russell, Ellen Berscheid, Elaine Walster, Paul Amato, and Ayala Malach Pines. Sociologists Erving Goffman and Lyn Lofland wrote groundbreaking books on the behavior of strangers in public, and I am grateful to have read them.

One or two couples in the book heard about my project and contacted me. But most I found through a relentless dragnet for compelling stories. I owe a few people a thousand thanks for helping to identify candidates for the book. Mike Holtzclaw, entertainment critic for the *Daily Press* of Newport News, Virginia, tracked down a terrific couple he'd briefly mentioned in a long-ago column. Ryan Brenizer, a phenomenal New York City photographer, put me in touch with a beautiful couple whose wedding he had just shot. Just when I was despairing of finding any couples who'd met at the Metropolitan Museum of Art, Lily Koppel, a fellow writer, offered up her charming parents.

I appreciated the hard work and dedication of two New York–based research interns in the summer of 2009, Amanda Martinez and Anthony Martin. Though still in college, they tirelessly worked the phones, the blogosphere, and their feet to hunt down leads. Thanks very much to Laura Harris and Ellen Locker, librarians, respectively, of the *New York Post* and *New York Daily News*, for letting me rummage through their newspapers' clip files. Thanks as well to Jonathan Pace of the New York Public Library, and to staff at the Library of Congress in Washington, D.C. I am grateful, too, to Laura Katz Smith, a curator at the Thomas J. Dodd Research Center at the University of Connecticut, Storrs, who miraculously turned up a copy of the spring 1951 schedule of the New York, New Haven, and Hartford Railroad line.

My agent, Andrew Blauner, believed in the book from day one, and his enthusiasm was wind at my back. Thanks very much to the team at Da Capo Press and especially my editor, Renée Sedliar, a poet with an eye for detail and an ear for the subtleties of language.

I thank my wife, Meg, and my children, Seth and Phoebe, who endured more absences than I would have liked. And thanks to my mother and father, whose own love story was the inspiration for this book. If my first book was a tribute to my father, this one is an homage to my mother, Stephanie, and her family's roots in New York City.

Most of all, I have to thank the couples who gave so much of their time and their hearts to this project. And that includes those remarkable couples whose stories I am so sorry I could not fit in this book. Though most didn't know me from Adam, they gamely took my first cold call and eventually spent hours on the phone, over e-mail, and in person answering what must have seemed like a barrage of questions about some of the most intimate moments in their lives. For their patience and trust, I am profoundly grateful. They did it not for themselves, I saw, but so that the world—and the cause of love—might be in some way richer for their stories.